MIDNIGHT
HOUR

Céleste perrino Walker

&

Eric Stoffle

a sycamore tree book
from

Pacific Press® Publishing Association
Nampa, Idaho
Oshawa, Ontario, Canada

Edited by Jerry D. Thomas
Designed by Robert Mason

Copyright © 1999 by
Pacific Press® Publishing Association
Printed in the United States of America
All Rights Reserved

ISBN 0-8163-1698-8

99 00 01 02 03 • 5 4 3 2 1

Dedication

This book is lovingly dedicated
to my Bhai,
Birendra Shrestha;
His wife, Sharmila; and their daughter, Elisa Marie.
From your Didi and Phuphu,
Céleste.

———————————

This book, this story, is dedicated to my grandmothers,
Marvel Castle and Clara Stoffle-Tarter,
who really know how to show rather than tell when it
comes to love.
Eric

Acknowledgment

I would like to thank my friend Kurt Matthews for his help with Amy's court scenes. And my friend Rich Edison for loaning me a book all about Ebola and USAMRIID, which helped in writing about the Cartier virus, which is fictional (aren't you glad?). CpW

Section I

Chaos and shock rocks the nation. Reeling from the assassination of their president, citizens who have gathered for the rally in the capital, and those across the country following the events with disbelief, look toward a future of uncertainty. Only one bright spot shines like a beacon to point the way—Donald Thurgood's miraculous recovery proves that "Someone" is still in control. Though most people are too stunned to venture more than mere speculation about the day's events and what the future holds, those who have reached any conclusions are careful to keep them quiet for the time being while they wait to see what will happen next.

In the confusion following the explosion, Dani Talbot and Mara Benneton are hustled through the congestion of the city into protective custody by the FBI. Randy Burton is rushed to the hospital, a hero for saving a busload of children and a failure for not succeeding in protecting the president . . . while Brian Willis mysteriously disappears without a trace.

Gavin Larson and his United Religious Coalition seem to be the only source of stability in a nation that is spiraling into turmoil. Does the nation need a spiritual rebirth to be saved?

Only one group of people truly realizes what is happening in the world. They are huddled around radios and television sets, watching with a mixture of worry and hope. They have expected these events for a long time, and they know what is coming. They have only one question—are they ready?

Chapter One

Saturday, November 20

Mara sat in a plush chair in the hotel room where she and Dani had been placed "under surveillance" by the FBI immediately following Jack's death and the explosion of the bus the day before. She massaged her temples, ignored her headache, and watched Dani sleep. The girl had dark smudges beneath her eyes, and her cheeks were hollow. Her face was pasty in the dim glow of the night light. In the seventeen hours since her father's death, she had not cried once.

Pushing herself up from the chair, Mara paced anxiously. It would be dawn soon, and she had to get out of this place. The face of the FBI director floated, detached and scornful, in her mind. What was his name? Eldrich? Albright? Something like that. After three hours of intense questioning, he had done all but come out and say that Dani was lying. He certainly did not act as though he placed any credibility in her at all. Yet, he had hustled them to this hotel room and stationed two agents at the only entrance to the room, and there was another in the lobby, for more security.

"We will discuss the details tomorrow," he had answered when she asked how long they were going to be detained there. *"After all, you are in no hurry. It will be impossible to book a flight out of this city for at least a week because of the backlog from the rally."*

Mara had hoped against all hope that he was wrong, but although she'd spent two hours on the phone with the airlines begging them to find her seats and some room in the cargo bay for a casket, she was empty-handed. They all assured her they were sorry, particularly in light of who she was and, more importantly, who she was traveling with, since Jack's heroism had made Dani instantly famous. The soonest, the very soonest, they could fly Mara and Dani out was a week from Monday. Jack's body could be squeezed in on a flight in the middle of the week, would that suit?

Not hardly, but she'd had no other choice. It was a week from Monday or at a later date. Fortunately, the man at the funeral parlor had been very sympathetic and understanding. He would keep Jack there as long as necessary, providing he obtained permission from the next of kin for embalming. He offered to make the arrangements with the airline for transportation of the body to a funeral home in Idaho where it would be held until they arrived to set up a funeral service. This, he informed her, was likely to be a large affair, considering that Jack was a police officer and had died such a heroic death, and did she want to authorize the funeral-home director on the receiving end to make all the necessary arrangements?

Her head whirling with the enormity of death and its obligations, Mara agreed weakly, gave him her UBC number, and hung up the phone. She would have preferred to tell Dani nothing. The girl didn't seem to want to talk much about Jack, and Mara was afraid that sooner or later she was going to melt down about it. She was keeping too much inside. It wasn't healthy. But the funeral director had wanted to come over immediately with the necessary papers to sign, so it couldn't be helped. At least that was out of the way.

Dani stirred, blinked, rubbed at her eyes, and slowly sat up, looking blankly around her. "Where am I?" she mumbled.

Mara walked over to the couch and sat down beside her, putting an arm around her shoulder even though Dani stiffened like an irritated feline. "We're at a hotel, remember? The FBI put us here? After the explosion yesterday?"

Dani stared owlishly at her. "You mean after that jerk at the FBI told me I was hallucinating about the Freedom Society?"

"Um, well, yeah," Mara agreed.

Dani shook off her arm. "Is there anything to eat here?"

Mara shrugged. "I don't think so. But there's a little kitchen. I'll run out and get a few things."

It was almost a relief to get away from Dani. She had no trouble talking the agent at the door into letting her go, but the respite was too brief. There was a corner store just a few blocks down, and she stocked up on healthy breakfast items. She was back at the hotel within fifteen minutes.

"Would you like an egg?" she asked, emptying the grocery bags onto the counter and moving around the kitchen swiftly, finding juice glasses and plates and eating utensils.

"I guess," Dani said, flipping through the paper that one of the agents had brought her while Mara was gone. Besides grunting an answer now and then, she said very little the entire time Mara fixed and then served her breakfast. Mostly, she read the paper or stared into space.

With nothing to distract her mind, Mara found herself replaying the events from the day before over and over, and she couldn't help wondering what had happened to the man who had saved the children. His name was Burton. Randy Burton. She'd treated him until the paramedics arrived.

Maybe she could go see him. It would get her out of the

hotel for a while and let Dani have some private time to reflect. Well, it was a good excuse, anyway. It took her three phone calls to find out where he was, and she reflected that all this dodging around was making her into a pretty good sleuth.

She cleared her throat and Dani glanced up, bored. "I'm going to go and visit someone," she announced.

"Who?" Dani asked bluntly.

"Randy Burton."

"You mean the guy from the bus?"

"Yeah. He's at the Washington Hospital Center."

"Oh." All right. When will you be back?"

"In a couple hours at the most," Mara replied. "I just want to say Hi and Thanks. I don't know the man. I doubt we'll talk too long. Then I might go do some research at the Library of Congress."

Quickly she gathered her coat, wallet, mittens, and a scarf. Dani watched her go, with no emotion displayed on her face. "I'll be back soon," Mara promised.

She walked out onto the street with a feeling of release. She was free for a couple of hours, and it felt wonderful. She started to the curb to hail a cab then changed her mind. *I'll walk to the hospital*, she decided. Turning the corner and heading toward the Washington Hospital Center, she didn't see the two men, dressed in dark colors, carrying ski masks and guns, enter the hotel lobby she'd just left. If she had, she would have run in terror.

* * *

In the comfort of his limousine, Gavin Larson read Saturday's paper, the entire first section of which had been devoted to President Fairfield's assassination. The vice president's death from the epidemic was analyzed as a background for the real story: The United States had neither a president nor vice president at the moment.

As he read on, he found himself feeling very pleased. Things were happening just as he had envisioned them. Early that morning, Speaker Thurgood had been summoned to an emergency session of Congress, where it was formally announced that the speaker was to become the next president of the United States. His swearing in was set for ten o'clock Monday morning. Gavin stared out the window and imagined what it would be like to be the president of the United States. He could accomplish so much. But could he really do much in that position? Not as much as he needed to. He would be bound by the office and constantly under the scrutiny of the press. He would have the greatest power in the world, yet not the freedom to use it, and so, in his heart of hearts, he knew he was more powerful where he was.

"Excuse me, Mr. Larson, we're on Blair Road, near the park."

Gavin pushed a button, lowering the privacy window. "Stop long enough to let that man in." He wiggled a finger at the side of the road. "Drive on as soon as he is inside."

A moment later, Gunnar Dietrich sat comfortably inside the limousine, with the privacy window rolled up.

"I'm not happy about meeting so soon," Gavin said. "You probably should have left the country for a while."

Dietrich chuckled dryly. "That's the nice thing about having the director of the FBI on the payroll, isn't it, though?"

Gavin gave him a narrow look. "I prefer to be cautious. It's taken a great deal of planning to get us this far. I don't need someone accidentally making a disaster of everything."

"Don't worry about me. I'm good at what I do."

"You're also arrogant, which is how you managed to let the girl get away. A pregnant seventeen-year-old girl, and you can't get your hands on her." Gavin shook his head disgustedly. "So don't try to convince me. We've been extremely lucky so far, though. In other words, I could be more paranoid and, consequently, more upset.

"If the vice president had not died from this disease, you would have had to kill him, and it would have been much more difficult to kill both the president and vice president at the same time, no matter how much money or resources I might have at my disposal. Speaking of which, without Shultz's monetary contributions, I don't have the money to cover any failures."

Dietrich nodded but chose not to defend himself. Gavin felt confident, and he couldn't be happier the VP had died a week earlier. The timing was perfect, and it really didn't matter to the VP. He would have been dead on this day either way.

"There *is* a matter that concerns me," Dietrich said, cocking his head to look at Gavin from the corner of his eye. "Randy Burton is still alive. Should I take care of him as I did with Watters?"

"No. It's not necessary at this point. You know that Aldridge doesn't trust me, Dietrich. That's why he insisted we let Burton in on this in the first place. He was protecting himself. At the last moment, he could have stepped in and taken credit for uncovering a plot to kill the president. Now, of course, he'll let the blame rest on Burton."

Frowning, Dietrich stared straight ahead, setting his jaw. "It nearly ruined everything," he said. "If you two want to have your petty rivalries, fine, but don't let them involve me. Burton got close. He got real close, and it got Scarpetti killed. Any closer, and he might have saved the president too. If that had happened, Kent Aldridge would have become the most distinguished FBI director since Hoover. We could all be sitting in prison right now."

Gavin shrugged. "But it didn't happen that way, did it?"

"No, it didn't! But it was awful close! I don't have any use for the FBI, but when they're in the game, they play hardball! Kent Aldridge is dangerous. He couldn't lose, and he knew it.

You just got lucky. Now let me off in Piney Creek Park."

They rode in silence for several more minutes. Gavin folded his paper and put it away, "I want that child, Dietrich. Whatever else you do from this point, make sure you don't foul this up. That girl promised her child as a token of her commitment to the Cause. And I want that child in my possession."

"Why is this particular child so important?"

Gavin turned cool eyes on Dietrich. For a long moment he didn't speak. How much could he tell? A series of visions, or, rather, vivid dreams had given him a sense of the future and had also left him deeply troubled. That uneasy feeling suddenly swallowed him again, and he felt himself yanked backward in time—willingly or unwillingly, he wasn't sure. But in the next instant he saw scenes from thousands of years ago of people making offerings to God. *"Fire,"* he heard himself mutter. When the scenes cleared from his mind, he said to Dietrich, "Because it is an offering."

"An offering? To whom?"

Gavin ignored him. "I want you to get the girl and bring her to me, alive, of course, at least until the child is born. If you do your job well, you will be rewarded far more than you could ever imagine."

For the first time, Dietrich looked pleased and also a bit excited about the unspecified prospects beyond what he was already earning for his work. "That I will do. You have no reason to worry."

Gavin had to restrain himself from reminding Dietrich again of his past failure. The limo rolled to a stop, and Dietrich opened his door and stepped out. He didn't look back as he walked away.

* * *

Dietrich needed a place to stay, a motel where there were many people, so he drove toward Baltimore. Finding the girl was his next priority, and he knew it would not be difficult. Then he remembered Gavin's reaction when he asked why he wanted the child so badly. Behind Gavin's eyes, it was as if his mind had gone someplace else. He had started to say something. *Through fire? Was that it?*

It interested him that for a moment in Gavin's car, Gavin appeared as weak and vulnerable as any man, as if he himself were actually serving someone else, someone who made him nearly tremble. He had never seen Gavin that way, and even though it had lasted for only the briefest of moments, Dietrich recognized it. It was something to keep in mind.

He booked a room in a Marriott under the false name of Ted Hauffmeyer, using a UBC issued under the same name. It was an identity he had never used before. This was another reason he didn't like the fact the FBI was involved. If Aldridge wanted to keep an eye on him, he'd have agents working overtime monitoring UBC and credit-card transactions. And he especially didn't like the idea of the country going completely to the UBC system. It would considerably restrict his freedom and anonymity.

Once he was settled in, he changed and left, returned to his car, and backtracked to Washington. He was walking toward the hospital when he saw the woman doctor from Vermont. She turned and walked away without seeing him.

* * *

Mara Benneton stood on the threshold of the door to Randy Burton's hospital room and knocked then felt foolish because he couldn't hear her. Head swathed in bandages, he was watching the afternoon news. It was close-captioned. Vases of daisies, chrysanthemums, roses, and carnations occupied all available surface space. Bright helium balloons were tied to the bedrail and chairs. Hundreds of cards decorated the walls, like an enormous decoupage of thanksgiving.

She cradled a bouquet of flowers a little tighter and stepped into the room. Standing awkwardly beside his bed, she reached out hesitantly and touched his arm. He jumped, and his eyes were wide as he turned to her. After a second, recognition swept over his face.

"Hi," he said. "For me?" He indicated the flowers.

Mara glanced at them. "Oh, yeah, for you," she said, handing him the bouquet.

His fingers moved nervously over the flowers, and he watched her face, waiting. Mara opened her mouth to speak and then clamped it shut again. Glancing at him sideways, she found his clear blue eyes studying her, curious. It was more than a curious look, though; he seemed to enjoy looking at her. Suddenly embarrassed, he looked away and pointed to a pad of writing paper and a pen on the bedside stand. Apparently people used it to communicate with him.

"No, thanks," Mara said, her hands trying to keep up with her words in the best pidgin sign language she could manage. "Um, I just wanted to see how you were doing."

"I'm fine," he said. "I was really lucky." He hesitated. "No, luck had nothing to do with it. Fortunate is a better word. There's no damage the doctors can't fix."

"What you did was very brave," she said, signing. She felt tears sting her eyes and wondered in mortification if she might break down and cry in front of him. "Very brave. I wanted to thank you. For all the people you saved."

He reached out and placed one hand over hers silencing her words. She felt a jolt like electricity run up her arm. "I just did my job," he said firmly. "Maybe it seemed brave to you and all those people watching. But it was just my job. I don't know if I would have done the same thing if it wasn't in the line of duty. I'd certainly like to think so." He shook his head gingerly. "I just don't know. I feel like I failed. If I had done my job better, I might have prevented it altogether, and President Fairfield would still be alive. I didn't figure it out in time. So I appreciate your sentiments, but I'm no hero. It makes me uncomfortable to think about it. Now, do you think we can talk about something else?"

Mara swallowed the rebuff and wished for a quick escape from the room. "Sure. How 'bout those Bills?" she said flippantly, trying to cover her discomfort.

His eyes locked with hers, and for an agonizing second nothing happened. She thought it would be a good idea to leave if she couldn't say the right thing; she hadn't come to make him more miserable.

Quite unexpectedly, she caught a faint twinkle in his eyes, and then he couldn't help himself and laughed out loud. Mara relaxed slightly. Suddenly he seemed more . . . human. "Aw, come on, you don't really follow football, do you?" His smile was contagious. "Besides, don't you know what BILLS stand for? Boy-I-Love-Losing-Superbowls. They haven't got a chance even if they do make it."

Mara chuckled. "OK, you've got me. I'm not much of a football fan," she signed.

"Now I'm curious. What are you into?" He was watching her intently, but it didn't bother her.

She shrugged one shoulder. "I don't know. Helping, I guess." Hesitating, she picked up the pen and paper. *I work at a welfare clinic in Vermont.*

"What do you do for fun?"

Mara smiled and pointed again at the paper. "I told you." *I work at a welfare clinic.*

"Ah, a workaholic," he said, defining her life in one word.

"A lot of good it's done me," she said, knowing the bitterness in her voice was lost on him. "Lately I think I missed out on a lot. Now maybe it's too late to catch up." The puzzled look on his face told her she had either said too much or her sign language wasn't making sense.

"Why do you think it's too late?" he asked.

Mara looked around and glanced at her watch. "I'm prob-

ably not supposed to stay here too long and tire you out. Maybe
I should be going."

"Sit," Randy said, tightening his grip on her hand. "Please."

Obediently, Mara pulled a chair over and seated herself
next to his bed. "Now what do you mean you think it's too
late? You haven't got only six months to live, have you?" He
was serious and concerned. Mara shook her head. Relieved,
he leaned toward her until his head almost touched hers.
"Have *I* got six months to live?"

Mara choked back a horrified laugh. "I don't think it's anything to joke about!"

"Are you going to tell me?"

"My sign language isn't that good."

He pushed the pad of paper toward her. "So write it down.
Come on. I want to know."

Mara hesitated and then took the pad. She wrote: *I've been
reading my Bible a lot lately, and I think the world will end
soon. And I'm not sure I'm ready.* The pen wavered over the
paper, and then she set it down and handed the pad to him,
waiting nervously while he read.

You think I'm crazy, her hands signed.

"No, I think you may be right," came his quiet reply. "My
sister, Lynn, gave me a Bible awhile back, and I started reading it too. I thought the same thing." Reaching over to his
bedside stand, he rummaged under a stack of papers and
pulled out a Bible, whose paper covers had been torn off. "Look
here," he said, flipping the pages to the end.

His fingers followed the words, and Mara bent forward to
look at them. "But woe to the earth and the sea, because the
devil has gone down to you! He is filled with fury, because he
knows that his time is short." He looked up. "I think that's
where we are now."

Randy gestured above him to the screen of the television,
which was tuned to CNN. Mara didn't need the sound to recognize yet another disaster being reported. The news was full

of them these days. He regarded her soberly. "The time is short."

Mara felt a chill chase up and down her spine as he confirmed her thoughts. It was one thing to secretly believe something, but it was quite another to have someone agree with you—out loud.

The silence between them lengthened, but it was not an uneasy silence. It was comforting to be lost in your thoughts and know they were shared. Mara brushed a strand of red hair back behind one ear and smiled slightly. It was as if on this shelf of common ground they had found a place to stand together and become friends. And she wasn't sure why, but being friends with Randy Burton was something she wanted very much.

"A penny for your thoughts," he offered.

Mara laughed. "They'd cost a lot more than that," she said. Taking the pad, she wrote, *I'd probably better get going, though. I wanted to drop by the Library of Congress before I go back to my hotel, and I don't dare leave Dani alone too long, or she might run away again. At least now, she'd have a harder time of it.*

"The pregnant girl?" Randy asked. "The one who's father was shot and killed by Scarpetti?" Suddenly, Randy's expression shifted from warmth to anger; then he looked both saddened and full of admiration for Jack Talbot. "I heard he was a policeman from Idaho. Was that true? He saved my life, Mara."

Yes, that was Dani. Her father was a policeman. She ran away from me once. She's got good reason, I suppose. It's not safe for her here in Washington. She knows too much about the assassination attempt. The FBI have her under protective custody until we can book a flight out of the city. I'm going to fly with her back to her home in Idaho.

"Soon?"

Mara thought she could detect a hint of disappointment in

his voice, and her heart jumped. *As soon as we can*, she wrote. *All the flights have been booked pretty solid for the next week getting people who came for the rally out of here. It's been a madhouse. There's just no way to leave. The airlines have been very sympathetic, though. They think they will be able to fly us out a week from Monday. That's the soonest they can manage unless someone cancels.*

Just as she lifted her pen from the paper and her eyes to his face, she realized they were no longer alone. Randy was looking over her shoulder. Mara turned to see who had entered the room, and her heart dropped. A pretty young woman and an elderly lady hung back as if they were afraid they might be disturbing something. Randy's wife? Girlfriend? Mara leapt to her feet, flushing with embarrassment.

"Lynn!" Randy said. "Alice. I'm so glad you came."

The young woman skirted the bed and leaned over to hug Randy for what seemed an eternity. When she straightened up, Mara could see she was crying. The elderly woman looked on compassionately.

"Has Alice been taking care of you, Sis?" Randy asked, but Mara didn't catch the rest of the exchange. The woman was his *sister.* Suddenly she felt much better, relieved. The elderly woman, Alice, stepped closer to the bed, and Mara began to feel like an outsider. She moved toward the door, but Randy called her back.

"Where are my manners? You'd think they'd been dislocated like my knee. Mara Benneton, this is my sister, Lynn, and her friend, *our* friend, Alice Nolan. She's been giving Lynn Bible studies and, well, just being friendly." His voice softened as he looked at the woman, and she smiled warmly. "She's got a soft spot for people who are hurting in many ways."

"I wish you could help Dani," Mara blurted out and then felt foolish. As if Dani would accept help from anyone. Alice was, as Randy had said, a Christian, and Dani seemed to object particularly to Christians.

"I would be happy to help in any way I could," Alice said hastily. She scribbled her name, address, and a phone number, using Randy's pad of paper, and handed the information to Mara. "You tell your friend to get in touch with me if she needs anything—food, shelter, clothes, or just a sympathetic ear. I'm a member of the Remnant Church, so if I can't help her, others will be able to. And they would love to."

"Alice is a real good listener," Lynn added shyly. Her eyes crept up and met Mara's. They were filled with curiosity. Mara decided she liked Lynn.

Mara smiled at Alice. "Thanks, I'll tell her. That's very kind." Mara placed the paper in a pocket of her coat and stood uncertainly. "It was nice meeting you—all of you," she said, sure she was blushing.

"It was nice meeting you too," Randy agreed. "You'll come back, won't you?"

"Sure," Mara said. "I'll come back."

"You keep reading your Bible, and the next time you come, we'll talk about it some more. OK?"

Mara nodded. "OK. Bye." Before she convinced herself she really didn't need to leave immediately, she forced her feet to carry her to the door. By a comparable effort of will, she also managed not to look back. Why did she always feel so immature around nice men? Suddenly, she was that gawky high school girl who could never get a date and lost all power of reason and intellect around boys. Emotions could be such powerful things.

* * *

At four in the afternoon, the limo pulled into Donald Thurgood's circular driveway. Secret Service agents poured out of the house, and there were others roaming the perimeter or stationed across the street. Two Suburbans were in the driveway ahead of Gavin, and two agents, a man and woman, made his driver stay put while others opened Gavin's door asking for identification. The woman radioed the house, and Gavin was cleared.

Thurgood met Gavin at the front door and led him to the study. Donald Thurgood looked healthier than Gavin had ever seen him, even considering he had worked for the man for over a decade.

"Sit, Gavin." Thurgood made a couple of drinks and brought one to Gavin. "Cheers."

"Cheers," Gavin said, smiling. He looked around. "Packing?"

"Not me. No professional movers, either. Secret Service seems to be able to do just about everything."

"Except," Gavin reminded Thurgood with a wink, "protect the president."

Thurgood sank into his leather recliner. "Right. There is that. They're smarting pretty badly over it too."

"I'd like to imagine." Gavin chuckled. Thurgood didn't.

"It's not so amusing when you're the one who's supposed to be protected next," Thurgood pointed out.

"Ah, right. I see your point," Gavin said with amusement. "To be sworn in as president of the United States . . . I can just imagine how you will feel Monday morning, Donald." He narrowed his eyes suddenly. "You won't forget me, will you?"

"Just how should I remember you?" Thurgood replied warily.

"Chief of Staff. I want to be the right hand of the man with the power."

"That will mean replacing Walt Harburg, of course," Thurgood said.

"I'm well aware of that, Donald. But this should not be difficult. He did lose his president. No one will question your replacing him first thing with someone who is as competent as me."

"You're a powerful man, Gavin. Wouldn't it be better for

you to stay clear of an office and continue to lead the Coalition? I'm not sure what I expected at the rally, Friday, but I know I didn't expect such a turnout. There must have been over a million people on the Mall and the surrounding park areas, all the way to the Lincoln Memorial. Full media coverage too."

"I will still head the Coalition."

"That would be a severe conflict of interest."

Gavin eyed Thurgood for a long moment. "You know, Donald, I get the impression you are not pleased with the prospect of having me nearby. Have you forgotten already how you came to be in this remarkable position?"

For a defiant moment, Thurgood stared across at Gavin then lowered his eyes. Thurgood had never been a puppet to any man, woman, or organization; he had survived so long in Congress by unquestionable integrity and sheer determination. His honesty was legendary. Service to the American people had always been his desire, never service to himself. But the presidency was in his grasp, closer than he had ever dreamed possible. He had held this dream dear to his heart in his earlier years, but he was beaten twice in presidential primaries because he lacked the funds for a truly effective campaign.

Yes, he had to admit to himself, the reason he would be sworn in as president of the United States on Monday was because of Gavin Larson. He was to become president but not the president he could have been.

"Maybe I won't take an office after all," Gavin conceded shrewdly. "Chief of Staff might be too restrictive." He grinned across at Thurgood, pleased to death with himself. Oh, how easily he could manipulate the next president. "I will let you know what I plan to do, Donald." He set his glass on the table beside his chair and stood. "Don't rule anything out. Walt Harburg's job is safe for a while, but when I come to you with my decision, be ready—and willing?"

Thurgood nodded. As he stood, Gavin thought the man didn't look as strong and confident as he had just a few minutes earlier. He looked rather weak and timid, and Gavin decided what he had come to do had been successfully accomplished. He owned the president, and the president would do whatever Gavin wanted. Gavin felt so good about the arrangement he put his arm around Thurgood as they walked to the front door.

* * *

Mara made her way out of the hospital. Standing on the curb, she tried to decide whether or not she should walk. It was tempting to call a cab but also dangerous, she had found out. She zipped up her coat and determined to walk. It would be a long walk. Coming here it hadn't seemed so bad; now she was tired, and the cold felt . . . colder. She just wanted to get back and rest.

Even though Randy Burton had heroically saved many lives, he had been taken to the Washington Hospital Center, far removed from the scene of the blast. Emergency personnel had radioed every hospital in between and were told the same thing each time: full to capacity. Scores of people attending the rally had collapsed from dehydration. Several had had heart attacks and some strokes. The brutal crush of people, the sheer mass of bodies, made rescue extremely difficult. Most were taken to the closest hospital, filling those nearest the Mall first. Fortunately, the people sick from the virus had already been transferred to special containment centers, or there would have been no room at any hospital.

Mara dodged a drunk sprawled across the sidewalk and then stopped. His coat was hanging open, exposing his bare chest to the bitter temperature. Quickly, she bent down, and holding her breath against the alcoholic vapors wafting over her with each breath he exhaled, she buttoned his coat. Unknowing and uncaring, he rolled over and embraced the sidewalk. Mara walked on.

As she passed the stone façade of a Catholic church, its bells tolled "Praise to the Lord." Changing her direction, she ran up the steps and into the church. The interior was dimly lighted, and her footsteps echoed as she made her way up a side aisle and to an alcove shining with the flickering lights of hundreds of candles. The church smelled strongly of incense, wood polish, and beeswax. And there was a musty, underlying smell of age.

Mara noticed that the coin boxes had been replaced with a black box whose high-tech appearance contrasted the age-old traditions of the church. She stepped closer to the box and noticed it was for UBC cards. Fishing hers out of her wallet, she swiped it through the machine and waited for it to be processed.

When asked how many candles she wished to purchase, she entered the number five and waited. A receipt churned out, and she pocketed it. A buzz accompanied the *kachink* of the match box unlatching. Mara selected one of the long matchsticks and held it to a burning candle to ignite it. Then, choosing five candles, she lighted them and knelt to pray before an altar of the Virgin Mary.

She looked at the statue a long time. She wanted to pray— for herself, for Dani, for Randy, for Amy, and for Jack's soul. But not a word left her lips. They were jammed up inside her, and all she could do was kneel and stare at the statue of Mary. Blessed Mary who deserved no prayers, who could answer no prayers, who was just as dead as Jack Talbot.

Where was he? Where was she? What was on the other side of death? Were they there already? In heaven? Waiting for the rest of them? Or were they just sleeping as Dani claimed.

"My father's not in heaven," Dani had insisted bitterly. "My father is sleeping."

"Dani, you're wrong," Mara had tried to comfort Dani more for her sake than the girl's. "He was a good man. He will be in heaven."

"I didn't say he wouldn't be in heaven," Dani argued. "Just that he isn't there now."

"Why on earth do you think your father is in purgatory after what he did? The man gave his life to save others. He's not in purgatory," Mara insisted.

"He's not in purgatory either," Dani had told her, getting belligerent and frustrated at the same time. "He's just sleeping. In his casket. Until Jesus comes back. Don't you know anything?"

And Mara had for once shut her mouth. Maybe she didn't know anything after all. It wouldn't be the first Catholic doctrine she'd held dear that didn't stand up under close scrutiny. But where did you go about finding the answers so you could know, if not everything, then a reasonable amount? She was sick of being made a fool of by a sarcastic, caustic, seventeen-year-old self-professed unbeliever.

And she was still tired of it. As all the foundational rocks of Catholicism crumbled around her, she felt dizzy and disoriented. She sagged against the railing. A metallic ping jolted her head up.

An old priest had entered the area where the candles were. He was taking out the metal tabs that remained in the votive holders after the candle had burned up, replacing them with fresh candles. He had a kind face and watery blue eyes. A halo of white hair ringed his head, and while she watched him, he met her gaze and smiled.

"Can I help you, my daughter?" he asked gently.

Mara was tempted to tell him; he was a priest, and she trusted him. Or did she? As the words formed in her mind, she suddenly decided not to tell him about her questions. "No, thank you, Father. I think I'll have to figure this one out on my own."

"We're never alone, my dear. The angels and saints and our dear mother, Mary, are always there to help us. Ask them for help, but also, don't be afraid to confide in an old priest. I just might be able to help too."

Mara nodded and avoided his eyes. He only meant to help, but she sensed that if she opened up to him, he would make light of her intense quest for knowledge, for truth. In her experience, it was not a quality nurtured by the Catholic Church. "Thank you, Father," she said.

Standing, she made her way back out of the church. A priest entered the confessional box, and a parishioner followed. Otherwise, the great vaulted interior of the church was empty except for a man dressed in black. His face was averted. He bowed his closely shaved head as she passed him. Walking by she could clearly see a tattoo of broken barbed wire on the wrist of one of his hands, now clasped in prayer.

Like frozen snapshots ripping in quick succession through her mind, she replayed the scene outside the clinic. A man walking across the street, shooting at her. The *ping* of the bullets as they slapped the car and the pavement. The taste of blood in her mouth, the way her nails broke as she clawed at the door of the car, trying to get in. The crazy careening of the car as she had punched the gas pedal racing death.

Her heartbeat was a dull whoosh in her ears as the memories flooded back. *Look up!* she thought, slowing her steps. *Look up, you coward!*

It was him.

She was sure of it. It was Dietrich. The man who had tried to kill her and Dani. Every muscle tense, she lengthened her stride until she was almost running. She wanted to look back, but fear froze her eyes straight ahead. The solid oak of the door was just a few feet ahead. Two strides, one stride.

Her fingers reached out and grabbed the iron handle, pushing the massive door open enough to allow her to squeeze through. She glanced over her shoulder before she allowed the door to close behind her. The man in the pew was gone.

She hunched her shoulders up and strode down the side-walk. A large black limousine was parked by the side of the street. Her surroundings felt surreal. As she walked, the limo pulled up to the sidewalk and crawled along beside her. She quickened her pace, and the limo sped up. Her heart caught in her throat as a darkened window slid down.

"Please, Dr. Benneton, there is no need for alarm." The man's head tipped to one side, catching the waning light of the cloudy day and highlighting his strong, handsome fea-tures and black hair. "Kent Aldridge, director of the FBI. I want to talk to you about the girl."

Mara's terror took a new twist. "FBI? What happened? Did Dani run away again? Is she OK? What is it?"

"Dr. Benneton, please, this is hardly the kind of thing we should be discussing on the street. Would you please get into the limo?" With a low hum, the dark window rose and the door opened.

Mara stepped hesitantly into the vehicle. She clutched her stomach, feeling queasy, and looked at the man opposite her. It was the same disdainful, skeptical face she remembered from the hours after the explosion and Jack's death. This was the "jerk" who had refused to believe Dani had been a mem-ber of the Freedom Society or that they had had any part in the assassination. He seemed to chalk her testimony up to the flighty nature of a teenager. Mara didn't trust him. "Well?"

Kent Aldridge arranged his hands on his lap calmly and composed his face before he spoke, giving Mara the distinct impression that what was going to come out of his mouth was well-rehearsed. "I'm afraid there has been an attempt on Miss Talbot. We are unsure if it was by the Freedom Society she *claims* to have been a member of or another party. However, my men acted quickly and were able to avert any disaster. She has been moved to a new location."

Mara let out her breath in relief and eyed him warily.

Throughout this whole ordeal it seemed that no one took Dani's story about the Freedom Society seriously. Whenever the subject came up it was downplayed, as if it was out of the question. "Where is she?"

He pursed his lips. "That is classified information."

"No kidding," Mara shot back, beginning to dislike him intensely. "But, I'm staying with her, like a guardian, remember? Since her father . . ."

"Yes, it was tragic, her father, already wounded in the service of his fellow man, giving his life like that to save those children." His tongue made a sympathetic clucking sound. "Tragic. However, we have decided that in Danielle's best interest, it would be better to separate the two of you. We have placed her, and I am here to take you to your new temporary residence."

"My new . . ." Mara's voice whistled off. Something was not right here, but she couldn't figure out what it was. Maybe her instincts were being tainted by the bad taste she had in her mouth talking to Aldridge. Maybe she was overreacting, paranoid. "I think I saw him just now," she said.

Aldridge straightened up, a keen light coming into his eyes like a hawk spying a squirrel. "Him? Who?"

"Dietrich. That killer, that's who," Mara snapped. "He was in the church just now."

Aldridge's eyelids dropped down, and he seemed to be thinking about something else. "Was he now. And you think he was following you?"

"What else am I supposed to think? That he just got religion?" She felt increasingly helpless and frustrated. "He's after Dani, and he thinks that he can get to her through me."

"Precisely why the two of you need to be separated," Aldridge agreed enthusiastically as if she were being difficult.

Mara hunched up into the corner of the plush limo and glared at Aldridge. This didn't seem to perturb him. He smiled faintly and hummed but had the vacant look of someone whose mind was occupied elsewhere. "Where am I going to stay now?"

"Hmm?" He started and then came to himself, as if just being reminded that there was someone else in the limo. "Oh, no need to concern yourself with the details, Mara, may I call you Mara?"

"Yes, there is," she said with forced politeness, "and no you may not. How, for instance, will I know how to get from one place to another if I don't know where I'm starting from?"

"Going? You won't be *going* anywhere," Aldridge said. "I don't want you to budge from your suite. That's precisely why I feel we're in the predicament we're in right now; you've been wandering around too much, being too visible. I don't know who is following you or why, but they are certainly not stupid. I will have a detail of agents stationed at the hotel, and they can fetch and carry for you anything your little heart desires."

Mara felt her body stiffen and expand with rage. "Do you mean to tell me I'm going to be a prisoner?" she asked hotly. "Stuffed away somewhere until Monday? I can't do that. I'll die!"

"Dr. Benneton," his voice was icy now, "if you don't, there is a good possibility that you *will* die, and then what good would you do Danielle?"

It seemed she had been defeated, and she sank against the upholstery, outwardly irritated, inwardly her mind churning out options. She could run. At the next stoplight she could bolt out of the car and run. Or she could try Dani's trick of running away later. Or she could call someone to rescue her. She could call . . . Who could she call?

Amy Cooper? Amy Cooper!

Like a poker player trying to hide a royal flush, Mara forced her features to remain the same. "I'm sorry if I've seemed difficult, Director Aldridge, but it's just that I don't know what I'm going to do with myself until Monday. I'll be so bored. What if . . ."

Aldridge regarded her benevolently, lifting his eyebrows in a patronizing expression of curiosity. "What if what?" he asked obligingly, taking the bait.

"Well, it's just that I've been doing a lot of research on this virus, and I think I could be of some help if I could study it further."

"I hardly see how this could affect your situation."

"What if," Mara continued, as if she hadn't heard him, "I was to go stay at Fort Detrick, at USAMRIID? I have colleagues there. I could work. You wouldn't have to worry about me or waste personnel trying to protect me. It would save the taxpayers' money for more important things, and I would have something to occupy my mind until I left. I might even be able to do some good."

Aldridge's eyes narrowed as he contemplated her suggestion. His face contorted, and she could see his mind chewing over the idea like a toothless dog with a grisly piece of meat. Either Director Aldridge wasn't a quick-witted man or he had too many different angles to consider. After an almost uncomfortable pause, he nodded. "I'll tell you what, Doctor. I will make the arrangements, but you will have to spend the night at the suite we have prepared first. If the folk at Fort Detrick agree, I will have someone pick you up in the morning and take you over. You can stay there until your flight leaves on Monday."

Yes! Mara thought. Fort Detrick wasn't freedom, but it was certainly going to be easier to construct and execute whatever plan she came up with from there than it would be from some confining hotel suite at some unknown location in the city. She settled back in her seat and then remembered the slip of paper Alice had given her for Dani. She pulled it out of her pocket and handed it to Director Aldridge. She didn't totally trust him, but there wasn't any other opportunity to get the note to Dani.

"Director Aldridge, I wonder if you might do me a favor?

Would you see that Dani gets this? It's a referral for a woman obstetrician I know here in D.C. in case she needs to see one, you know, if there's an emergency. This woman is good." Mara felt guilty for the deception as Aldridge took the note without interest, but she hoped that Dani would get the message: *Run away. Run to Alice.*

"Certainly," Aldridge murmured. He settled back in his seat and paid her no further attention. Mara watched the scenes of the city flash past the window and tried to figure out what was bothering her about Director Aldridge, the Freedom Society, and Dietrich.

* * *

Dietrich recognized Director Aldridge's car immediately as it pulled away with Mara Benneton. This front-end approach of Kent Aldridge's frustrated him. He'd not kept his dislike of the FBI director a secret, as Gavin well knew, but he seemed to be having a difficult time convincing Gavin that Director Aldridge could be dangerous to them. He returned to his car and tried to catch up to Aldridge, but it was far too late, and the director's security team was too proficient not to notice a tail. He turned around and headed back to his hotel in Baltimore, remembering he could not be too careful.

* * *

Dani Talbot pushed herself up from the plush velvet couch and made her way to the massive hotel suite window that overlooked the city of Washington, D.C. The sky was a blur of steel gray, and a high wind whistled faintly past the window. Far below, it seemed as if the people scurried around like restless ants.

She touched her fingertips lightly on the glass of the window, just beyond which was freedom. Beginning to pace anxiously in front of the window, she wondered if she was ever going to experience that freedom again. It seemed ironic that here in the capital of the United States, the nucleus of freedom, she should be held captive. She seemed to be getting kicked from one disaster to another, always out of control of her life.

"It's for your own protection," the FBI director had told her. *"Just until you leave on Monday."*

But his eyes said something different. Dani had seen that look many times on Dietrich's face, and she knew exactly what it meant. He was hiding something. In the aftershock of fear, when the FBI agents wrestled two intruders to the ground and hustled her out to a waiting car, she had followed them blindly. She trusted they had her best interests in mind. After all, they had put their own lives at stake protecting her.

But why was their car waiting?

And how had they procured this suite so quickly?

There had been no hesitation about where to bring her. Less than thirty minutes from the time of the attack she had been comfortably ensconced in this nice suite. Agents were stationed at the doors, and that should have made her feel safe. Instead, it made her feel like a prisoner. Security was much tighter. They told her she couldn't leave, and she was sure the rooms were bugged, but in her amateur inspection, she had been unable to find out for sure. Or maybe she'd just seen too many movies.

What she didn't understand was why they wanted her. If they were the Freedom Society, then she could understand, but this was the FBI. What did they want with a pregnant teenager? Even if they had known who she was in the Freedom Society, the only thing they would want her for would be as an accomplice to Shultz's murder. And so far she had been unable to get anyone to believe she had even witnessed Stan Shultz's murder despite the fact that she matched the description of a witness seen fleeing the scene. It was as if they didn't *want* to know what she knew about Shultz's murder or the Freedom Society's involvement in the assassination.

The other concern preying on her mind was Mara. She said she was going to visit the man who had saved the school children, and then she was going to do some research. She was supposed to be back, and yet no one had spoken of her. Was she coming back? What had happened to her? What would she do when she returned to the hotel room and found Dani and the agents gone?

Thinking about Mara brought to mind her father, and Dani felt the same dull ache in the pit of her stomach that she had felt almost constantly since the shooting. She hadn't cried, even though Mara and others encouraged her to. What they didn't realize was that she *couldn't* cry. She didn't *want* to cry.

Her father had done exactly what he had wanted to do, disregarding what was best for her from the beginning, just like he always had. Now, here she was stuck in Washington, D.C., at the mercy of the FBI to protect her from the Freedom Society they didn't believe she belonged to. And why? Because her father had been more interested in saving a bunch of kids than in protecting his daughter and her baby.

No, she wasn't about to cry.

Dani's head throbbed with the beginnings of a hormone headache, and her hips ached from standing too long. She made her way into the kitchenette and drew a glass of cold water from the tap. Even the flat taste of city water seemed refreshing. She decided to try to stop thinking for a while, take a shower to relax, and get some sleep. Tomorrow she would figure out what to do about her current predicament.

2—M.H.

Chapter Two

Sunday, November 21

Mara tried to relax in the plush leather interior of the limo. This time an agent rode with her and Director Aldridge. He maintained a polite silence. Aldridge, beyond a few clipped words of greeting, ignored her as well. Mara felt knots twisting in her stomach that had nothing to do with the lack of sleep she'd gotten the night before in the luxurious hotel suite they'd put her up in. Or the fact that she'd had nothing more for breakfast than a perfect orange from the overflowing fruit basket in her room.

Aldridge cleared his throat and looked at her. "Dr. Benneton, how well do you know Colonel Cooper?"

Mara shrugged. "We were good friends in college. We studied together a lot. Ate pizza. Pulled pranks. Like all college kids."

"Was Colonel Cooper a religious woman?"

"Religious? Amy?" Mara thought back. "I think her family was Methodist, but from what I understand, they didn't go to church for the religion. It was more of a society thing. You know, contacts and appearances and that sort of thing. It looked good, and her family was pretty well off, so they did what looked good."

He nodded as if he understood. "And now, would you say she's religious now?"

Mara tried to follow his line of reasoning. She recalled with clarity her conversation with Amy at the Mall. *"We've started going to church. We think God is trying to tell the country something."* Somehow she didn't think it was in Amy's best interest for her to tell Aldridge that.

"Amy was an old college friend," she answered vaguely. "We've hardly kept in touch at all these past few years. I am not privy to her religious convictions. I'm really not the best person to ask. Why do you want to know?" she finished boldly.

Aldridge scrutinized her face carefully. "Let's just say that while you're there, we would appreciate it if you would keep your eyes and ears open and pass on any information you think we might be interested in knowing. In exchange for your safety, and Dani's safety, for the next week. That's not too much to ask, is it?"

Mara bit back the sharp retort on the tip of her tongue and swallowed hard to keep her anger in check. "Are you threatening me?" she asked.

"Threatening?" His face showed mild surprise at the very suggestion. "Not at all. We are exchanging services." He smiled broadly. "Safety for information. Are we clear, Doctor?"

Mara nodded stiffly. She was clear. She was very clear.

* * *

Not being able to hear was the worst physical impediment he'd ever had to endure, even if the doctors did think it was temporary. Worse than not being able to hold a normal conversation had been not being aware of who came and went unless he saw them. Sleep was difficult not only because he was already well rested after the first day but because he couldn't convince himself to be so vulnerable. A nurse could drop a food tray beside his bed, and he would never know it.

And that was not all that disturbed him. His dreams, when he finally slept, were nightmares that magnified his inability to save the president from the tragic bombing that had taken her life. Yet, he was left in complete and total silence to relive it over and over, until the enormous weight of failure brought him slowly out of his troubled sleep.

The only bright spots in his life had been seeing Lynn, Alice . . . and Mara. Lynn came to visit often, sometimes with Alice, who assured him repeatedly he was a hero, apologizing upon entering and before leaving for the rotten things she'd thought of him. Alice had taken Lynn in, for which he was extremely grateful. He was also happy that Lynn's withdrawal symptoms where diminishing and that she seemed well on her way to beating her heroin addiction. Lynn had told him how constantly she and Alice were praying about it, and she could feel how much God was helping her.

Another of the more significant benefits of Lynn's and Alice's visits were the prayers they continually sent heavenward on his behalf. They prayed with him and for him all the time, for which he was grateful. He wasn't always sure how to react, but he decided it was important for him to allow God to work in his life, if that's what God wanted to do.

It was Sunday afternoon, shortly after Lynn had left to return to Alice's apartment. Randy was trying to read a paperback novel when the door opened and Kent Aldridge stepped in, striding over immediately to shake Randy's hand.

"Sorry I haven't been here before now," Aldridge said. "It's been a madhouse since Friday."

Randy's guilt intensified upon seeing the director. After getting most of what Aldridge had said by reading his lips, he looked away. "I can't believe how badly I failed, Mr. Aldridge.

My job was to keep my eyes and ears open in the Freedom Society and identify and stop any terrorism. I allowed President Fairfield to die. I let down the country and the Bureau."

Aldridge took out a pen and paper. *You're too hard on yourself, Burton. You saved the lives of twenty-five children. You're an excellent agent.*

Randy shook his head doubtfully.

We'll talk about this later. Right now, I need you to dictate everything that happened since you last reported to Dave Watters. Two agents right outside the door will fill out the 302s.

"Have you found the man who killed President Fairfield?" Randy asked, realizing the Bureau may be taking his statement to present to the grand jury because it already had the terrorist in custody.

Aldridge shook his head. *I'll talk to you later.* Then he turned and strode out of the room, and two agents he did not recognize entered and began to set up for a lengthy debriefing session. Randy wondered if he was up to it.

It took a few moments for it to sink in—he'd just had a visit from the director of the FBI. Had he been more successful in the field, he might have considered it an honor. But feeling that he had failed, it was more like pouring salt on an open wound. Director Aldridge had managed to come and go without giving Randy any clear idea what he was truly thinking.

The agents, a man and woman, pulled chairs up beside each other, set a recorder on the table, and got their paperwork in order. They introduced themselves as Agents Janet Roddrick and Paul Miller. Before the session began, Miller pulled a Snickers bar from his jacket pocket and unwrapped it. Roddrick looked annoyed.

"Sorry, but I haven't eaten since six o'clock this morning," Miller said. "Where's the trash, Burton?"

"Use the one next to my bed."

Miller nodded. "Thanks." He stood up, knelt down ponderously, and deposited the wrapper. Roddrick did not attempt to conceal her annoyance with the interruption.

Then for nearly two hours, Randy related his investigation into the Freedom Society's activities, reviewing his statement three times to make sure nothing had been overlooked and that the facts were clear.

At the end of the interview, Roddrick stood and pocketed the tape recorder while Miller moved their chairs.

"Has anyone heard from Brian Willis?" Randy asked.

Roddrick shrugged and shook her head.

"Be sure you thoroughly investigate Gavin Larson. That's where Willis was headed when I let him out of the car. From what he told me, I'm pretty sure there was a connection between Larson and the Freedom Society."

"Don't worry, Burton, we'll look into it. The entire WMFO (Washington Metropolitan Field Office) is working on this case, and Director Aldridge is supervising everything," Miller said.

As the two agents left, Randy thought he should feel better, but he didn't.

* * *

Yesterday and the day before had been a blur. Just now, he was finally thinking straight. The trauma of being imprisoned had turned him into a wreck, and for some time after the explosion that took President Fairfield's life, he had been in a daze. Then had come confusion, panic, and finally anger.

Sometime during Saturday night, he had awakened in the unheated, abandoned warehouse office, and for some time he thought over all that had taken place, and he tried to put it all into some kind of perspective, but it wasn't easy. Nothing flowed logically; everything was disjointed.

And then as he lay on his cot, he thought he saw it all so clearly, as if God had come to him and helped him to understand.

The rules as you know them have been changed. The devil knows his time is short, and he will unleash his fury on you in the last days.

Brian's heart quickened. Then he felt that God had impressed him with this message: *I will sustain all who love Me.*

Brian rested better after those few moments Saturday night. After he had awakened on Sunday, however, he began to worry more deeply about his family. He had not been given a chance to call Ann, though he had asked repeatedly for two days. Now, his worries were much more intense than they had been. Before, he had assumed it was all some huge, royal mistake that he'd been kidnapped. But after last night, he knew he was really imprisoned for his beliefs and that it wasn't merely by Gavin's doing that he was here. It was the devil's will.

Feeling more in control in the morning, Brian swung his legs to the floor and sat up. It had been a rough two days, and he reeked. His mouth tasted foul, and his clothes were stale and wrinkled. And for the first time, he realized he was alone. There were no other sounds save the occasional creaks and groans of the warehouse. As he considered each of these things, he came to the conclusion he was more a hostage than a prisoner of the law.

Gavin, what have you done?

Brian's next thoughts centered on his family. He imagined that Ann was worried sick by now, and he couldn't bear the thought of what his children must be thinking. He hoped Ann was calm and was protecting Matt and Hannah from worry. But he had to find some way to talk to her, to let her know he was alive but in trouble. Contacting a lawyer would help, but right now he didn't think that would be possible.

He didn't hear the guard until he unlocked the door. The man was clean-cut, tall, and wore an army cap. His eyes were quick as they glanced over the room before resting on Brian. He entered, wearing a holster but no gun, which made Brian curious, until he saw the second guard outside the door. They were very cautious, competent-looking men and treated him as if he were dangerous. He looked from the one outside to the one who'd come into the room. "Can either one of you tell me . . . why have I been kidnapped?"

The man in the baseball cap barely glanced at him as he looked around the room. He went back to the door and accepted a bag of food from KFC and a paper cup and put the bag on the cot and set the cup on the floor. Then he headed out without speaking. Brian noticed the broken-wire tattoo— *a member of the Freedom Society.*

"Wait a minute," Brian shouted.

Baseball cap turned around. "Yah?"

"Why am I here?"

"Mister, I don't know. All I know is we're supposed to keep an eye on you," he said before closing the door behind him.

Brian jumped off the bed just as the door latched. "Wait! I need to let my family know I'm all right! Come on," he yelled, "give me a phone!"

* * *

Colonel Amy Cooper, M.D., poured another cup of coffee and shuffled papers on her desk. Any minute now, Derek would be knocking on her door to let her know Mara Benneton had arrived. She'd been briefed the evening before, at home, much to her husband, Ray's, consternation, about Mara and asked to allow her to stay at Fort Detrick until a week from Monday. Mara had asked to help however she could in researching and studying the virus.

Amy ran her fingers through her short black hair and rested her head in her hands. Lately things had been going from bad to worse at USAMRIID, and the effects were beginning to show on Amy. Always thin, she had begun to drop weight she couldn't afford to lose. Ray kept after her to go

AWOL. They would disappear, he promised. Get away. Somewhere this virus hadn't touched.

If Amy had believed that such a place truly existed, she would have been more than tempted. But this was no time to run away from her problems. This one would just follow them wherever they went, and eventually it would overcome them whatever they did. No, the best thing she could do was to try her very hardest to beat this virus, to stop it for good. And she wasn't a quitter.

The anticipated knock startled her, and she jumped to her feet, sending her chair flying backward into the wall. She clasped her hands together to prevent the tremors she got in the morning from drinking too much coffee. Maybe the people at that new church she and Ray had begun going to were right. Maybe coffee was bad for you. She put the thought out of her mind, arranged her face into a welcoming smile, and opened her door.

Beyond Derek stood Mara, pale and nervous, flanked by two FBI agents, one of them Director Kent Aldridge. She had to give the man credit; he took his responsibility seriously, handling matters personally. Amy hoped Mara got the mute message she shot the first time their eyes locked. *Pretend we haven't seen each other in years,* she begged silently. No one could find out that they had, in reality, met not quite a week before at the Mall.

"Mara, how very nice to see you again. It's been such a *long* time." Amy's voice was warm and meant to sound like the voice of someone meeting an old, but distant, friend.

"Amy, I'm so sorry we didn't stay in touch. We've got so much to talk about," Mara replied, catching her pass and running with it.

"Director Aldridge," Amy said, reaching out to shake his hand. "Always glad to be of service, sir."

"Colonel Cooper, I thought of you immediately when Dr. Benneton suggested she would like to help in any way she could with this virus. I didn't realize the two of you had gone to college together."

And you still wouldn't know that if you hadn't checked it out, Amy thought angrily. *Why you think that will be of some use to you is what I want to know.* "Yes, we were in the same graduating class. We lost track of each other after school, though, didn't we, Mara? It's too bad. We had some fun times in college. Remember that cadaver . . . some other time. I don't want to spoil breakfast for you gentlemen. Mara, if you want to come with me, Private Grosse will take your bags to where you'll be bunking, and I will give you a tour of the facility. Is there anything further I can do for you gentlemen before we go?"

Amy paused a moment, hoping that Aldridge and his man would decide that there wasn't anything else to interest them there. The silence became uncomfortable before Aldridge cleared his throat. "That will be all, Colonel. You will be sure to keep in touch with me and let me know if there is anything the Bureau can do to assist in Dr. Benneton's comfort? Anything at all."

"I certainly will, sir," Amy assured him. "Goodbye." Then taking Mara firmly by the elbow, she steered her down the hallway in the opposite direction from the FBI men, leaving Derek to deal with Mara's bags and the FBI director.

"What was that all about back there . . ." Mara began, but Amy cut her off.

"*Shhhh,* not here." They continued along the corridor in silence until they reached an unused lab. "This is the electron microscopy lab," Amy recited, in the monotone voice of a bored teacher.

Once inside the lab, Amy turned to face Mara. "We have to talk."

"Apparently," Mara agreed. "What's going on here?"

"Look, I can't explain everything to you. It's just not feasible or safe." Amy dropped her voice to a guarded whisper.

"But I can tell you that someone has an ulterior motive for bringing you here. I just can't figure out what it is."

"Then how do you know that?" Mara countered.

"I told you. I can't explain everything. You're just going to have to trust me on this one." She sighed deeply and searched Mara's face. "For all I know, you are in on this thing too."

"What thing? What are you talking about?" Mara's voice rose in frustration, and Amy shushed her. "Listen, Amy, I've been through the wringer since last week, and my patience is just about gone. Now I have to figure out some way to get an innocent girl away from the FBI and back to her home state. I know they're watching me, and I'm sure they're watching her. I just don't have that many options. You were one of them. That's why I'm here. I convinced them that I could help you with the virus and they wouldn't have to baby-sit me. Now they want me to watch you and report back to them like some little spy."

Amy slumped as if a heavyweight had delivered a punch to her solar plexus. She staggered over to a lab chair and sank down, not trusting her legs to hold her. "They what? Why do they want you to watch me?"

"They want to know how religious you are. Why would they want to know about your religion?"

"Religious?" The full impact of the word barely made it past Amy's consciousness before another thought took its place. "They know," she whispered. "They know about the Remnant Believers."

Mara moved in closer, and Amy looked up, sure her fright showed in her eyes. "Look, they don't *know* anything yet," Mara pointed out. "If they did, they wouldn't want me to snoop around for them. But I think you can be sure they suspect something. What's this all about, anyway?"

"It's the United Religious Coalition," Amy said, resignation in her voice. "I keep them informed about the progress of the disease. At least I did. Lately I've been having second thoughts. I'm not sure that what I'm doing for them is right. It must have made them suspicious."

"But what's the FBI got to do with it?" Mara asked.

"It's Aldridge. He's one of Larson's puppets. Only I think he's got other plans for himself." Amy looked up fearfully. "What are you going to tell the FBI?"

Mara shook her head stubbornly. "Nothing. I'm going to tell them nothing."

Amy's hands were shaking when she reached out and gripped Mara's forearm. "Thank you. I'll figure some way out of this. For right now, let's see what we can do for you. What girl are you talking about?"

Amy listened carefully as Mara filled her in on the details of Dani and the assassination of the president and the Freedom Society's involvement. While Mara talked, Amy forced herself to listen with intense concentration, catching every detail, a discipline she had learned in the military that had served her well more than once.

"He acts as if Dani is lying about the Freedom Society being involved," Mara was saying.

Amy held up her hands like a distraught traffic cop. "Wait! The Freedom Society?"

"Yes, they are responsible for assassinating the president. Dani saw their plans, and her boyfriend, who murdered that millionaire a few weeks back, was supposed to be in on it. He told her."

"But the Freedom Society is the United Religious Coalition's strong arm, so . . ."

"So, if the FBI director is working with the United Religious Coalition, then he wouldn't *want* evidence that would implicate the Freedom Society in the death of the president," Mara finished for her. Her face fell as she thought about what she'd just said. "So that's why he wants to keep Dani 'protected.' But what's he going to do with her? Will he kill her?"

Amy shrugged. "There's no telling. Maybe he wants to use

her to blackmail Larson or as a bargaining chip. Like I said, I think he's got other plans for himself. I think his motive is money. "

"What can I do?" Mara asked.

"Nothing right now," Amy replied. "But we'll think of something. Come on. I'll show you the layout here, and I'll get you into the computer system. Maybe that will be useful somehow. Right now I just don't know. I'll have to think about it."

Mara grabbed her arm. "Amy, thank you."

Amy smiled slightly. "Don't thank me now. We haven't won yet."

Chapter Three

Monday, November 22

Pope John Innocent Xavier woke from a peaceful slumber with a start of panic. He looked around to see what might have awakened him, but he could locate nothing amiss in the Lincoln Room, where guests stayed at the White House. He swung his legs over the side of the bed and sat for a moment, his head still swimming with the remnants of a dream that was beginning to come back to him.

He had been at the Vatican, presiding over High Mass. As he looked out at his congregation, the view suddenly opened up and expanded so that he could see not only those worshiping in the pews in front of him but all the faithful throughout the world. As he watched, a plague of locusts had descended upon his people, biting them and covering them with sores. His people cried out for relief from the plague.

The memory of their anguish burned in his mind and caused him to writhe in agony. His breathing came in short, racing puffs, and he clutched his heart as though it might fail. Fortunately, it had only been a dream.

"My little father?" a sweet voice asked, and his old heart skipped a beat.

"Blessed Mother of God," he whispered in Latin as he slid from the bed and onto his knees. "*Totus tuus.* I am yours."

Feeling warmth and light bathe him, he reverently lifted his eyes from the floor, unable to stifle a gasp at the sight of Mary. Striking in beauty and youth, she bore herself with regal grace. Her garments were so bright it was hard to make out any distinction beyond the fact that they were all white, seemingly made of light. A gentle breeze caressed his face.

"Do not be afraid," she said. "I come to you as a loving mother. I have something very important to tell you about your dream."

"The plague of locusts?" he asked, fear filling his heart. The dream had been prophetic!

"Yes, the locusts. My Son will send them upon the people. He is very angry, my little father. He is very angry at His people. They refuse to obey Him. They have turned against Him and must be punished."

"No!" The word was wrenched from the lips of the old pope, and he struggled to rise from his knees, but the apparition held up her hands sternly to stay him. "Please, you must stop Him. I will entreat the people to change their wicked, idolatrous ways. You must give me time. Mercy, sweet Mother!"

Mary smiled gently. "How well you intercede for your people, my little father. You shall have time. Even now the plague of locusts has begun to smite the people, but I will give you time to speak to them, to entreat them to obey my Son. You must do this immediately. I cannot hold back the hand of my Son's vengeance for long. Act quickly. I will come to you again."

The light faded, and Mary was gone. As Pope Xavier slumped to the floor beside his bed, he realized that the room without her presence seemed draped in gloom and foreboding. How he wished she had taken him with her! Forcing himself onto his feet, he thought frantically that he had a lot of work ahead of him.

He picked up the smart-looking, black, trimline phone on the table beside his bed. "This is Pope Xavier," he told the operator who answered. "Please put me through to Donald Thurgood. Immediately."

* * *

Monday morning found Gavin Larson slow to rise. He'd drunk too much the night before, celebrating. The lights were still on in his suite. Apparently he'd passed out. He didn't appreciate the condition it left him in. He rarely allowed himself to lose control.

The telephone rang. He reached to answer it, and Thurgood was on the line. "Yes?" he growled.

"My swearing in has been postponed until Wednesday. The networks are carrying it right now."

Gavin swore as he found the remote and switched on the television. "Where are you? At home?"

"The Service has moved me into the White House."

At least things were proceeding, Gavin thought, although obviously they were not moving along as quickly as he'd hoped. It made him nervous. Johnson had been sworn in immediately after Kennedy's death. Thurgood should have become president at least that fast. He must consider, however, that it was quite a trauma for the American people to lose the president and vice president and have the Speaker of the House rise to the presidency so quickly. "Why the delay?"

"Security issues, I believe. The Secret Service is deeply concerned. They have not identified the terrorist responsible for blowing up the buses, and they're being extremely cautious."

"I don't care if it's a security concern or chaos that's causing the delay. This country needs a president immediately."

"This situation is unprecedented, Gavin. No one knows exactly what to do, and no one seems to be willing to take major steps. Rest assured that I will be the next president within the week."

Gavin clenched his jaw. What he needed was to have the president of the United States fire the director of the FBI right now.

"Gavin, there's something else. Pope Xavier called me quite early this morning in somewhat of a panic. He had a vision early this morning, from the Virgin Mary herself. It . . . it concerned him very deeply, and he would like to meet with us as soon as possible."

* * *

Thurgood ushered Pope Xavier into the Oval Office. Gavin followed the pope. He was taken by surprise when a Secret Service agent slipped in behind him and took a position by the door. The agent stared straight ahead as Gavin frowned on his way to the center of the room, where two blue couches sat facing each other. He, Thurgood, and His Excellency sat down at the same time. Thurgood noticed Gavin's discomfort at the presence of the Secret Service agent.

"It's a fact of life around here, Gavin. Secret Service agents follow me everywhere. Relax, they're loyal to the president and sworn to secrecy. They have to be here for my protection."

"But you are not the president, yet," Gavin reminded him.

"I know, but I'm the closest thing this country has got at the moment."

Gavin nodded, took another look at the agent, then turned to Pope Xavier. "Your Excellency, you have some concerns?"

Xavier nodded. "I do," he said gravely. "The Holy Mother visited me early this morning." His face shone as he described to them the beautiful vision he had witnessed. Gavin and

Thurgood listened with great interest. Gavin thought it good that this pope could speak fluent English, making an interpreter unnecessary and their meeting much easier to conduct. The story was eloquent and vividly told, and when Xavier finished, his eyes were moist from emotion.

After a moment, the corner of Gavin's mouth flinched. "The epidemic. This disease, you believe it cannot be cured?"

"Not by the hands of mortals. Precious Jesu is angry with us; this plague, this epidemic, is the wrath of God. Our only hope is in doing what the Blessed Mother has asked. She has vowed to protect us from the vengeance of her Son."

Gavin stood and walked behind the couch, deep in thought. "What should be done?" Xavier's presence was commanding, although his physical stature was merely average. The old man himself seemed to radiate, as if he had indeed been blessed by a supernatural presence.

"My son, you will agree that there is a certain group of people who are responsible for the wrath of the Holy Jesu." Xavier's face seemed carved of cold marble. "Those who call themselves by the name Remnant Believers are the enemies of the Holy One. They desire nothing more than to trample the holy law of God. It is their digression from the authority of the Catholic Church that has caused these worldwide problems, and the Holy Mother has assured me that it is they who are responsible for this terrible epidemic. We must unite our faithful and punish these pagan unbelievers."

Gavin ardently shook his head. "Your Excellency, we're not just talking about the Catholic Church here. We're talking about Protestants too. There are huge fundamental differences yet to be resolved. Certainly you can't expect the United Religious Coalition to readily embrace the theology of the Catholic Church. Since the Reformation, issues have separated our two faiths that have not yet been resolved."

The pope smiled benevolently, as though looking upon a small child of whom he was inordinately fond. "You forget, my son, that our faiths have united in many areas and made great gains over the last decade. Yes, there are areas that must still be considered. Our scholars still quibble about such things as merit, reward, purgatory, and indulgences; Marian devotion and the assistance of the saints in the lives of salvation; *but these are areas we can work on.* Let us build together on our common ground.

"You are a rational man, Mr. Larson. You and I, we desire the same things, I believe. I admit, unity can be a slow process. But we must concentrate on our common ground." Xavier stood abruptly and walked to Gavin with outstretched arms, grabbing him by the shoulders as a father would a son. "You have courted the alliance of the Catholic Church. As the emissary of God on earth, I have the authority to seal an alliance with your United Religious Coalition."

Gavin was stunned. Had he just heard what he thought he heard? Had the Catholic Church actually taken such a giant step of good faith?

"We have it in our power to reign supreme," Pope Xavier assured him. "We can claim the whole of the planet for our Blessed Mother."

"What can I do?" Gavin asked.

His Excellency smiled. "Already we have agreed on a common understanding of salvation. Let us now agree on a common day of worship. Let us please God by uniting on our most common institution and establish by law a day of worship—Sunday."

* * *

"I'm tired of this hospital, and I'd like to get out."

Lynn smiled. "*Shhhh,* lay back and be good. The doctor's coming." She unconsciously exaggerated her articulation. Randy didn't tell her that he could partially hear. It had come as a surprise to him, and as yet he was still worried there might be some serious damage. As soon as Dr. Hodges came, Lynn picked up her purse and left for the cafeteria.

"I think we'll take the bandages off tomorrow, Mr. Burton. How does that sound?" Hodges smiled at his witticism.

"Doctor, I heard that, and it wasn't that funny."

"What? You did, didn't you? Well, that's awfully promising. Let me remove the bandages now, then." He pulled a pair of bandage scissors from his lab coat pocket and began to unwrap Randy's head.

"I've been afraid to believe it, but I've been able to hear progressively better for the past two or three hours. I noticed a dramatic, steady improvement. Is that normal?"

"For one's hearing to come back so quickly?" Dr. Hodges shrugged. "Everyone is different. I'm not surprised at your recovery, but I am quite pleased. Your ankle and collarbone will, of course, need more time to repair themselves." Hodges did a thorough examination of Randy's ears and tested his hearing. He looked at the ankle and collarbone and arrived at a decision. "I think I will order an air cast for your ankle and a clavicle splint to restrict the movement of your arm as your collarbone heals. Let's plan on having you released tomorrow. All right?"

"Perfectly OK with me, doc." Randy couldn't suppress the huge grin on his face.

Ten minutes after the doctor left, Lynn returned and sat with Randy, and they talked for an hour before he went to sleep. And when he awoke, Alice was there.

"Lynn went for a walk," Alice said, smiling warmly as she watered his plants.

"The nurses do that, Alice."

"I know. I asked your nurse to allow me. She just left."

"How's Lynn?"

"Oh, she's fine, Randy. She's been an absolute joy to have around. So bright and so full of questions."

Randy watched his elderly friend for a few moments. "I

mean, how's her withdrawals? How's she doing? How is she handling things?"

Alice came over and gave his hand a squeeze. "Don't look so concerned. She's been fine. She still has some rough spells. I've seen her get so agitated she can't sit still. She paces around my apartment like a caged animal, but when those attacks come, we pray, and it's like a miracle. She calms down."

"She hasn't used?"

"Not that I know about. Really, Randy, stop worrying about Lynn. She's a strong girl, and she's developing a solid relationship with God that no one can touch, not even the devil. You know, I've watched Lynn when she has attacks, and she calls directly on God. Doesn't try to fight it herself. Just goes right to the source of the greatest power in the universe. It's comforting to know God is in control."

Randy looked at the ceiling and sighed. "I suppose we should all learn how to do that."

"Yes, I suppose we should," Alice agreed as she finished with a vase of carnations and daisies. She sat down next to the bed and looked deeply concerned. "Randy, have you heard from Brian? We haven't. It's been two days.'

"No. He hasn't been here, that I know about. I wonder if he got to Gavin Larson, and I wonder what Gavin Larson had to say." Suddenly he felt completely worthless having to stay in the hospital.

"Randy," Alice said, her voice suddenly very serious. "I— I'm also worried about Lynn."

"Oh? But you said Lynn was fine."

"I know. And Lynn is. It's me. Or . . . it's . . . my insecurities. In some ways Lynn scares me. She's so eager to learn about God, and she's understanding everything I tell her, and she's got this relationship with Him that's like nothing I've ever seen."

"She's not possessed, is she?"

Alice smiled, but she still looked very concerned. "No, she's a complete Christian, but she's yearning for more truth than I wonder if I'm capable of teaching her. I've taught her about God's love and grace. She's devoured the stories of Jesus and, although I hesitated to start so quickly, we've been reading through the Old Testament. The very first time I visited her, she gave up reading the Bible. Now she has nearly read it completely through. I think she understands much of it better than I do."

"Perhaps she's been without any direction in her life for so long she's going overboard. Perhaps all this studying is just something to burn off energy. She'll probably get tired of it."

Alice smiled tolerantly.

"You don't think so."

Alice shook her head. "No, I don't."

Randy raised himself up on an elbow. "What is it, then?"

Alice drew a deep breath, exhaling slowly. "I don't know quite how to explain it, but I think God is giving Lynn insights into the last days. She seems to understand so much. In fact, she's understanding far more than I have explained to her. Yet I'm the only person she's been learning from."

"She's just fixated," Randy concluded. "Like I said, it's only a diversion."

"I don't believe you, Randy Burton! You *are* arrogant, aren't you? Are you telling me your sister is not bright enough to reason? Or are you telling me that because you may not feel her passion or don't have the same relationship she has with God, you can't possibly validate her experience?"

"I'm sorry. I didn't mean it like that. Of course I believe in Lynn. She's all I've got."

Alice stood. "Then treat her better than a child!" she snapped back. The room fell silent for a few moments. "Lynn understands prophecy better than I do, better than my pastor does too. It hasn't even been two weeks since she began studying. Are you aware that many of the events that have taken place fit into the prophecy of the end times recorded in the Bible?"

"I've felt that way, yes. But I don't know much about the Bible."

"Well, Lynn does. She needs to learn more, though. She thirsts for it. She fully understands the grace of God. She seems to grasp the magnitude of God's love, just like I believe Mary did as she sat at Jesus' feet. But now she needs to know how it all fits into the story."

Randy frowned. He suddenly felt as if he were the child here, not Lynn, certainly not Alice. And he was still smarting from Alice's reproach. "What do you mean, 'the story'?"

"The great controversy between God and Satan," Alice said patiently.

"I don't understand. Why is understanding this 'controversy' so important?"

Alice sat back down. "There must be a purpose for everything, don't you think? That's the way life works. For instance, God had a purpose for us when He created us. He didn't just do it because He was bored. Unfortunately, His original purpose for us was sidetracked by sin. Although He still has His original purpose in mind for us, He has to deal with the sin issue first."

"Like good versus evil."

"Yes, something like that but much, much more. Those cliché stories, like Star Wars, for instance, show the fight between 'good' and 'evil' but don't mention God, whose very nature is love. Even His judgments, punishments, and rewards are made out of that love. We like to think of good winning just because it's right, but all the good in the universe won't save us if we don't have a relationship with God and accept the sacrifice He made for us."

He thought of Mara and wished she could be there hearing what he was hearing. She'd probably understand even more of it than he did. Still, if she ever came back to see him, he could try to explain it. "Why do you say that?"

"Randy, I—I'm not sure how to explain it exactly . . . OK,

for a real close-to-home example, let's say that Lynn tried to quit heroin on her own because she knew it was the right thing to do. Do you think she could have done as well as she's doing now? I don't think so. That time she used it again after deciding to quit perhaps would have made her give up despite knowing she was doing the 'right' thing or the 'good' thing. Even if she were just a 'Christian' she might have given up. But I believe we owe her success to the fact that she accepted Jesus into her heart, and although she knows she's a sinner, she also knows without a shadow of a doubt that God loves her no matter what. To me, that shows God's grace at work, and it shows how we should accept His grace."

Frowning, Randy concentrated on digesting this. To him, it seemed either too simple or that there should be a catch somewhere. In one way it seemed genuine, but in other ways it seemed to mean people weren't accountable for their sins. "I can see a lot of criminals preaching this concept of grace."

"True, maybe it doesn't seem authentic."

"So, can we convince other people, even ourselves, we're Christians and still live however we want?"

"Apart from God? Is that what you mean? Sinfully and harmfully?"

"Yeah, I guess."

"The best example I can give you is your sister. She couldn't be developing a pure relationship with God and keep rationalizing drug use. After a while, one or the other would have to go. Randy, I can tell you this: She's fervently decided to stick with God."

* * *

"Larson, this is Gunnar. Kent Aldridge still has the girl in his custody, as you are well aware."

"Yes."

"FBI agents were guarding her at the hotel when my men

tried to get to her on Saturday, and soon after they tried, she was moved to another location. Aldridge is using her to bargain with. There's no reason for him not to turn over the girl to you."

Gavin was silent on the line for a few moments. "It appears as though you were right, Gunnar. We cannot trust him any further. I am also concerned that Brian Willis was helping Burton in his investigation. Willis might have given Burton enough information to convince the attorney general to launch an investigation."

"Then he should be killed, shouldn't he?"

"At the moment, it depends on who Aldridge is loyal to. Burton and the girl, Dani Talbot, are either assets or liabilities to him. With them, Aldridge has leverage. He has evidence against the Freedom Society to launch a full-scale investigation and file a string of indictments that could reach all the way to me. Without Dani Talbot, he's vulnerable, and he knows it. He might also have enough evidence with Burton to incriminate me."

"I've told you, the only person Aldridge is working for is himself."

Although the observation angered Gavin, Dietrich was right. It had become blatantly obvious Aldridge was holding the girl to extort money from Gavin. He could never have gained control of the White House without Kent Aldridge's help, yet he had miscalculated that Aldridge's only motive would turn out to be greed. "Kent Aldridge is not protecting Dani Talbot to build a case against me, Dietrich, not yet. He's holding her because she's worth a great deal to me. I'm sure he'll want to make a trade—for the right price."

"Do you have any idea where he might be holding the girl?"

"None. Not since he moved her after your failed abduction."

"I'm doing what I can to locate her. But you must understand that Aldridge has the resources of the FBI at his disposal, as well as influence within the Justice Department. If I feel any agency is using all its resources to come after me, I'm going to disappear, and then you're on your own."

"I understand your desire to protect yourself, Dietrich, but I can guarantee that your rewards will far outweigh the risks you may have to take. I also want *you* to understand that what we are in is a delicate situation. If you find the girl, hide her until you have notified me. I cannot afford to have the Freedom Society implicated in the president's assassination, and she can obviously do us a great deal of harm. Once Thurgood is sworn in, he will have the power to fire Aldridge or put enough pressure on the Justice Department to remove him from office."

"Aldridge knows this, of course," Dietrich said.

"Of course. He has to know he must work quickly. But he's greedy, and that will make him predictable, I think. Every move of his that we can counter will weaken him."

It was after 7:00 p.m. when Dietrich got off the phone with Gavin. He dialed into his ISP and downloaded several messages under a Freedom Society account. He scrolled quickly through the UBC statement information. Their plant at the bank had gotten him everything he asked for.

Am I through? She asked hopefully in the message.

"No one is ever *through* working for the Freedom Society," he said out loud as he disconnected from the Internet.

He studied the credit information, along with a map of the District of Columbia, Maryland, and Virginia. Most of what he discovered was useless. In fact, nearly all of it. But he did find one small coincidence in the charges. Shuffling them together, he moved them out of the way and lay down. He wasn't going to chase Kent Aldridge around. He was going to keep his eyes open, and then he would make his move.

* * *

Brian was left alone Sunday night and for most of the day

Monday. It had been a restless night, and several times he awoke and lay on his cot thinking and listening. He never heard a soul. He began to wonder if he'd been left completely alone in the warehouse, but that seemed unreasonable. He never for an instant believed he was alone enough to attempt to escape. But toying with the idea over and over gave him motivation to check things out, just to be sure. He knew he would have hated not doing anything.

So at 3:00 a.m., he put his feet on the floor and crept over to the door and tried the knob. Locked. Of course. He examined the door frame and found it wasn't terribly solid; he could probably pry it open if he had something to pry with. The door itself contained a frosted-glass window, which could be easily broken. And cause a ton of racket, he knew. He wouldn't have a chance of escape then. He settled back on the heels of his socked feet and contemplated his situation. Could he chance an escape? Having a family, what could he risk when he really had no idea what was happening?

He pounded loudly on the door, but the noise didn't seem to rouse anyone.

He could try kicking the door open, but it swung to the inside, and he didn't think he would have the leverage to splinter the jamb. Grabbing a blanket from the cot, he wrapped it around his fist and abruptly broke the glass, not taking time to think about the consequences. Now that he was committed, he reasoned, he was relieved of further deliberation.

The warehouse was as large and empty as he had imagined it. Light came from rows of windows high on the walls. His feet barely whispered on his way down the stairs. A quick glance around outside the office hadn't located his shoes, nor were they lying underneath the stairway.

Concrete met him at the bottom of the stairs. Cold stung the soles of his feet and chilled his spine, not that he wasn't already trembling. Still, he seemed to be alone, and he trotted off, looking for a way out. He was beginning to feel better, sensing now that he had done the right thing by trying to escape.

He wasn't sure of the time of day. The opaque light filtering through the high windows told him there was either a cloud cover or it was near dusk. He trotted down the long, empty warehouse, hardly making a noise, his senses detecting no guards, no Freedom Society goons, no one. He was actually going to be free and able to call his wife! For a brief moment he allowed himself to think it was possible.

At the end of the warehouse were two doors, wide and tall enough to allow tractor-trailer rigs to drive through side by side. Remembering what sounded like a corridor when he was brought here, Brian concluded he had headed in the opposite direction than he had come in from, otherwise he would have come to the corridor instead of the massive doors.

The doors were secured with a heavy chain, but a smaller access door just to the right of them looked promising. Not surprisingly, it was also locked. After five minutes of searching, he found a rusted tire iron and pried the latch, popping the door open. A wall of frigid air sucked his breath away.

But he was free!

* * *

Dani sat at the little kitchen table in her suite and stared at the piece of paper in her hand. *Alice Nolan.* The name sounded familiar. An obstetrician, Aldridge had told her. Mara referred her. And Mara sent her regrets, but she had work to do at Fort Detrick, so she wouldn't be joining Dani at the suite. They would catch up later at the airport when they flew out to Idaho together.

That just didn't sound like Mara. But apparently it was true, because although she'd waited, trying to decide what to do, an entire day had gone by and Mara had still not arrived. Aldridge, for once, seemed to be telling the truth.

Dani had been placated by plenty of people in her life, and

this sure felt like more of the same. Aldridge's oily voice and his patronizing manner made her uncomfortable. Something was fishy here. She'd been trying for hours to figure out just what it was. It was so hard to separate everything in her head. Her memories were jumbled and disjointed. Scenes from the last few days would pop into her mind, unbidden.

"He's down! He's been shot! I want two men fully protected out there immediately. Bring him back. Rogers, your team covers them."

"Daddy? Daddy!"

"Make way. Give them some room. Is he alive?"

"I'm sorry. I'm so sorry."

Dani shook her head fiercely. This wasn't getting her anywhere. She stared again at the paper. Why would Mara refer her to an obstetrician? She forced her mind back. The last time she'd seen Mara she had been on her way to see Randy Burton at the Washington Hospital Center. Had she met an obstetrician there? Unlikely.

Maybe this was Mara's way of getting her a message. Go to the hospital. Pretend you need to see an obstetrician. She fiddled with the paper. It might just work. If she could get them to take her to the Washington Hospital Center, she could talk to Randy Burton. Maybe he could help her.

Quickly she went to her duffel bag and retrieved Shon's picture and his letters. They were the only personal items she had. She stuffed them, with her father's UBC card, beneath the waistband of her maternity pants in the small of her back. Taking a glass of water, she spilled it on the floor at her feet. Then she grabbed the edge of the couch and moaned loudly.

An agent rapped on the door and tentatively cracked it open. "Miss Talbot?"

Dani sagged against the couch. "Help me," she panted. "Help me. My baby! There's something wrong! It's too early! The baby is coming. My water broke. Call an ambulance!"

"Oh, man," the agent said, throwing the door open and sprinting across the room to support her. "Not now. This can't happen now. O'Shea! Bring a car around. We've got to get her to a hospital *now!*"

"Please," Dani pleaded. "I have to go to the Washington Hospital Center. My doctor is there. Please make them take me there." She groaned again and clutched her abdomen.

"Ma'am, the Washington Hospital Center is not the closest hospital," the agent said, helping to ease her into a sitting position on the couch. "I'm sure we can find a closer hospital."

Dani infused her voice with panic. "But my doctor is there. She's the best doctor. She'll help me. She has to. It's not time yet. The baby is too early. Please, I want to see her. Please don't let my baby die."

"OK, OK, please just calm down," the agent tried to reassure her.

Dani continued to make noises as though she was in great agony while they carried her firemanstyle down the elevator and out to the street where a dark sedan was waiting. The agent who had found her, whose last name was Christopher, rode with her in the back of the car. She supposed the others would follow.

Dani grabbed the agent's hand and squeezed as she pretended to have another contraction, putting on what she believed was an Emmy-winning performance. When the "pain" subsided, she turned to the agent. "Mr. Christopher, do you have any children?"

"Two girls," he replied, pale despite a healthy tan. "Twins. They'll be a year old next month."

"Were you there? When they were born?"

"Yes, I . . . my wife had a C-section, and I watched. The nurses let me help clean the babies up after they were all checked out."

Dani grimaced. "Then you know what it's like," she gasped, squeezing his hand.

Christopher squeezed back. "Yeah, I know. My wife told me all about it. She was in labor for ten hours before they decided to take the babies. She didn't do labor well. You just hang in there. We'll be at the hospital soon, and they'll take good care of you. What did you say the name of that doctor of yours was?"

"Nolan. Dr. Nolan."

They arrived at the emergency room, having called ahead, and a gurney with a compliment of orderlies was waiting. Dani was pulled from the car and strapped to a gurney almost before the car completed its stop. The agents were left to deal with admissions as Dani was wheeled into a cubicle to await a doctor who was on his way down from the maternity floor.

"You jest wait here, hon. I'll be right back. The doctor will be here right quick and ya'll be just fine." The nurse went from the cubicle, drawing the curtain behind her.

Dani unstrapped herself and scrambled awkwardly off the gurney. She could hear the sound of raised voices outside near the admissions area. "I want someone in there with her," Christopher was saying.

"I'm sorry, sir," a man's voice replied in sterile, controlled tones. "but she will need to be examined, and I cannot have someone in the room with her during the examination unless she approves. She has rights."

Christopher swore. Peeking out of the curtain Dani could see a long corridor stretching off in both directions. She chose the direction away from Christopher. At the end of the corridor was a staircase. Looking over her shoulder to be sure she hadn't been seen, Dani shoved the door open and began to climb the stairs.

* * *

After leaving the White House, Gavin instructed his driver to head for the abandoned industrial park where Brian Willis was being held. Gavin had not yet decided what to do about him. He liked Brian and felt discouraged that Brian had so animatedly opposed him. Gavin felt he could have made excellent use of Brian's personality and expertise as the Coalition's growth exploded. People had always been drawn to him, and to have had Brian working for him now would make political changes go along much smoother.

But such an idea was absolute nonsense now. Brian was nothing if not a man of conviction, and he would certainly not give up trying to bring Gavin to some kind of justice. Gavin shook his head sadly, wondering how he would have to deal with the Willis problem.

As Gavin's limo came to a stop at the warehouse, two of Dietrich's men ran out. They were surprised to see the car and looked ready to use their weapons. Gavin slid out.

"What's happened?"

"Willis has escaped!" the man in the baseball cap yelled.

"You fools! Can't you do anything right?"

The two men pivoted on their heels and disappeared back inside the warehouse. Gavin ran after them, pulling his cellular phone from his overcoat and punching in numbers. "Dietrich, Willis has escaped! Get over here!"

Dietrich was already on his way, and the Legacy squealed around the warehouse a few seconds after Gavin's call. His men must have already alerted him, Gavin thought. Dietrich bolted into the warehouse and caught up to Gavin at the office in which Willis had been held.

Gavin threw up his arms and began kicking glass off the landing in a rage. "Dietrich! Your people are fools! You've failed to bring me the girl, and you've managed to foul up a task as simple as detaining one man for a couple of days! You've done nothing but fail to carry out my orders!"

Dietrich's veins swelled. He whirled around and trotted down the stairs. Baseball cap ran up from the far end of the warehouse.

3—M.H.

"We found where he left the building."

"Good, track him down. I've got more people coming." Then he grabbed the man's arm like a vise and pulled him off balance. "You blow it again, I'll kill you!"

The man's eyes distended, and the bill of his cap actually trembled. "Y-yes, sir!"

Dietrich shoved him away and began pacing.

"And what do you plan to do about Brian Willis when you find him?" Gavin asked.

Dietrich half-smiled. "He's a liability. I think he should be eliminated."

Gavin lowered his eyes, then looked at Dietrich again, and nodded sadly. "Yes. Yes, of course. He will only cause trouble."

Dietrich gestured lightly with his right hand. "Then I will simply have him killed once he is found."

* * *

Brian came up against a high chain-link fence with strands of razor wire running along the top. Pausing to catch his breath, he sank down on his haunches. His breath clouded the air, and his feet were in a great deal of pain. He slid down to the ground and pulled his right foot up, discovering deep lacerations on his sole. The left foot appeared to be just as badly cut and bruised. Both socks were shredded, and it was hard to tell just how badly his feet were torn up through all the blood and dirt as the last of daylight faded away. He must have run through some broken glass somewhere, but he had not realized it then.

"Oh, God, please help me. I've got to get away. I've got to find a phone somewhere." Brain bowed his head. Then, a minute later, he stood up and began running again, choosing to go left.

After several minutes, he came to a cut in the fence barely large enough to fit through. Wiggling through the hole, he ran down an embankment, hit dirt and rocks, and slowed down. With agonizing determination, he picked his way over the rocks. Twenty minutes later, he found himself among a community of box shelters, a few fires, and a dozen or more homeless people. Walking tentatively to the nearest fire, he stretched out his hands toward it.

Four people in tattered, threadbare clothes hovered over the fire barrel. First one, then another, and another raised vacant eyes to him.

"Hello."

"Mmm," one grunted, light reflecting off his smudged face.

Brian gave a shaky smile. "Mind if I share your fire?"

"Naaaw," the same man said.

"Thanks." Brian rubbed his hands over the flame as he surveyed the faces of his new friends: three men and one woman, all with greasy hair and grimy faces.

"You've got a limp, looks like. Where'd your shoes go? Get 'em stole?" the woman asked.

"N—well, yeah, I guess I did."

"Figured." Her grin was toothless. "Bedda git yuh some, or your feet'll freeze."

"Thanks." Brian began to worry that he'd already been discovered missing, and if he didn't get farther away, he'd be captured again. "Look, I need your help. I don't know where I am. Where's the nearest phone?"

"You runnin' from the po' leese?"

"No," Brian said to the woman.

"You look like you are."

"Look, I just need a phone. You're right, I'm running, but not from the police. Someone else is after me, and if they catch me, they'll probably kill me because I'm trying to escape. Do you understand? I need to find someone who will help me!" Brian's voice echoed in the chilly air, and he noticed more dirty faces peering at him.

Suddenly, he thought he heard tires screeching to a halt

somewhere up along the fence. They were closer than he thought.

* * *

Dani didn't have time to wander aimlessly around the hospital hoping to stumble across Randy Burton's room, so she picked up a courtesy phone and waited for the operator to pick up. "Can I help you?"

"Yes, I'm looking for Randy Burton's room."

"Room 118 on the Med/Surg floor."

"Thank you." Dani followed the brightly colored maps on the walls and easily found it. She slipped inside and closed the door behind her. He looked away from the television. At that moment, she fully realized the predicament she'd gotten herself into. The man was deaf, and she didn't know sign language. Then she spotted a pad of paper and a pen on his bedside table.

"Hold on," she muttered under her breath as she grabbed the pad and pen, "and I'll tell you who I am so you won't freak out."

"I know who you are," Burton said quietly.

Dani gasped. "You can hear me?"

"Yes. My hearing came back."

"Oh, I'm so glad. Can you help me? FBI agents are going to be looking for me any minute. They've been holding me in a hotel room. They wouldn't believe that I was part of the Freedom Society or that it was responsible for the assassination of President Fairfield or for Stan Shultz's murder either."

"*Whaa*—? I don't understand. The FBI wouldn't believe you?"

"No, that man, Aldridge, he thinks I'm making it all up. He put me in a hotel with guards and said it was for my 'protection' until he has done a thorough investigation and understands exactly what has happened. What is there to straighten out? The Freedom Society was responsible, but he won't even listen to me." Dani glanced uneasily toward the door.

"Look, do you have any idea where I can go? Mara had the FBI give me this," she handed him the piece of paper. "She said it was a doctor, but I don't need a doctor. I need someone to stay with until I can get out of D.C."

Burton glanced at the paper. "This is Alice. She's not a doctor, but she'll take care of you." He gave her all the change he had stashed in a drawer beside his bed. "Get out of here as fast as you can. Go find a phone and call Alice. Tell her to come pick you up. My sister, Lynn, is staying with her too. She might answer the phone. But she'll help you too. Explain everything to them. Just stay clear of the FBI. Understand? I don't know if I can do much to help you from here, but I'll try."

Dani smiled for the first time since her father had been killed. "Thank you." She began to turn away, but Randy stopped her.

"Wait, take my jacket from the closet. Dump yours in a trash basket somewhere."

"Thank you." Dani opened the closet doors. She pulled off her threadbare coat and slipped into the airy lightness of his down jacket. "Thank you so much."

"Your father saved my life," Burton said softly. "He saved the lives of all those children. I'd help you in any case, but I owe it to him to do what I can for you. I owe him more than that. Now, go! Those guys aren't going to be put off for long."

Dani opened the door and glanced up and down the hallway. There was no sign of the FBI, but she wasn't going to take any chances. She entered a door marked "Locker Room." Inside were a few rows of lockers, some showers, one of which was occupied, bathroom stalls, and benches. On one bench was a crumpled uniform, a pair of nurse's ugly, white, crepe-soled shoes, white stockings, and a totebag holding a hair-brush, blow dryer, and other personal items. The owner of

⌄ₒ was apparently the shower occupant.

ᴅani quickly shed her maternity pants and pulled on the wrinkled white ones on the bench. They wouldn't pull up over her belly so she rolled up the waistband and snugged them up beneath it. The shoes were several sizes too large, but they would do.

She left the locker room and made her way to the elevator and down to the lobby moments before the nurse emerged from the shower. Only once did she stiffen and hold her breath. A man in a dark suit was at the far end of the hallway. She ducked her head and tried not to hurry as she approached the huge automatic doors at the front of the hospital. They opened with a whoosh of air that seemed to pull her outside.

Shielding the side of her face that was nearest to the road, she hurried down the street. She went three blocks before she felt safe enough to stop at a Quik Stop and make the phone call. She dropped the coins into the machine, her fingers blue with cold. The phone rang only once before it was answered.

"Hello?"

"Hi, can I talk to Alice Nolan, please?"

"This is Alice," the friendly voice said.

"Alice, my name is Dani Talbot. I need your help."

* * *

"Waaaaahhhhh!" a baby bawled. Dan Reiss rolled over and glanced at the luminous numbers on the alarm clock on his windowsill. Two in the morning. It was the third time the baby had woken up since being put to bed by its mother at eight the previous evening. Dan groaned and thought about trying to go back to sleep, but as the baby continued to cry, he shoved himself out of bed and made his way down the hall.

As he reached the door, the shadowy figure of the baby's mother met him. "Don't worry, Jenna, I'll take him," Dan assured her. She smiled gratefully at him in the semidarkness. Her eyelids drooped with fatigue.

"Thank you, Pastor," she murmured.

The baby, an eighteen-month-old boy, stood at the crib railing, looking toward the door and howling mightily. When he saw Dan, he stopped and regarded him with curiosity. "Come here, Cody," Dan crooned.

He picked the wiggling baby up and carried him to the rocking chair, dodging Cody's sleeping brothers as he went. They slept soundlessly on the floor, camped out in their sleeping bags. His sister, Jules, had the only bed in the little room. She slept so deeply she never heard Cody cry.

Dan settled himself into the rocking chair and held Cody against his shoulder. The baby burrowed into Dan's flannel robe as he sucked on his thumb and clutched his battered "lambie," a piece of sheepskin torn off from the one he slept on. Dan rocked back and forth while he rubbed the baby's back.

He was certainly not used to this new routine. He wondered if he ever would be used to it. Life had changed for him so drastically it was as though a bomb had been dropped in the middle of his peaceful existence. Families who were having trouble making it on their own had begun to arrive in a steady stream. Within four days, his house was filled to capacity and bursting at the seams. Something had to be done because more were asking to come every day, and he couldn't refuse them. Everything had happened so fast he just hadn't been able to come up with any answers to the problems that had quickly followed.

"Lord," he prayed, "what should I do? I know you are sending me these people for a reason, some of them aren't even Remnant Believers. I'm just not sure what You want me to do with all of them."

And then an idea came to him so swiftly that it took his breath away. What if they pooled their assets, sold his house and any other extraneous possessions, and bought one or two houses that would accommodate everyone? They could live communally like the early apostles. The reasonable side of him saw this as an answer directly from the throne of heaven. The unreasonable side of him groaned in protest.

In the chaos of his house since the "occupation," he had been mentally reeling. A dedicated bachelor who grew up as an only child, his first impulse was to flee from his own house in search of the tiniest space in which he could experience the peace of life he was so accustomed to. Part of him wanted God to suggest a place he could send them to . . . away, so that he could return to his quiet life.

He laid his head on the back of the rocker. Cody's head now bobbed heavily, and Dan suspected the boy had fallen asleep. "Lord, cut this selfishness from my heart," Dan pleaded. "I know this feeling isn't from You. It's from Satan, and I have no part with him. My life is Yours. It is in Your hands. Give me a heart of sharing and unity and tolerance. In the name of Jesus I ask, Amen."

Rising clumsily from the rocker, he carefully made his way to the crib and placed Cody gently down into it. The baby stirred, found his thumb again, and began to suck lustily. Dan covered him with a baby quilt and tiptoed out of the room. Back in his own room sleep eluded him for an hour while his mind worked feverishly on the details of his new plan.

* * *

As soon as Dani was out the door, Randy dialed the switchboard at the J. Edgar Hoover Building and asked for Director Aldridge.

"I'm sorry, he's not in."

Randy hung up and lay back on the bed, a million thoughts spinning through his mind as he went over again what he knew about the Freedom Society and the events that had led up to Fairfield's assassination. He remembered Dani's expression and tone of voice when she told him about Aldridge. There was no way she had contrived her behavior; she was truly frightened, and he believed she was telling him the truth as she saw it.

But why wasn't Aldridge taking her seriously? She might have misunderstood Aldridge's motives for keeping her in a safe house. It was quite possible Director Aldridge had very good reasons for keeping her under FBI protection. Possibly he was even now building a case against the Freedom Society and planned for Dani to be his key witness.

Randy's eyes began flitting around the room, and he felt his body become tense, his arms and legs grow as stiff as tree limbs. Heavy and firm, frustration seemed to suddenly be smothering him. Taking several deep breaths, he closed his eyes and lay back, willing himself to relax. He needed to be up, moving, and doing his job.

The anxiety attack seemed to have passed for a while. He studied the ceiling. An orderly stepped inside to empty the trash receptacles. He carried a cellular phone on his belt. *Everyone seems to have a cell phone,* Randy thought.

"Excuse me, Mr. Burton."

Randy turned his head. The orderly was puzzling over something in his hand he'd knocked off the bed while emptying the bedside trash can. "I've worked this floor a couple of years, and I ain't seen anything like this before. Did you lose a button . . . or something that sort of *looks* like a button?"

"I don't think so. What do you have?"

The orderly handed over the item. He chuckled and said it looked like a bug, like the things spies use to eavesdrop. Randy didn't even have to look at it closely to know that it was a tiny microphone/transmitter. "*There* it is!" he exclaimed for the orderly's benefit. Inside, he began to feel outrage.

The orderly shrugged. "Too bad. I thought it was a bug. I got a friend who is into spies and all that techno junk. Thought I had something."

As soon as the orderly left, Randy turned the television on and used a rubber band to hold the tiny microphone against the speaker attached to the bed. Then he turned up the TV volume and dialed Alice's number. "Alice, there's trouble. Is Lynn with you?" He spoke as low as possible.

"No, she's out giving some Bible studies. Why? What's wrong?"

"Did you get a call from a young woman named Dani Talbot?"

"Yes, just a few minutes ago. She's coming right here. I promised to pay her cab fare when she arrived."

"Good. Listen carefully. I think she may be in danger. I don't know how much, but since she knows so much about President Fairfield's assassination, there is a good chance her life is at stake. I want you two to get out of your apartment as soon as she arrives."

"Oh, Randy, not again!"

"Just do it, Alice. If it's nothing, I'll apologize profusely later. I apologize now. But please, be on your way out as *soon* as Dani gets there. Then go get Lynn."

Alice thought for a moment. "Well, let me tell you where I'm go—"

"No! Don't say a word."

"But—"

"Go where you were Thursday night, and I'll meet you there as soon as possible. If you notice anything strange or suspicious, leave that place too."

Again there was a pause. "OK, I will," Alice said just before she hung up.

Randy put the receiver back with a vaguely uncomfortable feeling, unable to shake the feeling that Alice, Dani, and Lynn were still in trouble. He turned down the TV volume but left the microphone attached to the speaker. It occurred to him that the bug was probably transmitting to a remote recording device, because nothing unusual had happened once the microphone was discovered. It made good sense. The bug was too small to send a signal very far, and the hospital was littered with equipment that would cause interference. It had to be a remote that was picked up periodically, he decided.

He lay back again and tried to relax. He sent up a brief prayer to God, as odd as it felt to do. Some preconceptions he had toward God and Christianity made him uncomfortable about making God a central part of his life, central enough or close enough to have a profound relationship. It just didn't appear to be as natural for him as it was for Lynn.

Chapter Four

Wednesday, November 24

Mara looked over Amy's shoulder at the loopy strands of the virus. The pictures on the left were Ebola Zaire, the ones on the right were the new virus, called Cartier's virus after the index patient. The photos were nearly identical.

"See these?" Amy slapped down another set of photos that resembled chocolate-chip cookies that were mostly chocolate chips. The "chips" were blocks, like crystals, of pure, unadulterated virus. "Cells, loaded with inclusion bodies."

"They're preparing to hatch out," Mara murmured under her breath. When a virus grew in a cell, crystalloids, or bricks, appeared in the middle of the cell. Then they began to move to the surface of the cell preparing to "hatch." As the brick touched the inner surface of the cell wall, it shattered into hundreds of individual viruses, which were shaped like threads. These pushed their way through the cell wall like worms coming out of moist earth after a heavy rain. The moving bricks distorted the cell shape, making it bulge and swell until the cell finally popped and died, releasing the virus threads into the bloodstream of the host where they could multiply and take over more cells.

Mara felt her hands clutch the edge of the desk, and she must have turned a little green around the gills.

"Major puker factor, huh?" Amy said sympathetically, describing the gut-wrenching tightening that occurs deep inside as a result of an expressible fear. "Don't worry, these are just pictures. You can't catch it from this."

"Yeah, but I've been *working* with this stuff, Amy. I've had my *hands* in blood that was loaded with this virus. How come I'm not sick?"

Amy shrugged. "I don't know. No one knows yet. That's what you're supposed to help me find out." She laid down an armload of files on the desk in front of Mara. "Here are all the reports, everything that's been written on this thing. Even stuff that hasn't been released yet. Why don't you see what you can find out? I've got a martial arts class." She grinned. "Time to go throw some soldiers around. I'll be back in an hour, and we can go over this."

Mara nodded. "OK." But her mind wasn't really on the virus anymore. She was more concerned than ever about Dani. Where was she? Had she gotten away from the FBI? And if so, where had she gone? Had she gotten the hint about Alice?

Shaking these thoughts out of her head, she flipped open the first file and began to read about the Cartier virus. Outside the small office where she worked, soldiers passed by in the hallway, going about their business at USAMRIID. There were soldiers everywhere. And security measures.

No wonder Aldridge had been willing to let her come here. It was impossible to get out, and it saved him the headache of watching her for a week. Now he could concentrate on Dani. She felt an inescapable urge to do *something*. To find the girl. To rescue her. She almost laughed at herself.

She was a doctor. At least she had been until this whole

mess started. She was totally unprepared to fight a battle of wits against the FBI. Not that, at the moment, she had much choice. She had been placed in a very unenviable position, and she would have resented it except that for some reason she believed she really could help, despite the odds. After all, she'd come this far, and that had been against a killer like Dietrich. Surely the FBI couldn't be worse than he was.

Thinking of Dietrich reminded her that he was still out there. He wouldn't have gone away, and that meant that once she got out of here and away from the FBI, she still had to watch out for him. But first she had to think of some way out of here.

She slammed the folders shut with disgust. It was useless to try to concentrate on the virus. Right now she was consumed with trying to find a way to get Dani and get out of the state. But how?

The security at Fort Detrick wasn't particularly tight, but it had been stepped up. She couldn't just walk out of the place.

But Amy could.

Or drive out anyway. If she had a passenger in the trunk, would anyone know?

"No," Amy said, when Mara voiced her plan after she'd returned from her class, her hair still wet from a hasty shower. "They don't check my trunk every time I come and go. You could get out that way. No one would know how you got out unless they saw you, and we could get around that. But where do you want me to take you? We still haven't found your friend."

"I know this guy," Mara started and ignored the blush she felt creeping up her cheeks. "He works for the FBI. He's the one who saved those kids on the bus. I treated him while we were waiting for the paramedics to arrive, and then I visited him. He's a good man. Maybe he can find out where Dani is being held and help me find her."

Amy shrugged. "OK, sure, but where is this guy?"

Mara sighed with relief. "At the Washington Hospital Center."

"When do you want to do this?"

"This afternoon. There's no time to waste. I think Dani might be in danger."

* * *

Randy jumped when the phone on his bedside table rang. He hesitated to pick it up. It had occurred to him that if someone had gone to the trouble of planting a listening device in his room, his phone was likely tapped as well.

"Randy?" a female voice asked tentatively. "It's Mara."

Randy sat up. "Mara? Hi. How are you? When are you coming to visit?"

"Randy, I have to talk to you. It's important." Her voice sounded urgent, and his heart rate accelerated. "I was so afraid you wouldn't have your hearing back. I'm glad you are able to talk on the phone."

He was able to hold a conversation, but was it a good idea over the phone?

"I'm sorry, Mara, but the nurse is here with my medicine," he lied glibly. "Let me take your number, and I'll call you back in a minute. OK?"

He heard her cover the phone with her hand and talk to someone before she came back on and gave him a number. "It'll be just a few minutes. OK?"

Randy rang his call bell and waited impatiently for a nurse. "Yes, Mr. Burton?"

"There was a guy in here just a little while ago, had a cell phone on him. He just left a few minutes ago. Could you ask him to come back here for a moment?"

"Is there anything wrong?"

"No, nothing like that."

The nurse shrugged and went in search of Jeffery, the orderly. He arrived ten minutes later. "Yes, sir?"

"Jeffery, I would really appreciate it if I could use your cellular phone."

* * *

Mara never would have thought that she'd be grateful to be inside the trunk of a car, any car. It was uncomfortable, certainly, and she'd had a moment of panic when Amy slammed it shut, but she had mastered that. She repeated the twenty-third Psalm and practiced deep breathing. Slowly in and out, in and out.

Before Amy had closed the trunk, they prayed together.

"Dear God," Amy said, her head bowed, a peaceful look on her face. "Please help Mara to get out of here safely. You know that Dani is depending on her. Please blind the soldiers at the gate like you did the mobs in the Bible who were bent on harm. Help her to find Dani, and help them to get somewhere safe. Amen."

Mara had marveled at what Director Aldridge would have called Amy's *religiousness*. Was Amy religious? Mara still didn't know. But Amy was certainly a different person than the one she remembered from college. And this woman had a deep and growing relationship with her heavenly Father.

Mara felt something in the trunk dig into her ribs as the car slowed down. She could hear the murmur of voices, and she stifled a shriek of surprise when a palm slapped the trunk before Amy accelerated and left Fort Detrick. They'd made it. She was free.

Tears of gratitude spilled onto her cheeks, and she felt her limbs trembling with release. By the time Amy pulled over on a dirt road to let her out of the trunk, she was shaking uncontrollably and hyperventilating. Amy helped her out of the trunk, and Mara sank onto the shoulder of the road trying to catch her breath.

"It's OK," Amy repeated over and over. "We made it. You're safe now."

But she wasn't safe now. She was less safe than she had been fifteen minutes earlier. But she was *free*. And that made all the difference. Slowly her breathing eased up, and she staggered onto her feet, leaning heavily against Amy, who helped her into the passenger seat.

"Are you going to be OK?" Amy asked with a worried glance before she pulled back out onto the road.

Mara took a deep breath and wiped her mouth with the back of her hand. "Yeah, I'll be fine. 'Even though I walk through the valley of the shadow of death, I will fear no evil,' remember?" She gave Amy more of a grimace than a smile, but Amy reached over and squeezed her hand.

"That's right. 'The Lord is my light and my salvation—whom shall I fear? The Lord is the stronghold of my life—of whom shall I be afraid?'" Amy quoted. "Now, I've got to get you to Randy Burton, so I can be on time for my weekly interview with Greg Harrison to keep the American public informed about the virus. Otherwise, Aldridge might be able to pin your disappearance on me."

Mara nodded and clutched an army knapsack to her stomach. Inside were an ankle brace and collarbone brace she had pilfered from the medical supplies at Fort Detrick. Randy had asked for them, and she had a suspicion that he planned to break out of the hospital. The thought excited and terrified her. What had she gotten herself into?

* * *

Mara entered the room a little shaken but with her arms full and a ghost of a smile for Randy.

"Hiya," Randy said, grinning.

"What's that look for?"

Randy eased himself into a sitting position and let Mara

lay the medical gear on the foot of his bed. "What look?"

"Cat-that-ate-the-mouse grin. You know what I'm talking about."

"Well . . . let's see. I'm getting my own personal physician. She's very kind, obviously intelligent and thoughtful, and she's extremely attractive." Randy shrugged. "What kind of look should I have?"

Mara's mouth fell open. If she had planned to say something, she'd completely forgotten it.

Randy was struck most by her clear blue eyes, now open so wide he felt somewhat guilty because he suddenly felt for all the world that he'd ambushed her. But the fact was, he would not have wanted to miss those eyes for anything. They were amazing. And they weren't upset with him. "I'm sorry. I probably shouldn't have been so forward."

Mara blinked. The first time in about a minute. Then she smiled while Randy's face turned deeply red. "Who said I was complaining?"

"Well, OK then, let's get me out of here," Randy said.

"I take it you're leaving against doctor's orders?"

Randy shrugged. "Whoever Dani is running from may know that she took a cab from here. It wouldn't have taken them but a few minutes to figure out that it dropped her off at Alice's place. Dani is confused and frightened. She doesn't know who she can trust. I have to leave and make sure she's all right."

"Dani is with Alice?" Mara gasped. "That's a relief. I wasn't sure how to go about finding her. But I don't know if it's a good idea to leave the hospital. I understand how you feel, Randy, but it's policy. Doctors can't have their patients leaving the hospital whenever they feel up to it."

Seeing Mara's anxiety took Randy down a notch from the high he was riding on getting out of this place. He hadn't realized how tired he was of being here, and now with the inconsistencies in the FBI's investigation, the unwillingness to pursue Gavin Larson, or to provide him information about

Brian Willis had made him increasingly uneasy. The final straw had been the visit from Dani and her insistence that the FBI was not seriously investigating the Freedom Society. He really needed to find out some answers for himself. He certainly couldn't do it in here. Mara must have felt the same kind of confusion and worry.

"Listen, Mara,"—Randy's voice became grave—"it's not safe here. If you're not comfortable with my leaving now, then I'll do this myself."

Mara stiffened. Randy thought she looked as if she were emotionally bottoming out. The dark circles underneath her eyes plainly showed how little rest she'd gotten lately. "Why is everything so messed up?" she moaned, rubbing both hands over her face and taking a long, deep breath. "Somebody's got to stick to the rules. But nobody is, not even your FBI."

"What do you mean?"

"I called from Fort Dietrich because that's where the FBI director allowed me to go. It was a mutual decision. Although he claims it is for my protection, I think he really wants to keep me away from Dani. That and he wants to keep me in some kind of custody without me actually feeling I'm being detained against my will. It's the same thing he was doing to Dani." Mara looked Randy in the eyes. "Do you know why?"

Randy shrugged. "I have no idea. If you haven't been formally charged, then it's illegal for him to hold you against your will." Randy smiled. "Which I guess gives you more freedom than I've got right now."

Mara laughed lightly. "I get the point."

"Show me how to work these braces, OK? And we'll go find her."

"I'm ready. *Uh-hmm,* but you're not. You need to get some clothes on before we brace your ankle and deal with your collarbone. I'll just go outside." Mara gathered his clothes from the closet and laid them on the bed.

"Could you check something out for me, Mara?" Randy asked.

"Yes?"

"I discovered a hidden microphone in my room earlier. It was very small, so its transmitter range is somewhat limited, meaning that somewhere outside this room but not too far away there's a minireel. I want to find it before we leave."

"You dress, I'll look," Mara said as she stepped outside his room. Five minutes later, she entered and shut the door, frantically looking around. "Aldridge is coming down the hall! What do I do? He can't see me here!"

"Did you find the minireel?" Randy had his jeans on and was trying to slip into his shirt.

Mara held up a small black box and wiggled it in the air for him while her eyes darted around for likely hiding places. "I found this above the nurses station. Shouldn't the tape be running, though?"

"It's voice activated." He pulled the tiny microphone out from under his pillow. "Look at it now. It should be running. Now hurry, you can hide in the bathroom while I talk to Aldridge." He didn't have to suggest the idea twice; it was the only possible hiding place.

Mara barely closed the bathroom door when Aldridge entered the room. Randy didn't have much time to notice. He was too busy trying to get under the covers.

Aldridge knocked on his way in, two agents right behind him. "How's your hearing, Burton?"

"Good. Real good." Randy carefully watched Kent Aldridge's expression. He was again struck by the man's physical presence. He was tall, wide in the shoulders, and athletic looking.

"How is the investigation going?" Randy asked.

Aldridge spoke to an agent on his security detail then closed the door for privacy. "We are still working on it. You know the Bureau likes to be sure it has the right person before it begins making arrests."

"Then you have developed some leads. You know who is responsible."

Aldridge waved his right hand and shook his head. "Now, I didn't say we have a suspect. I'm saying that this investigation will be thorough right from the beginning. All agents on the case have been instructed to be meticulous and precise in their investigations. The wreckage of both buses has been moved to the lab where the best scientists and technicians are carefully looking for physical evidence. I have over two hundred agents assigned to this case. Because of its high profile nature, I don't want agents affecting poor investigations. I want a solid, airtight case when we're finished.

"Yet you haven't focused on the Freedom Society. Why not seize the Freedom Society's assets and investigate the heart out of the organization? I believe I found enough evidence for a federal magistrate to issue a search warrant."

Aldridge's eyes narrowed for a fraction of a second; then he smiled rather condescendingly. "You must realize, Burton, that this is a delicate issue. I don't believe we have enough probable cause for freezing the Freedom Society organization. If we were wrong and subsequently violated people's civil rights on such a massive scale, the American people would be outraged. Already the president's murder has caused uncertainty in the economy. The stock market has yet to recover from the plunge it took the day after the assassination, and along with fears about this seemingly incurable disease, these things are frightening the American people."

"Then take that chance. This is the murder of the president of the United States we're talking about!"

"All the more reason to do it right the first time."

Randy shook his head with a silly half-smile. "You're protecting the Society, aren't you?"

"What?" Aldridge said with just enough disbelief to come off genuinely offended and justifiably outraged. "I *can* have you dismissed from the Bureau."

"Then we would hash this out in an Office of Professional Responsibility investigation, which I am sure you will want to avoid. All I want to know is why the Freedom Society is not the target of a full-scale investigation. I believe there are other witnesses who can support my undercover investigation. Isn't that true?"

Aldridge shook his head and began to chuckle. He wagged his finger at Randy. "You've spoken to the girl, Dani Talbot."

Randy ignored the comment. He was almost certain Aldridge knew that Dani had come to the hospital to see him.

"Considering your performance while undercover within the Freedom Society, I think an investigation into your dismissal would glide through the OPR."

Randy shook his head out of disbelief. "What are you talking about? You want to place blame for President Fairfield's murder on me?"

"I think it's possible to make that happen. Yes. Let's say, for instance, the investigation established that you were the last person to have been in contact with SAC Dave Watters, who was running your undercover operation. Then, the day before the president is assassinated, Agent Watters is found dead. That leaves just you who supposedly figures out that the Freedom Society is planning to assassinate President Fairfield. You claim you were frantically trying to find out what the Freedom Society was planning to do, but there is in fact no evidence the Freedom Society was even involved. Unfortunately, or maybe *conveniently for you* is a better choice of words, you were the only person to escape the explosion on the bus."

Randy trembled with rage. "I risked my life going undercover! Assign more agents to finding a man named Gunnar Dietrich, and you'll have even more evidence the Freedom Society assassinated the president. You might even get more information than you bargained for."

"Meaning precisely?"

"I also believe a thorough investigation of Gavin Larson will prove he played a large role in the assassination. Do you still have a man named Leaman in custody? I left him hand-cuffed in my house before I left it Thursday evening. If you still have him or know his whereabouts, question him exten-sively about his involvement in the assassination. I've already given you enough information to charge him with conspiracy to assassinate the president of the United States. Use his tes-timony. Cut a deal with him for more names." Why, Randy thought, was Aldridge seemingly uninterested in focusing the investigative power of the FBI on the Freedom Society?

"Burton, I am going to request an investigation from the OPR into your conduct before you are put back on active duty. Pending the outcome of an OPR investigation, you will be suspended from duty."

Randy stared at the director. "I can't believe this!"

Aldridge moved toward the door. "It would be in your best interest not to talk to anyone about your suspicions or inves-tigation. No one. Is that clear?"

"Is that a threat?"

"Take it however you want, Burton. If you obtain any more evidence, it comes to me first."

Randy waited a full minute after Aldridge left to call Mara out of the bathroom. In the meantime, he pulled his shirt on.

"I can't believe what I just heard," Mara said, coming around the bed and grabbing the air cast for Randy's ankle.

"Neither can I. I couldn't begin to tell you what he is up to."

"He must know Dani escaped him."

"I think he does. It's possible he was fishing for informa-tion about where she might have gone. Once I told him there were others who could testify to the Freedom Society's involve-ment in President Fairfield's assassination, he was positive that I was referring to Dani or at least knew something of what she knew.

Mara suddenly looked up from Randy's ankle, her eyes wide. "Are they going to check for that minireel while they're here? What happens if they don't find it?"

"Right! Let's get out of here."

Mara finished up with the soft cervical collar for Randy's fractured collarbone and helped adjust the height of the crutches. Randy stood up and took a few test steps.

"There, how did I look?"

"Pitiful," she grinned. "I've got the minireel and . . . where's your coat?"

"I gave it to Dani. I'll brave the weather without complaint if it means getting out of here."

Mara walked him out of the room. Aldridge and his security detail were standing in the corridor not more than fifty feet way. Aldridge was on his cellular phone with his back turned to Randy and Mara. They walked in the opposite direction slowly and stiff with fear.

"Should we borrow a wheelchair?" Randy whispered. "I thought that's how patients were supposed to exit a hospital."

"Well, silly, if we weren't trying to pretend you're not a patient, that would be a grand idea, wouldn't it?"

Randy grimaced. "No wonder my career as an FBI agent feels like it's over."

Once inside an elevator, Mara slumped against the wall. "I've had too much excitement for one day, I think."

Randy smiled.

As they headed across the main lobby, four agents were entering through the front doors. Two of them, one female and the other male, Randy recognized immediately. He changed course in the next step to put a wall between the agents and Mara and him and almost ran into an espresso kiosk.

"What's the matter?"

"Agents Roddrick and Miller. They were in my hospital room a couple of days ago to ask me questions. I think they must have been the ones who planted the microphone. I'll bet the minireel has just recently been discovered missing."

"What are we going to do?" Mara acted as if she were going to place a coffee order.

"I don't know," Randy whispered back. "Pray, maybe?"

"I've been doing that already."

"Then pray more, I guess." Randy turned around to face the kiosk with Mara. There was no place for them to go and certainly no way he could run. *I haven't done anything wrong. I haven't done a thing wrong,* he thought. *Dear God, Mara and I need Your help. I know You've helped me before, even when I haven't asked and when I didn't really care. What will happen to Lynn and Dani if Mara and I are not able to help them?*

All of a sudden laughter erupted nearby. Randy, who'd had his head bowed and eyes closed without even realizing he had done so, jerked his head up. A group of people, many of them college age, with songbooks and guitars were huddled not ten feet away.

"Hi!" a tall, wide redheaded man said with the warmest smile Randy had ever seen. "Come with us."

"Uh, what?"

The redhead motioned Randy and Mara over. "Come with us. We're leaving."

"If you don't mind me asking, wh . . . where did you come from?" Randy asked. The group looked as if it had been in the hospital cheering patients up with song.

"Please, come with us. We're leaving now."

Randy glanced at Mara, and she shrugged. "I guess we go," she said.

"I guess."

As they fell in with the crowd of singers, Randy tried to locate the FBI agents he and Mara had seen earlier but found it was impossible to see through the singing group. Then it dawned on him that the group's average height was well over his own height. They all walked outside into the cool evening air. Once outside, the singing group let Randy and Mara walk ahead.

"That was very opportune," Mara commented.

They turned around to thank the singers, although Randy wasn't sure how to explain their thanks. But he never had to because the group was gone.

Mara's mouth had fallen wide open. "Randy, did you see a van or bus parked out here to pick them up?"

Randy shook his head. "No. There wasn't one." Completely baffled, he aimed a crutch at a taxi. "But let's get out of here while we can."

Mara held Randy's crutches while he slid inside, then she climbed in and sat close. Randy took her hand, leaned over, and gave her a kiss. "We made it. I was afraid we wouldn't."

* * *

Dani struggled to tuck her legs up under her on the worn loveseat in the basement of the church Alice Nolan had taken her to. She pulled the cuffs of her sweater down over her hands farther and pretended she wasn't watching Alice Nolan and Lynn Burton. They were sitting at a folding table with their heads together over a Bible, talking earnestly. Every now and then they looked toward the stairs that led to the door as though they were expecting someone.

Dani was glad she'd come to Alice. For the first time since she'd stayed with Mara in the beginning, she felt safe again. From the moment she'd met Alice, there had been a connection, and Dani was reminded of her Grandma Talbot who had died when she was ten.

Alice was very much like her, bristling with mothering instincts and capable ways. She had immediately taken over mothering Dani, buying her a nice pair of maternity leggings, thick and lined with fleece to keep her legs warm, and a big, men's lambswool sweater to replace the horrible, ill-fitting nurse's uniform she had taken. Dani was warm and grateful.

Lynn was nice, too, but shy and withdrawn. She had her

nose constantly in a book, usually the Bible. When she wasn't reading, she was talking about what she'd read to Alice. Dani didn't think she meant to be excluding, it was just that she seemed obsessed with what she was learning.

Presently they were in a deep discussion about angels and trumpets and things. Dani sighed and tried to tune them out. She had more important things to think about. Somehow she had to get herself back out West. She couldn't wait around for Mara to come and help her. Apparently Mara had better things to do. And she couldn't afford to stick around here. Who knew when Aldridge or Dietrich would track her down? It was too risky. She had to get out.

She'd mulled the idea over in her mind numerous times. She had only one option. She couldn't wait until Monday and take the flight she was booked on. The FBI would easily have that staked out. Her only other option was to try to get to her father's car and drive back to Idaho. No doubt Alice and Lynn would try to talk her out of it, but she had to be firm. Her baby was depending on her.

She dropped her legs to the floor and pushed herself out of the loveseat. Walking over to Alice and Lynn, the older woman looked up at her with a smile. "Would you like to go lie down, dear?" she asked sympathetically. "You look tired."

"Actually," Dani began, "I was thinking I really should be getting out of here. It's time for me to go home."

"Oh, dear," Alice fretted. "I don't think that's such a good idea."

Dani braced herself. She had known this was coming. "I'm sorry, Mrs. Nolan, but I don't agree with you. The longer I stay in one place, the easier it is for the FBI or the Freedom Society to track me down." She lowered her voice. "I know you mean well, and you've been so nice to me. But I can't stay here."

"Can't you at least wait until Randy gets here?" Lynn pleaded. "Maybe he can help you find a way to get back home."

Dani's protest was replaced with surprise. "Randy is coming here?"

Lynn nodded. "He told Alice that he would meet us here when he could."

"B-but, why do we have to stay here?" Dani sputtered.

Lynn shrugged her thin angular shoulders. "I'm not quite sure, but Alice said Randy seemed anxious. He said he suspected you might be in danger." She paused. "I'm afraid something might have happened to him," she added quietly. Dani intercepted a look of sympathy Alice shot Lynn, and she gulped back a question.

What had happened to him?

Dani felt herself begin to tremble. The walls felt close and confining. On the other side of them, somewhere, were Dietrich and Aldridge. Randy thought she was in danger. How much longer would it be before something really did happen to her? Dani gripped the table, her fingers white-knuckled.

"You've both been so good to me," she heard her voice say from far away, "but I can't stay here any longer. Who knows how much time I have before they get to me? I've got to go. Can you give me a ride to my father's car? I can take that and drive to Idaho. At least there, I should be safe. My mother is there, and so is my dad's pastor. Please," she begged with a catch in her voice. "I have to leave. Now!"

Alice and Lynn exchanged looks. "OK. You're right. You're probably safer going out there than you are here where everyone is looking for you. But first, Lynn and I would like to pray for you. God is still in control of this situation no matter how it seems to us. May we pray?"

Dani nodded numbly. Sure, what would it hurt? Let them pray and then she could get out of here. She bowed her head, but her mind wasn't on Alice's words.

"Dear heavenly Father, we ask for your protection for Danielle. We ask You to send Your holy angels to guard her. Keep her safe from the FBI and the Freedom Society. Please watch over Randy also, Lord."

"Yes, Lord," Lynn breathed, a catch in her voice.

"You know where he is right now. Keep him safe as well. I claim these precious ones for You, Lord. Keep them in the palm of Your hand, I pray. In the name of Your blessed Son, Jesus. Amen."

The slam of the door upstairs and a clatter of footsteps descending the stairs made Alice, Lynn, and Dani's heads snap up in unison. Dani read fear in the faces of the others.

"They've found me," she said dully.

"Not yet they haven't," Alice said, pushing them toward a small room adjacent to the large one they had been in. She pulled the door shut behind them and they searched the dark area for additional places to hide. Dani found one first, and Alice and Lynn followed her behind the piano.

"Alice?" A voice called. "Lynn?"

"Randy!" Lynn yelled, scrambling out from behind the piano. She reached the door in two leaps. "Randy! We're in here."

Dani and Alice sheepishly crawled out from behind the piano and stood uncertainly as Randy and Lynn embraced. A woman in back of Randy peered around him, her expression tired and worried.

"Mara!" Dani exclaimed. "How did you find me? Where have you been? What are you doing here?"

"Dani! I'm so glad I found you." Mara skirted Randy and Lynn, who were talking excitedly. She grabbed Dani's shoulders and embraced her warmly. "You have no idea. I was so afraid for you."

"What's happened? Where have you been?"

"There's no time for that now," Mara said. "We've got to get out of here."

"I was just going to leave," Dani agreed excitedly. "I've got my father's car."

"Have you?" Mara asked absently at first, then her head snapped up and she stared intently at Dani. "Your father's

car? I don't know. I'm sure they will have my car under surveillance. They might have your father's under surveillance
too. They'll know it's his."

"No, they won't," Dani argued. "It's not really his. He borrowed it. It's registered to his pastor, and they'll never know
that."

"His pastor? No, I don't suppose the Freedom Society or
even the FBI is that far ahead yet. It's definitely worth a try.
Where is the car parked?"

"Wait just a minute," Randy interrupted, stepping over to
them with a frown. "What are you two cooking up?"

"We're going to take Jack's car and drive to Idaho," Mara
responded, summarizing their decision. "Dani doesn't feel she's
safe here, and I agree. You do, too, so will you help us?"

Conflicting emotions struggled on Randy's face, but finally
he nodded. "Of course. I just hate to see you go that far away."
His voice was wistful and brought Dani up short. There was
something in the way he was looking at Mara that was familiar. It was in the eyes, maybe. Shon had looked at her like
that early in their relationship. But, Mara and Randy weren't
. . . Dani bit back a smile. Maybe they were.

"Uh, Mara, you don't have to come," Dani offered quickly.
"I can get back by myself. I'll be OK. Really."

"No way. You're pregnant, and you're in trouble. You need
someone to travel with you. What if you went into labor on
the road or something? No. It's settled. I'm going with you."
Mara set her jaw, and there was a stubborn gleam in her eye.

"Alice will drive you," Randy said with resignation. "I
would, but with this ankle, it's impossible. Mara, can I talk to
you alone for a minute?"

Dani shuffled off to one side and began to collect her things.
She willed herself not to stare at Mara and Randy but found
her eyes drifting toward them. They talked intently for several minutes. She saw Mara give Randy what looked like a
miniature tape recorder, then Randy said something, and

Mara was blushing. Randy leaned over and kissed her cheek. Dani tore her eyes off them and concentrated on putting her few belongings into a tote bag. Suddenly Mara was beside her.

"All set?" she asked with forced brightness.

"Yup, all set," Dani agreed. She paused to hug Randy and Lynn before following Mara and Alice up the stairs and out to the car. Her eyes were brimming with tears, but she blinked them back. There was nothing to cry about. She was going home, where it was safe.

* * *

Brian wasn't sure how to react, except to run. But where to? And for how long and how far could he go without shoes and his feet in such poor condition? He looked down at his feet, and when he looked up again, the woman was at his side.

"Ya need help." It wasn't a question. She grabbed his arm and pulled him into the darkness. "Hide here." She pointed at a run-down cardboard box, something that had gotten wet a few times. Inside were pieces of grungy cloth.

Brian hesitated.

"Aah, ain't nothin' ta worry about. I'll help yuh."

"Why?"

"Ain't time ta argue. They gonna kill yuh, ain't they? And yore feet ain't in no shape ta carry yuh."

Seeing Brian's hesitation, the woman reached up to his shoulders and physically urged him into the filthy shelter. Her touch felt gentle and remarkably firm, and Brian had neither the time nor the will to resist. As he curled up inside the box, which lay against a concrete wall, the homeless community flooded with armed men.

Brian peeked through a hole in the box and watched as much as he could see without moving. The severe profile of

Dietrich's face moved in and out of his line of sight. He had a good view of the barrel he had come to in the first place, which was now surrounded only by the homeless man and woman. The woman seemed remarkably stoical and collected. Though shaking from fear and cold, Brian was intrigued with her, for she seemed to have a lot of nerve.

Dietrich's eyes roamed over the homeless community, then he walked over to the fire. In the crisp air Brian could clearly make out the voices. "Did either of you see a man come through here wearing no coat or shoes?"

Brian watched and listened carefully, waiting for the woman to sharply deny it. But she said, "Yes, a man came here." That was all she said, though Dietrich was clearly expecting her to elaborate.

"So, where is he? Which way did he go?"

The woman shrugged.

Come on! Point! Tell him something; just get him to leave! Brian thought. She wasn't helping as much as she could be. Why go to all the trouble to hide him and then risk herself and him like that?

Dietrich's lips cracked a grin. "OK, spread out and search every square foot of this place. Turn it all upside down," he said to his men.

"Why you wanna wreck what these folks got, Mistah?" the woman asked as Brian worriedly covered his head with newspapers and pieces of cloth.

He listened to the men moving back and forth and wondered how many Dietrich had with him. More than the two who'd been his captors, he felt sure. Maybe six or eight now. He found himself praying suddenly, his mind reaching out to God for help but also for the ability to accept his fate in faith. It was impossible for him not to be found. *Impossible!* Stopping here and then trusting the homeless woman had turned out to be a foolish decision.

But as Dietrich's men moved in and out among the homeless community, Brian's hiding place was left completely alone. He felt as if a miracle were taking place. Several times footsteps grew loud as they approached and then faded away without anyone checking his hiding place. He continued to pray and thank God for divine protection.

Finally, when it appeared they were moving on, Brian relaxed. He allowed himself to think he would soon be able to see his family. He'd fooled them. God had protected him. The moment he felt safe, someone walked up and tore the top off the cardboard box. Baseball cap, his guard from the warehouse, stared down at him.

"Got him right here, boys." He waved his gun for Brian to come out. "You best get out of there."

Brian crawled out and was led to Dietrich, who stood near the fire barrel along with the homeless woman. The other homeless in the area had either faded into the shadows or, fearing trouble, had left the area altogether.

"Brian Willis," Dietrich said. "We've never met, but you've managed to cause me a lot of problems just the same."

Brian's eyes shifted from Dietrich to the woman. He felt betrayed. "Why didn't you help me more? You could have told them I had gone on. It's almost as if you wanted them to stay. Why?" Paralyzed with hopelessness, his eyes began to cloud. The faces of his children, Matthew and Hannah, were in his mind. How long before he saw them now? He'd been so close to being free a few minutes ago. The woman met his gaze. Even with the anger and sense of betrayal heavy within his chest, he couldn't transfer it through his eyes. Yet he couldn't look away, either. Oddly, the look she returned gave him a sense of comfort.

"It will be all right," the woman said, and Brian felt compelled to believe her. It also didn't occur to him that her English had improved. It didn't occur to anyone at the moment.

Brian said, "Dietrich, I would appreciate knowing why I have been kidnapped."

Dietrich raised an eyebrow. "Gavin Larson ordered it to keep you from talking to the police."

"And he's right, I would have gone to the police. But he can't hide me forever."

"I know. It's not a concern anymore." Dietrich lifted a gun and pointed it at Brian's face. "I am not taking you back."

Brian nearly lost his legs beneath him. "You're going to kill me in cold blood? Right here in front of these witnesses?"

"It doesn't matter, Willis. No one will believe them."

Brian looked from Dietrich to the homeless woman, his eyes accusing her of putting him in this position. She had been no help at all, and, in fact, if it hadn't been for her, he might very well have gotten away.

"I'm sorry, Brian," she said simply.

"You know my name?" Oddly, it was the first thought that came to his mind. He couldn't remember telling her who he was.

"Yes, I do," she said in a warm, comforting voice.

While Dietrich stood there with the gun in Brian's face, Brian focused his attention on the woman. "Do I know you?"

"No, but I know you. I know you are afraid and angry right now, but don't worry. God is with you and watches over you and has sent me to be a protector and comforter to you."

"You're an angel," Brian said. The woman smiled. "But why did you allow me to get caught?" All the power of an angel nearby and he was about ready to be shot down by a cold-blooded killer . . .

Dietrich pressed the gun against Brian's forehead. "This is all very insane. You two are crazy. She's not an angel, and no one is going to protect you. You're a dead man right now!"

Brian closed his eyes and stiffened, expecting the explosion of the gun and instant death, but nothing happened. When he opened his eyes, the woman, or angel, stood beside him with her hand clamped firmly over the gun, part of her palm wedged in front of the hammer. Dietrich glared at her with fury and warned her to get back or he'd kill her as well.

"Gunnar Dietrich, I don't think that will happen," the woman said. "I am here to protect Brian. You cannot do what you have come here to do."

"Oh, you don't think so, huh?" Dietrich tried to yank the woman off balance, but he couldn't budge her. She stood as solid as a mountain. "All right, I warned you to stay out of it," Dietrich said, and he pulled the trigger. The hammer snapped forward, but with the woman's hand in the way it was ineffectual. She calmly removed her hand, easing the hammer down.

Dietrich turned away as if giving up but then raised the gun swiftly and shot at Brian and the woman.

But he missed.

Neither Brian nor the woman stood in the same place. Now they were opposite the fire barrel. A dozen eyes blinked.

"Dietrich, you will not attempt to harm Brian any further, but you will take him with you. As you can see, I won't allow it."

"What? What do you mean, 'he can take me?'" Brian asked.

"Do not fear, Brian. Trust completely in God, and you will have peace, comfort, and understanding."

"I don't see how," Brian said.

The woman smiled and squeezed Brian's hand. "God has a plan for you, Brian. You may not understand it now, but you will."

Then, in a moment when everyone present felt they must have blinked, the dirty homeless woman—the angel, disappeared.

Dietrich avoided looking at Brian. He put away his gun and ordered his men to bring Brian, and they left the homeless community, piled into their vehicles, and drove back to the abandoned warehouse.

Brian was returned to the office and ordered to strip to his underwear as a deterrent to escaping again. Two guards with broken barbwire tattoos were stationed permanently outside the door, able to watch him constantly through the window-less frame that Brian had broken during his escape.

"Dietrich," Brian said, "I'd like to phone my family." Dietrich was on his way out the door. He paused and turned around.

"You know, Willis, if I could, I'd kill you just as soon as talk to you."

Brian spread his arms, hands open, completely vulnerable and humiliated. "Then do it, Dietrich. Kill me now. If I will never see my family again, then I have no reason to live."

Dietrich didn't hesitate. He grabbed his 9mm, aimed it at Brian's chest, and pulled the trigger in one fluid movement, as if the sudden action couldn't be deterred by either human hands or heavenly angels. The gun bellowed.

Scarcely a second later, Dietrich turned pale. *It was impossible!* Brian Willis stood in front of him, completely unharmed. Dietrich swallowed hard. "I may not be able to kill you, Willis, but you will never speak to your family again. Never!"

Dietrich's words cut Brian to the core, but he would not allow himself to accept their finality. "Then allow me to have a Bible. Give me that much, at least, or else I'll go crazy in here."

Dietrich took a moment to think this over then shook his head. "No, Willis, no Bible either." He walked out and shut the door. Brian listened to him descend the stairs.

Lying down on the cot, Brian spread the one blanket over him and let his mind drift through a million memories of home and family. Why had he spent so much time away from his wife and children? The time he had spent in the Coalition seemed like such an utter waste now, and he felt a deep rage toward Gavin Larson but also toward himself. Was there no way he could make up for the lost time now? He began to relax, and as his mind drifted toward sleep, he regretted not having a Bible to read for comfort.

Knowing he had read the Bible in its entirety and hundreds of individual texts over and over again, he thought he must be able to remember the words of his favorite texts. Eyes closed, he tried to remember a verse from James about faith that seemed to be nudging his conscious. *"Consider it pure joy, my brothers, whenever you face trials of many kinds, because you know that the testing of your faith develops perseverance. Perseverance must finish its work so that you may be mature and complete, not lacking anything."* It came from James. *James 1:2-4.*

Brian's eyes flashed open. "Oh, Jesus, You wanted me to remember this verse!"

One of the guards banged on the door. "What's going on in there?"

"Nothing. I'm talking to my Lord God," Brian said. He smiled and closed his eyes again. He visualized another text that had come to mind: " *'Blessed are you when people insult you, persecute you and falsely say all kinds of evil against you because of me. Rejoice and be glad, because great is your reward in heaven, for in the same way they persecuted the prophets who were before you.'* " This text was found in Matthew 5: 11, 12, and Brian could see the words clearly, as if he had a photographic memory. He chuckled as tears ran freely. "God has supercharged my memory," he said quietly.

Chapter Five

Thursday, November 25

Amy Cooper squeezed her husband, Ray's, hand as he climbed into the baptismal tank. She had never seen such a look of pure joy on his face. Tears streamed down her own cheeks. This was the most wonderful day of their lives. As soon as Ray was baptized, it would be her turn. Today they were making a stand for the truth and joining the church of the Remnant Believers.

They had been coming to the Remnant Believer's church for a couple of months, but after Gavin Larson's disturbing speech, they had really discussed what was happening in the world. To them there seemed to be two factions. On one hand was Gavin Larson's mainstream evangelical movement, which was merging with the Catholic Church; on the other was the Remnant Believers, who were being blamed for the wrath of God on His people. But all their study had only convinced them more that the Remnant Believers had the truth, a truth Gavin Larson was simultaneously watering down and reshaping to fit his agenda.

It would have been easy to join the Gavin Larson bandwagon, but by the time they reached that point, neither Amy nor Ray could do that with a clear conscience. The previous evening Pastor Ellis had come for the last in their Bible study series. After he left, they had stayed up all night long discussing what to do next. Joining the Remnant Believers would put them both in serious jeopardy.

Amy would be fired immediately if it were known that she was a member of that church. "There's too much for me to do still, Ray," she'd said. "There might be a chance for me to solve the puzzle of this virus and come up with a cure. I just don't think God wants me to leave yet. I've been praying for His will for me and asking for His heart, and I just don't think it is the right time for me to leave just now. I just won't tell anyone. They'll find out soon enough."

Ray had agreed, and they had decided that he should quit his job and go into full-time lay ministry with the help of Pastor Ellis and others, since the end seemed so close. Neither could see any advantages to his keeping his present job, but they prayed about that before the night was over too. In the morning, they had called Pastor Ellis and requested immediate baptism. He had happily agreed.

But it wasn't until later, when Amy reported to work, her hair still damp, that she realized just how dangerous and tenuous her position at the Fort was. Particularly in light of her accountability to Gavin Larson. She had tried to sever the connection, but Larson wouldn't be put off. Finally she had appealed to her superiors, but that hadn't worked either. Although he had yet to be sworn in, Donald Thurgood requested that she continue to work with Gavin Larson and supply him with any information he desired. He was cleared at the highest levels.

Amy decided that the best course of action was to keep her mouth shut and do what she was told. God had placed her in her position for some reason, and He was in control, after all. He could handle Gavin Larson. That wasn't her responsibility. Her primary responsibility was to try to find a cure for the virus.

She spent the remainder of the morning doing paperwork at her desk. After lunch she planned to go into Level 4 and do an autopsy on a soldier who had died early that morning in the Slammer—the holding area for those infected with the virus—displaying several symptoms in addition to the usual ones the virus produced. Colonel Gary Hudson would be accompanying her. She met him outside the locker room. Since there was only one and they both had to get changed, he motioned her to go ahead of him.

Amy felt her heart pick up some speed as she undressed and pulled on the sterile green scrub suit that was all she would wear beneath her bright blue Chemturion biological space suit. Ultraviolet light—which smashed viruses—streamed through a window in the door leading to Level 2. Amy tugged on the door. Negative air pressure, designed to suck air *into* the room rather than push it *out* of the room, held the door tightly, and she tugged harder until it opened. In Level 2 she put on a pair of white socks and then went through another door into Level 3.

This room was called the staging area. There was a desk, sink, and telephone. A few empty biohazard containers served as chairs. Amy found the bottle of baby powder and shook it onto her hands before pulling on yellow rubber latex gloves. Tearing off several strips of tape, she began to tape herself. She taped her gloves to her sleeve and her socks to her pant legs, making a seal. This was her first layer of protection against the hot agents in Level 4.

Amy was just zipping her space suit up when Colonel Hudson entered the room and began to repeat her procedures. Amy reached over to the wall and grabbed a coiled yellow air hose, plugging it into her suit. Immediately she heard the roar of flowing air, and the suit bloated up. The fog that had accumulated on her faceplate after she zipped up the suit vanished.

Amy fought to control the nervousness she always felt just before stepping into Level 4 while she waited for Hudson to finish suiting up. When he was ready, she picked up a pack of dissection tools and faced the stainless-steel door that led into an air lock and Level 4. She unplugged her air hose, unlatched the steel door, and entered the air lock. Hudson followed her, and the door closed behind them.

The air lock was stainless steel and lined with nozzles for spraying water and chemicals. This was the decon shower, which they would have to go through on the way out of Level 4. Amy crossed the air lock, opened the door, and stepped into the hot side.

On the other side of the door was a narrow cinder-block corridor. Hudson followed behind her as Amy entered the necropsy room—sometimes called the Submarine—where they were going to perform the autopsy. The cadaver was laid out on a stainless-steel table, covered with a sheet. They plugged in their air hoses, and Amy began laying out the instruments they would need.

"GLOVE UP," Hudson said, shouting, so Amy could hear him over the roar of air in her suit.

Amy pulled on another pair of latex rubber gloves over her spacesuit ones. Now she had three layers of protection against the hot agent. Hudson would be doing the autopsy. Amy was assisting. As he called for instruments, she placed them in his hand. They moved slowly, methodically. They could afford no mistakes.

She wasn't sure quite how it happened. Hudson was having trouble cutting through some tissue, and she moved her hand over to help when suddenly she felt a searing pain between her thumb and first finger. Looking down, she saw her hand drenched in blood, both her own bright red, and the dead soldier's nearly black. Hudson's scissors were embedded in her hand.

"OH, MAN! AMY, I'M SORRY!" Hudson shouted. She saw fear in his eyes. "MY HAND SLIPPED. I'M SO SORRY!"

"I'M GETTING OUT! FOLLOW ME. I'M GOING TO NEED HELP." Amy unplugged the air hose with her good hand and raced down the corridor to the air lock. Standing in the decon shower, she pulled the chain, and it started up. It would take seven minutes. And then another seven for Hudson. There was too much time to think.

What have I done? her mind screamed. *I've been exposed. Now they're going to send me to the Slammer. And then, in a couple weeks, I'll be in the Submarine, and they'll come and dissect me. Oh, Lord, how could this happen? I was just baptized this morning!*

That thought calmed her. She'd just been baptized. Everything was in God's hands. It was going to be OK. Everything was going to be OK. He was in charge.

The accident report concluded that Colonel Amy Cooper had been exposed to the Cartier virus. She was admitted to the Slammer, and Hudson promised to contact Ray. And Amy cradled her bandaged hand while she sang children's Bible verse songs to herself as she waited for sleep to come.

* * *

The interesting thing about life was how crazy it could become so quickly. And yet, no matter how crazy and mixed up it got, there were reasons to wear a smile and feel warm from the heart.

Mara was one of those reasons. Randy Burton missed Mara a lot, and it was something to feel good about because he knew these feelings were because of a deep, very real, connection they had both felt and that he had never experienced in his life. Remembering their brief moments together made his heart ache. He found himself thinking about her often. He wondered where she was and prayed for her safety every time she crossed his mind.

He'd been crazy, he told himself, to let her and Dani go alone. He should have insisted on accompanying them. As soon as she delivered Dani safely, he was going to talk her into coming back. Without her he felt lonely and detached. He knew he could never go back to the FBI. That world was far behind him, and there was too much going on in the Bureau that was confusing to him. Aldridge was running a shoddy investigation, as if he were trying to hide something in the confusion.

When he could drive, he had borrowed Alice's car. Returning to his house, he had a feeling that it had been searched— very carefully—and with everything replaced just as it had been found. There were special teams who did this kind of work. The operations were called "black bag jobs" and were performed by a highly skilled team who were part of the FBI's Special Operations Group. Each member of the team was a specialist and assigned a specific duty. The agents entered, searched through files, cataloged everything, took thorough pictures, downloaded computer hard drives, and left without leaving a trace they had ever been there.

Randy felt, more than found, evidence that it had happened. But he couldn't be positive. He was unsure what they were after and wished there was someone he could contact to find out what was going on. But FBI agents were extremely loyal. If they were led to believe he was an agent who'd gone bad, no one within the Agency would talk to him.

Randy packed his and Lynn's things. They hadn't had much. He had gone there from the Freedom Society, and Lynn had had few things with her when she came to live with him. Most of his stuff was stored in a storage unit in Virginia. It had been over a year since he'd opened the unit, and there was nothing there he needed right now. His life was too uncertain for him to rent an apartment.

He drove back to the church and unloaded with Lynn and Alice's help. With the last of the clothes stored in the pastor's office, Randy sank into a chair. "Thank you, Alice. I don't know where Lynn and I would be without your help."

"It's my pleasure to help."

Randy smiled. "Thank you. But now, I don't know what to do." He shrugged and gave Lynn a questioning look. "What about you?"

"I don't have any plans other than to continue doing God's work. I've got thirteen Bible studies going, and it's hard for me because I don't know that much about the Bible."

"You certainly know more than I do," Alice commented.

Lynn shook her head hopelessly. "I don't know about that. I just wish I knew more. It's all I can do to answer half of people's questions. Every time I leave someone's house, I have more questions that I had before I got there."

A little perplexed, Randy was watching his sister, still wrestling with her comment about the amount of Bible studies she was giving. "You have thirteen Bible studies? How? I mean, it's only been a few days, not even a week, before you started your first study!"

Lynn shrugged. "I don't know where they all came from. Right after you were hurt, the pastor got a call from someone who wasn't even a Remnant Believer asking about Bible studies. By the next morning, she had received thirty calls from people who had suddenly felt impressed to call."

"Yes," Alice agreed. "And since there were so many requests, the pastor was scrambling for people to give studies, and so Lynn and I volunteered."

"Are calls still coming in?" Randy asked.

"Yes, they are," a woman's rich speaking voice said from the doorway.

"Hi, Pastor James," Lynn said. "I'd like you to meet my brother, Randy."

Jenny James smiled warmly as Randy stood to shake her

hand. "I'm pleased to finally meet you, Randy."

"It's my pleasure."

Jenny James's hazel eyes sparkled. She was Randy's height and a little heavyset. "Lynn had asked me to come see you in the hospital, but I'm afraid I'm far too late for that now. I'm sorry."

"Oh, don't worry. I had plenty of company."

Section II

The United States Government swore into the presidency former Speaker of the House Donald Thurgood on Thursday, November 25. The amount of time the country had gone without a president was unprecedented, but so were the circumstances—and so were the events to come . . .

A press conference immediately followed, which Secret Service agents had made extremely secure. The obvious reason was a justifiably deep paranoia after President Fairfield's assassination. However another problem, and one much more obscure to outsiders, was the confusion within the ranks of the FBI and the channels of communication between the Secret Service agents and Bureau agents. The two agencies bustled with rumors about the lack of direction in the investigation of President Fairfield's assassination.

Oddly enough, SHAME was the code name assigned to the investigation of President Fairfield's assassination. Although Director Aldridge demanded that any investigation was to be headed up by his Bureau, agents in the field were inclined to ignore agency rivalries on this one. Despite their cooperative efforts, however, there were few developments in the case. All of which was terribly frustrating to the dedicated agents in both agencies.

The investigation bogged down and threatened to come to a complete standstill. FBI Director Aldridge gave high priority to seemingly dead-end leads while many agents were convinced they should be looking more closely at the Freedom Society.

Midnight Hour

Immediately after Thurgood became president, he instructed the attorney general, Collin Soran, to begin an investigation of Kent Aldridge. The request caught Soran by surprise, and he called a meeting of top Justice Department prosecutors to discuss Thurgood's request. He then returned a decision on the presidential order: The Justice Department did not feel it could investigate Director Aldridge without sufficient proof of wrongdoing.

Tension arose between the White House and the Justice Department. Thurgood called Soran directly, making a more forceful request for an investigation of Director Aldridge. Collin Soran became incensed, stating emphatically that he would not start an investigation without substantiation of some kind of misconduct by Director Aldridge.

Chapter Six

Friday, November 26

When President Thurgood received the second call from Soran, Gavin Larson was present in Thurgood's private office.

"Yes, Mr. Soran. I understand the law. I'll see that you have the evidence you need." Thurgood glanced at Gavin. Gavin nodded as Thurgood hung up.

From behind his desk, President Thurgood said, "To me, this all seems extremely risky. Aldridge, of course, can implicate us if he feels threatened."

"He can try," Gavin said. "And I'm sure he will. But I have a way to preempt Kent Aldridge."

Despite his powerful position, Thurgood appeared extremely uneasy. "How can you keep Aldridge from attacking us? He must have evidence of his own that could be damaging. As you've mentioned before, he is an intelligent man."

Gavin's jaw muscles worked, and he smiled smugly. "If the attorney general and the Justice Department want evidence to get an investigation off the ground, Brian Willis can give a deposition that will do it."

"Explain how Willis can help us, Gavin. I know Willis. He's a man who would never lie. He cannot be bought. Why, he even balked at the thought of continuing in the Coalition when you asked him."

"I remember, Donald. But I am not interested in buying lies from Brian Willis. Of course it would never work. And to threaten his life may be equally fruitless. But threatening him with the lives of his family is an efficient means of coercion, don't you think?"

Thurgood frowned. "What about your giving orders for Dietrich to kill Brian? If he had succeeded, you wouldn't have this option. All these variables concern me. I'm not comfortable with problems that neither you, Dietrich, nor I seem to have any control over."

Gavin remained silent for a moment. He did not appreciate Thurgood's doubts, and it concerned him deeply when people became so easily shaken by obstacles. Problems caused weaker people to doubt, and doubt bred fear for one's personal well-being over the interests of the majority.

"Donald, learn to trust me, will you? When I was your aide, you followed my advice and trusted my judgment without question. I wish you would do the same now."

Soberly, Thurgood shook his head. "Look at the changes, Gavin. Look at where I am and where you are, for heaven's sake." He stood and walked from behind his desk, looking deeply thoughtful and concerned. "I hold the fate of this great country in my hands. My decisions affect more than two hundred million people. And look at you . . . the most influential spiritual leader in the world! It makes our existence before now seem very trivial, doesn't it? But if you think about it, everything we have done up until now has been in preparation for this very moment. Let's not do anything to jeopardize the trust of the American people."

After a protracted, uncomfortable silence for President

Thurgood as he studied Gavin's eyes, Gavin threw back his head and howled with laughter. "Oh, you small-minded man." His black eyes pierced Thurgood, and the older man jerked from Gavin's insult. "How stupid are you? Donald, you have served this country for more than a quarter of a century and yet you are as blind and naïve as everyone else." His laugh died away slowly, under Thurgood's flustered and confused stare.

Gavin's voice shifted to a more concrete and sinister pitch. Thurgood retreated, almost scurried, behind his desk for protection. "How long have you trusted me? Years. And this is the way you repay me for my support. How many times do I have to remind you how you became the president of the United States? How many times, Donald?"

As Thurgood's blood pressure rose, Gavin lightly shook his head, wearing an odd smile, his chin down, his pupils shaded ominously by lowered lids. Thurgood didn't speak, couldn't speak really. He was too stunned. "You, of course, want to know what I was referring to when I called you naïve." Gavin stood and walked toward the desk. "Maybe it's time I introduced you to your role in the future. Up until now, you've been stumbling along quite myopically, Donald. You have trusted to your education, instincts, and minor attention to spiritual matters to guide you through life and years in Congress."

"Yes, I have served my country. I've done it well and certainly not by stumbling around unwittingly. And certainly not myopically, as you believe. My long tenure in Congress proves my constituents have considered me a wise and dedicated public servant. So how dare you speak to me as if I were some kind of baffoon!"

"Then wake up!" Gavin snapped. "Remember why you're here! And remember that no matter who you are, if you're not in a position of power, you can do nothing! A dead man cannot lead this country, and that's just what you would be now if you had not been healed! A few short weeks ago, you were making peace with God. A man limited by death. But now look at where you are! Even as millions of people watched you decay, I had a different insight into your future."

"Are you telling me you knew that I would not die, that God was certainly going to heal me? You're a lunatic, Gavin. I am not someone you can fool. Don't try to make me believe that God has blessed you with prophetic visions. You may be a spiritual leader, but you are by no means a spiritual man. That I discovered a long time ago." Thurgood snapped contemptuously as he stormed out of the room.

* * *

It was a beautiful place. The light was warm and the air so alive with purity that each breath was like taking a deep draught from a mountain waterfall. There were trees, and he could hear birds, but they were on the fringes of his consciousness, beautiful but unimportant. He walked, at least it felt like walking, only there was a bounce in his step that hadn't been there since he was a boy. No pain nagged at his old joints. He stood straight and tall, striding with excitement and purpose. Where was she? He knew she was here.

"Here I am, my little father." Her voice sparkled like chimes. It echoed like the rich peal of bells ringing through the thin air on an icy day in Rome, clear and perfect.

"Mother?" he asked, and turning he saw her. She was seated beneath a tree. Her arms wrapped around her body, her youthful face sad. As he drew nearer he could see tears staining her perfect cheeks. "Mother!" he exclaimed in dismay. "Why do you cry?"

"I weep for my people," she replied, "who weep not for themselves. They do not love me, for they do not do as I ask." She lifted her eyes to him, and there was a hint of reproach in their blue, fathomless depths. "Why do you allow them to delay? Do *you* not love me?"

Xavier felt a shooting pain, like a knife driven deep in his breast at the very thought. "Oh no, Mother, please do not suggest such a thing! I would do anything for you. I would die for you. I am yours alone."

"Then why?" she asked, fresh tears spilling down her cheeks. "Why do you not force them to listen? The time is so short. My Son grows angrier every day. I cannot hold Him back from seeking vengeance upon my stubborn people, and I do not want to see them harmed. They are my children. Each one of them is precious." She reached out a hand and caressed his jaw. "But, you, my little father, are the most precious of them all. You will make them see the urgency, will you not?"

He reached up to lay his hand on her own and found it warm and soft beneath his touch. Tears broke his voice. "Yes, Mother, yes. I am sorry there has been a delay at all, but you must know that the very men who will help me are in the midst of great change. Soon they will be in position to urge the people, with me, to appease the Mighty Jesu and follow His will for their lives."

Suddenly the holy mother's face grew dark with anger, and terror struck Xavier's heart. In a tightly controlled voice she said, "That they may know that what I have told you is true and that they will heed your voice and save themselves, I will make this vow to you. Because of the hardness of their hearts, I will cause the western coast of the United States to fall into the sea."

Xavier fell to his knees, stricken with the magnitude of the destruction this would cause. He clutched at the hem of her shining garment. "Mercy, my mother," he pleaded. "Mercy for your people. Give me time."

Mary nodded and smiled. But her smile was sad and never reached her eyes. "Very well. You may tell them they have 72 hours." She laid a warm hand upon his shoulder. "My son, you have served me well," she said. "I see that you have done all that is within your power. My favor rests upon you. Go in peace." As she spoke, her voice became distant, and the light faded.

The trees, birds, and indigo sky were gone. Pope Xavier jerked up from his bed, reaching, grasping, but his fingers met only thin air. She was gone and the beautiful light with her.

"Mother," he whispered hoarsely. "Don't leave me, Mother." He lay back on his bed, aware now that his pillow was wet with tears. The lovely feeling of youth had vanished, and in its place were the perpetual pains that assailed his old frame daily. He rolled over and peered far-sightedly at the clock. He knew without looking that it would be four o'clock, the time when the Holy Mother usually visited him.

He thought about calling Gavin Larson at this hour. He had not been pleased the last time. Since discussing the Sunday law, little had happened to institute it. Pope Xavier, unfamiliar with the wheels of politics, found them to grind frustratingly slow. From what he had been told, by Larson and even by President Thurgood himself, there was little that could be done, short of a national emergency, that would make them move any quicker.

The old pope swung his arthritic legs over the side of the bed and pushed himself up into a sitting position. He paused a moment as his blood pressure adjusted to the new position. Then he picked up the phone and dialed Gavin Larson's number. Something must be done immediately to prevent the tragedy the Holy Mother had warned of.

"I must speak to you immediately," he said tersely after announcing himself to the sleepy voice of Larson. "There is to be an earthquake that will cause the whole of your West Coast to fall into the sea."

"Wha—" Larson was obviously struggling to comprehend. "How do you know this?"

"Our Holy Mother came to me in a vision. She is not happy about how slowly things are progressing. The Sunday law must be passed *immediately*." Pope Xavier spoke so forcefully that spittle spewed out of his mouth and sprayed the phone.

"These things take time, Your Eminence," Larson said, frustration mounting in his voice. "We barely have a new president. It's impossible to move so quickly."

"We don't have time. Only 72 hours. That is all she has given us. Seventy-two hours before the destruction of your West Coast. Surely you can do something to save those people."

There was silence on Larson's end. Then, "I'll see what I can do. But I can't make any promises. Meet President Thurgood and me in the Oval Office this morning at 7. I'll inform the president of the meeting, but you're going to have to convince him of the urgency."

Pope Xavier readied himself and spent the remainder of the morning at his prayers. When he rose from his knees to meet with President Thurgood and Gavin Larson, he had steeled himself to be polite but firm. He was not asking for favors. He was insisting on instituting the policy already agreed upon.

President Thurgood rose respectfully, but Larson remained seated when Pope Xavier was ushered into the Oval Office. "Please, Your Excellency, be seated. Help yourself to breakfast. I asked my personal secretary to arrange for some bagels and such. Nothing? A shame. Forgive me, but I'm famished. Please go ahead. Gavin tells me that you've had another vision?"

Pope Xavier ignored the cynical smile Larson was trying to hide and concentrated on the president as he covered a bagel with jam and helped himself to a plate of scrambled eggs. "Our Holy Mother visits me often, but this time she was most severe. She is angry that we have not instituted the policies *agreed upon in this very room* which will appease her Son. He will not stay His hand much longer."

"But, Your Excellency," Thurgood protested, licking jam off his fingers and trying to look indulgent at the same time, "surely you understand that these things take time. I've only just become president. The country hasn't recovered from the whirlwind of events of the last month yet. I am hardly in a position to push through what is bound to be a rather controversial bill. Let me build some support first. Then the bill will breeze through without a hitch. The country will not even murmur a protest, I promise you."

"Seventy two hours," Pope Xavier said, setting his mouth in a hard line. "That is all the Holy Mother allows you to do as she asks. After that she will cause the West Coast of America to fall into the sea."

"You can't be serious." Thurgood looked from the pope to Gavin and back to the pope.

"I assure you, I am. She says in this way she will prove to you that what she says is true, and she hopes very much that you will save these people from such a terrible fate by following through on your promise."

Thurgood sat back in his chair, a defeated slump to his shoulders. "Surely you can't be serious. I haven't the means or the resources. I especially don't have the time."

Pope Xavier sat forward in his chair. "It is a national emergency, is it not?"

"No one will believe anything of the sort," Larson spoke up, his voice laced with ridicule. "Look, Your Excellency, we're doing the best we can, and we want to work with you on this, but you have to be patient. We have our own concerns at the moment, which are a bit more pressing. After that, we will be more than happy to cooperate with you to our mutual advantage."

Pope Xavier rose. "You do not believe the Holy Mother." Neither man disputed the statement. Pope Xavier sighed heavily. "When you see that I am telling the truth, I will be willing to help in any way I can." Gathering his robes about him with great dignity, Pope Xavier turned and made his way from the room. A stony-faced security guard opened the door for him.

Maybe Thurgood and Larson were willing to allow thousands of innocent people to perish without so much as lifting a finger, but Pope Xavier definitely was not. Television would help him to warn the American people. *They deserve at least a chance to know what is coming*, he decided. *And may God have mercy on their souls.*

* * *

Randy got out of Alice's car and limped up to the massive J. Edgar Hoover Building, a structure that looked like a couple of offset building blocks. Inside, it quickly became obvious he was to get no farther than the front desk.

"Is Director Aldridge in?"

"Yes, sir," The receptionist replied politely. "But he will not see anyone without an appointment."

"My name is Randy Burton. I'm an agent . . . or I used to be an agent," he added.

"Then you know it's impossible to see Director Aldridge, Mr. Burton."

"Do you know who I am?"

"Yes. You're the agent who failed to save the president. Everyone in the Bureau knows who you are."

"A few days ago I was being called a hero for saving those children. Now I'm a pariah. Doesn't it seem strange to anyone that the investigation of the president's assassination is going nowhere? Why is that? It seems I'm the only person who knows the investigation is being led in circles. I was in an undercover operation that was blown right from the beginning because of someone higher up. Someone higher up than me or Special Agent Dave Watters knew what was going on. Someone who was working for Freedom Society as well." He unloaded his suspicions as if she were his only hope. It would have been worthless prattle if she were merely a receptionist, but she was an agent. If he could just get her to question some of the things he was telling her.

"Mr. Burton. I'm going to have to ask you to leave."

"Please, you have to listen to me," Randy protested.

The agent's response, of course, was to ignore him. Left with his last option, he reached inside his jacket and pulled out a manila envelope. This grabbed the agent's attention, and she watched him carefully.

"Don't worry, I haven't flipped out. This isn't a bomb."

She spared him an unfriendly smile.

"I think Aldridge will want this, so be sure he gets it."

Randy left the package in the agent's hands and walked briskly out of FBI headquarters for the last time.

* * *

"What do you suppose that was about?" Gavin asked as he watched the video monitor that ran a live feed from the lobby. Shortly after his meeting with the pope and Thurgood, he had insisted on a meeting with Aldridge.

"That was Randy Burton. I don't believe you know him. But he's the one who saved the children."

"Ah. So that's him."

"Every agent in the Bureau believes he's crazy. No one will listen to him. If he gets to be a problem for me, I will do something about it, I can assure you," Aldridge smiled. "What exactly have you come to discuss? It wasn't Burton."

"No. I want to ask about the girl, Dani Talbot. I want her turned over to me."

Aldridge stared at Gavin.

Gavin proceeded with his bluff. "I'm willing to pay a great deal for her."

"I can imagine. She could cause you a great deal of frustration, knowing as much as she does about the Freedom Society and its connection to your United Religious Coalition."

"Then, let's make a deal. I know you have no altruistic views. You are merely interested in money, and I am willing to pay you two million dollars if you will agree to stop interfering."

"And you?" Aldridge asked. "What are you truly interested in? Something more idealistic? Don't try to fool me as you have fooled yourself, Gavin. You are no more altruistic than I am. You just disguise it well enough to fool even yourself."

Gavin's eyebrows raised. He made a move to extract himself from the chair and leave. "I'm growing tired of these games, Aldridge. I'm willing to offer you a great deal of money. Otherwise President Thurgood will press for your removal regardless of the Attorney General's advice."

"I hardly think of that as a threat." Aldridge smiled. "You have much more to lose should your involvement in President Fairfield's assassination be uncovered."

Gavin laughed aloud as he walked across the office. "You don't have enough evidence to touch me, Aldridge. You said yourself no one will believe Randy Burton. That leaves you with one witness, Dani Talbot." Before opening the director's door, he turned and said, "But you don't even have her anymore, do you?"

Gavin's comment stung Aldridge, and it probably would have made him angrier than it did if he hadn't been concerned about the package he saw Randy Burton hand to the agent at the receptionist's desk. Whatever it contained, he had a feeling it wasn't going to be good news. As soon as Gavin closed the door, Aldridge dialed the front desk.

"That package Burton left. Was it for me? Yes, I was watching. I'd like it brought to me right away. Right, make sure it's not a bomb. Thank you."

The package arrived fifteen minutes later. Aldridge found a single microcassette tape inside, along with a note assuring him he only had a copy of the original. He shook his head in disbelief. *More problems. That's what I need.*

* * *

Mara sat in the sun room of the old farmhouse and soaked up the bright rays that filtered in the somewhat grimy windows and splashed across the worn hardwood floors where two toddlers played with snap-blocks. She wished the events of the last month would seep into her conscience as easily as the sun drenched the room. As she stared at the peeling paint on the window casings, she tried to untangle the mess of scenes her memory had captured, but she couldn't do it. They were too knotted, too distorted and confused.

The days since she and Dani had left Washington to come here to Idaho were equally jumbled. Days and nights spent on the road, driving to near exhaustion. Still, they had pressed on. Talking out loud to each other and singing at the top of their lungs to keep awake. They'd eaten nothing but junk food purchased at convenience stores along the way. When they had finally staggered out of the car at Dan Reiss's house, they had both been near collapse. Mara had slept thirty of the preceding forty-eight hours. Dani was still asleep.

A hand touched her shoulder gently, and she started and looked up. Dan Reiss stood there looking rumpled and sleepy. "How are you this morning. Mara, is it? It means 'bitter,' you know. 'When they came to Marah, they could not drink its water because it was bitter. That is why the place is called Marah.' It's in the Bible," he finished lamely, seeming to realize that what he'd just said might not be considered a compliment of any kind.

Mara smiled. "I'm not surprised I've never heard that. The whole inside of the Bible seems to have changed from the last time I read it."

"I'm sorry," Dan tried to apologize. "I'm so tired I'm barely aware of what I'm saying. I didn't mean to imply—"

"Of course you didn't," Mara interrupted hastily.

Dan sat down beside her and scrubbed his bristly face with his hands. "I never realized how exhausting it is to take care of small children. I'm up most of the night, and I don't even get a break during the day. It's just such a constant drain on me."

"How old are your little ones?"

His eyes widened. "Oh, they're not mine!" he exclaimed. "I've just been trying to help some of the mothers take care of the children. One little fellow in particular is such a live wire." He slumped back against the sofa, arms dangling by his sides. "You know," he said thoughtfully, "I never really appreciated mothers before. I never empathized with them. I sure do now."

Mara smiled. "I think I know what you mean. Only I entered parenthood at the teenager stage. It's been quite an experience."

Dan turned toward her, some of the fatigue in his face replaced by curiosity. "Tell me what happened."

"Where do I start?"

"At the beginning?" he suggested.

Mara took a deep breath and attempted to reconstruct the events leading up the present moment. She found Dan Reiss a good listener. He asked pertinent questions that helped to focus her, and in expressing all that had happened out loud to someone, she felt a release inside her as she talked. When she finished, Dan Reiss didn't seem like a stranger anymore. "You know," she confided, "even with all this going on, I was amazed to find that I began to have feelings for someone." She stopped, not sure she could go on.

"Randy Burton?" Dan guessed and then smiled at the shock that Mara felt.

"Was it that obvious?" she laughed, trying to cover her embarrassment. "When I left him at that church, I would have done anything to stay. It was the hardest thing I've ever done. I just wanted to get away from all this craziness, just the two of us, and get to know each other like normal people do. But there was just no time. And I don't know if he feels the same way about me or not.

"I told him that I plan to come back to D.C. just as soon as Dani is settled here. I think I owe it to myself to find out if there is anything there." Mara felt her eyes fill with tears. "But then I look around at what is happening in the world, and I wonder if there is any sense in even going back. I mean, it sure doesn't look like the world is going to last long enough for it to matter much either way."

Dan laid his head back on the sofa and closed his eyes. "You wouldn't believe how that very thing has been weighing on my mind," he confessed. "I feel the Lord has given me the responsibility for these people. But we have no source of income. The families living here have no jobs. We're slowly eating up everyone's liquidated assets. What happens now? Will the world end before or after the money runs out and we starve?" He sat forward and cradled his head in his hands. "I don't know," he muttered thickly. "I just don't know any more."

And suddenly he wasn't talking to her anymore, and Mara felt her spine tingle in awe. He was talking to *God*. Just as if He was his very best friend in all the world.

"Lord, You promised that our bread and water will be sure. What will we do? We have no more resources. In a couple of months when we run out of funds, how will we eat? I'm not as concerned about myself as I am about these children, Lord. I am clinging to You! I trust You! I have faith that You will provide for us even if I don't know how. Strengthen me, Lord. Give me even more faith."

Dan lapsed into silence, and Mara waited respectfully, not sure whether she should bow her head and fold her hands. Finally she cleared her throat, and he started and looked at her. "I'm sorry. Did you say something?"

Mara shook her head dumbly. Then she plucked up her courage and asked, "How can you do that? Talk to God like that? Aren't you being a little presumptuous?"

Dan looked puzzled. "How so?"

"Well, I mean, the way you were talking to Him, it was like you were on intimate terms or something."

"But I am," Dan said, smiling broadly. "He is my God, my Best Friend, my Comfort, my Redeemer. We're on the most intimate terms possible. He's everything to me. Absolutely everything."

"You'll have to excuse me, I don't mean to be disrespectful, Father Reiss, it's just that I've been brought up to believe that you should make requests of God through saints and apostles and Mary. I've been talking to God myself lately, but I've felt rather guilty doing it."

"First, please don't call me father. The Bible says, 'Do not call anyone on earth 'Father,' for you have one Father, and he is in heaven.' My title is Pastor, and you can call me either Pastor Reiss or Pastor Dan. And second, my dear girl," here he took her hands and smiled at her gently, "you don't need any intercessor to approach God except Jesus, and He is your Friend and Brother. Go boldly to God, and talk to Him as you would your parents or friends. He loves you far more than any earthly person does."

Mara felt tears spring up in her eyes and spill down her cheeks. His words tore down walls that others had painstakingly built in her heart. Suddenly she felt free, and she could feel God's love for her surround her with its strength and acceptance. "Thank You," she whispered.

"You're welcome," Dan replied.

Mara giggled. "I wasn't talking to you," she teased.

Dan laughed heartily. "Then they will say that you are as crazy as I am. Come on. I'm famished. Let's see what we can rustle up for breakfast."

"Pastor Reiss?" A young woman whose face was drawn deeply with fatigue stood hesitantly in the doorway between the sun room and the living room. "I think you should come see this."

Mara followed Dan into the living room where several adults she did not know were clustered around a television set. On the screen, a reporter was speaking to the pope.

"Your Excellency, first let me say that I am honored that you have agreed to come on camera with your fantastic story. I fully realize that under normal circumstances you would never grant an interview, but I hope that following your announcement, you will allow me to ask you a few brief questions." The pope's head nodded tersely. Clearly he was barely tolerating the experience. "Now, from what I understand, you have some very disturbing news from heaven itself? Would you please tell our viewers what that news is?"

The pope glanced around, trying to locate the appropriate camera. When he found it, he stared long and hard into it before speaking. "Our Holy Mother Mary has appeared to me in a vision. She says our Lord is angry with His people because they do not obey His laws. He will destroy the earth if we will not listen to His voice and obey His commands. The Blessed Mother has promised to intercede for us, to stay His hand of vengeance. This great plague the population of the world is now beginning to suffer with will also grow unless our Lord is not obeyed.

"I have urged the fathers of this glorious country, America, the land of liberty and freedom, to join the entire world in honoring the Lord on His Holy day, Sunday. But these leaders have been slow to comply in instituting this law, and our Holy Mother fears that we do not take her seriously. She has given seventy-two hours for us to come together as a nation and as a world to demonstrate our faithfulness and obedience. That time frame ends Monday morning. If we have not shown our unfailing devotion, she has promised to cut off the West Coast of the United States and throw it into the sea, and as a further reminder, people will continue to die from this dreadful disease."

A collective gasp fluttered around the room, and Mara felt her knees weaken. She sank into a chair and crossed herself. The television reporter composed himself with great effort. "Am I to understand correctly that Mary, the mother of Jesus Christ, will send—what—an earthquake? And the entire West Coast will be lost?"

Pope Xavier nodded gravely. "It breaks the heart of this old man to say these words, and I urge you, citizens of the United States, people all over the world, to please go to your churches and repent of your misguided ways. And to the faithful on the West Coast of America, please come out and be safe, my people."

While the television program went to a commercial, the people gathered in the room began to talk excitedly at once. Dan held up his hands for silence. "Please, let's get some perspective here. Let's not panic. We know that we are living in the very last days. The Bible tells us that "The coming of the lawless one will be in accordance with the work of Satan, displayed in all kinds of counterfeit miracles, signs and wonders, and in every sort of evil that deceives those who are perishing. They perish because they refused to love the truth and so be saved. For this reason God sends them a powerful delusion so that they will believe the lie and so that all will be condemned who have not believed the truth but have delighted in wickedness."

"Now, let's test what we just heard against what we know from the Bible. First, we know that God's holy day is Sabbath, Saturday, so He would not ask us to keep Sunday. Second, if God had a message for us, He would give it to us Himself. Mary is dead, and the Bible says that the dead know not anything. So, we know that this 'Mary' is a deception of Satan."

Walking over to the television set, he turned it off. Every eye in the room was on him, and the silence was staggering. Emotions struggled on his face, and he began to cry. Mara who was usually uncomfortable at any display of emotion, particularly by men, found that instead she was touched and somewhat thrilled. "We're going home so very *soon*. I'm ready, aren't you? Come, let's pray together and praise our God."

* * *

Pastor Jenny James burst into her office, her face pallid. She pulled a television on a rollaway stand away from the wall.

"What's the matter?" Randy set his Bible down.

"I can't believe they're doing this. I just can't believe it! I knew it was possible, but . . ." Jenny rambled on as Randy helped her plug the set in.

Finally, he caught her eyes and held her gaze. "Tell me, what's got you so spooked?"

"Earlier the pope said that unless everyone agreed to worship on Sunday, the entire West Coast would drop into the ocean. Can you believe that?" Pastor Jenny turned on the small television. "I want to see what the news has to say about it."

Randy laughed. "Now that's rich. Don't tell me you actually believe that."

Pastor Jenny scowled. "I do take it seriously. With all that has happened these past two weeks, you bet I'm spooked. Who would have thought the president would have been assassinated? Since then, Gavin Larson has become a Protestant religious icon. His United Religious Coalition has been assimilating nearly all the Protestant denominations. And he's formed an alliance with the pope. All of a sudden there's this one huge religious organization, with Gavin Larson and the pope leading it."

"OK, so it's a big political beast. But we're talking about a cataclysmic natural event. There is no way the West Coast can be covered by water because the pope or anyone else says so."

"Maybe you're right, Randy, but I'm still worried. There are so many strange, horrible things happening lately that it's hard not to believe the end of the world is coming, especially if you read Revelation."

Randy looked down at his Bible and felt a faint chill. His logical mind resisted the urge to believe that events were coming to pass as prophesied, but he did, in fact, believe. Down in his gut he knew these were the last days. He thought about Brian Willis and their dinner, where Brian was reading a book about Revelation. Where was Brian, and why hadn't he heard anything from him or about him?

CNN returned from a commercial just as Lynn entered the office. "Alice is shopping for groceries," she said.

"Are you all right, Randy?" Jenny asked. "You look pale."

"Uh, yeah. I was just thinking about Brian Willis. I really should be trying to figure out what happened to him after President Fairfield was killed. I asked Aldridge about him, but I haven't heard a thing, and I'm afraid I left it at that. If Aldridge knows, I'm sure it's in his best interest not to allow Brian a chance to tell what he knows about Fairfield's assassination."

"Do you think something bad has happened to Brian?" Lynn asked.

"I'm afraid so. I just should have done something before now."

"Right, like how? You almost got killed yourself, and you just got out of the hospital. I think it's pretty obvious why you haven't been 'doing' anything. You can't save the world." Lynn sat beside Randy and put an arm around his shoulders. "Can you?"

"No, I can't. But there are things I *can* do. It's important that I do them. Besides, what else is there for me to do? I'm no longer a federal agent."

"It would probably be good for you anyway."

"What's that supposed to mean, Lynn?"

"It means that it would help take your mind off Mara too. I assume you know what I mean." Lynn smiled and squeezed Randy's shoulders.

Pastor Jenny suddenly shushed them and turned the television volume up. They watched in complete silence as the tape of Pope Xavier was replayed and analyzed by a variety of religious and political experts.

"What does it mean, Pastor Jenny?" Lynn asked when CNN moved on to other news, none of which appeared to be positive. Reports about the continually spreading epidemic nearly saturated what was left of the news, and what wasn't concerning the disease was distributed among a dozen or more catastrophes around the globe.

Jenny turned solemn, fearful eyes on Lynn. "It means the

time for Jesus' second coming is drawing near."

Lynn and Randy looked at each other.

Randy cleared his throat. "I've got to find Brian Willis." He used the pastor's phone and dialed information for a Chicago number. He wrote down a number and dialed again.

"Mrs. Willis?"

"Yes, this is she."

"Mrs. Willis, my name is Randy Burton. I'm a friend of your husband. We went to First Christian together our senior year. I met him again just recently. Before the United Religious Coalition rally." Brian sensed worry and tension on the line. "Mrs. Willis?"

"Oh yes, I'm so relieved someone has called me who knows something about Brian. I haven't heard from him for over a week. The police, well, the police don't know what happened to him . . ."

"I'm afraid I don't know, either, ma'am. I was hoping you had heard."

"Oh, God. Please, no," Ann Willis cried hopelessly. "I can't go on much longer not knowing something. Why doesn't anyone know?"

"Let me ask you. Have you talked to Gavin Larson? Has he given any indication that he knows what happened to Brian?"

"Mr. Burton, I've left dozens of messages with Gavin's secretary and Brian's secretary. They don't know, either. Gavin hasn't called me personally, but he has returned a message that he doesn't know Brian's whereabouts, either. He says that as soon as he knows something, he'll call me."

Randy was about to ask if she really believed Gavin was telling the truth, but he didn't want to cause her more anxiety than she already felt. He assured her that he would do all he could to find Brian, and he slowly hung up.

Little did he know how long it would take.

Chapter Seven

Saturday, November 27

To Dani, living with Pastor Reiss and all those other people in that rambling farmhouse was very similar to living with her parents. She was told she could come and go as she pleased and no one, not even Mara, questioned her. On Saturday while everyone in the house was having a church service, she went to visit her mother, who was living in a small house in Meridian.

Marilyn seemed the same as ever, except that she was really excited about some meetings she'd been going to. She invited Dani to one, and Dani had been about to turn down the invitation thinking it was a religious meeting, when her mother smiled slyly and said, "I've seen your father."

Dani stared at her blankly. "What do you mean you've seen Dad?"

Marilyn shrugged. "He's come to the meetings. He apologized to me for the way he treated me in our marriage and said I had every right to leave and he didn't blame me a bit.

He took responsibility for everything and said he wished he could go back and change everything. I wasn't the only one who heard him. He apologized in front of everyone."

She leaned forward and took Dani's hands in her own, which were covered with rings. A purple crystal dangled from a black cord around her neck, and a small leather pouch, fastened with a Chinese coin which had a square hole in the center of it, hung from her neck by a piece of jute. "He wants to see you. He says he has a message for you."

"A message? For me?" Dani squeaked. Her stomach felt extremely queasy, and she was torn between feeling like she shouldn't have come and a curiosity about what her father wanted to say to her. She didn't really believe in ghosts, but . . .

She looked at her mother. "When is it?"

"Oh, right now, honey. In fact, if I don't get going, I'll be late. Are you coming or what?"

"Uh-I-uh, hadn't planned . . ." Dani stammered.

"Dani," her mother said, barely able to hide her impatience, "you know your father and I didn't get along much toward the end of our marriage, but I tell you, he's a changed man. And I can tell he's worried about you. I think what he has to say is very important. He seemed extremely eager to talk to you. Will you come?"

Dani pushed herself off the couch. "Yeah, sure, Mom. I'll come." She swallowed back a lump of fear that wedged itself in her throat as she followed her mother out to the car. Little was said during the drive. Dani's mother put a CD of forest sounds and synthesized music into the car stereo and hummed along as she drove. Every now and then she looked over at Dani and patted her hand, smiling warmly.

Dani wasn't sure where she expected the meeting to take place, but she couldn't help a rush of surprise when her mother pulled the car into the parking lot of a DoubleTree Inn near the Boise River. "Come on, honey, we're going to be late, and I hate to interrupt."

Dani struggled to keep pace with her mother as she nearly sprinted across the parking lot. Marilyn pulled out a couple of hundred-dollar bills with a flourish and handed them to an attendant holding an offering plate stuffed with similar bills. The entire act seemed like a performance. Inside, they were ushered into a large conference room jammed with people. Dani's mother quickly pulled her toward two empty chairs. A sophisticated business-type woman was at a podium speaking to those present, and Dani looked around in confusion, sure they had entered the wrong conference room.

"That's Elizabeth Nelson," her mother whispered, nodding at the woman at the podium. "She's a channeler and very well off. Her son married Chakktra—you know, the singer. She came and did a concert here once. It was divine. Of course, it cost a bundle to get in, and there were hordes outside just clamoring to get even a peek at her, but as I always say, money has its rewards." She smiled smugly.

Elizabeth Nelson hardly looked the part of a hokey, crystal ball-carrying, palm-reading medium. She looked . . . normal. Not a thing about her seemed mysterious. Her brown hair was cut in a chin-length bob a smidgen too short to flatter her rather round face. Her suit was a businesslike brown and black, obviously expensive and tailored to broaden her shoulders and balance her sleekly camouflaged, but rather wide, hips. Her high heels were neither too flat and sensible nor overly spiky and high.

"The spirits are here," she was saying in a voice that was devoid of dramatic expression. In the same tone, she could announce the weather conditions outside and no one would dispute her. "Make yourselves known to those present," she said with authority.

The room was silent, and then she spoke again. "Rose Taylor? Are you attending?" An exclamation of surprise and anxiety met her question, and an angular woman with long black hair rose to her feet, half-supported by two young girls who resembled her.

"Yes," she said in a shaky voice. "I'm here."

Dani's mother leaned over and hissed in her ear. "Her husband died two months ago of lung cancer. He never smoked a day in his life, but she was a chain smoker. When he got cancer she quit, but by then it was too late. She's been trying to reach him since he died, but he hasn't come to a meeting yet." Her mother's eyes snapped with excitement, and Dani felt her skin prickle. Then she added, as an afterthought, "He owned a Fortune 500 company."

"Rose?" a man's voice asked, and Dani noticed suddenly that there was a man standing in the middle of the aisle who hadn't been there before. "Honey, I miss you so much. And I want you to know that I forgive you for killing me." At these words the woman, who was shaky to begin with, fainted, sagging between the two sobbing girls supporting her. "Goodbye girls," he said, blowing them a kiss. "I miss you both, and I love you." Attendants came to help the girls carry their mother out into the waiting room where she could recover. Dani looked for the man, but he was gone.

The meeting went on like that. The spirits of those departed would make themselves known, and there would be an exchange, sometimes tearful, sometimes joyful, but always emotional. During scheduled breaks the members of the audience talked among themselves about the encounters. Many of them conversed with Elizabeth Nelson. Most of them seemed to know each other, and several greeted her mother.

"This is the daughter your husband wants to talk with?" they would ask. "You must be one special lady. Your father really loves you."

Dani squirmed uncomfortably in her chair, enduring the introductions and the uncomfortable knowledge that everyone in the room probably knew more about her than she knew about them. Before she had time to reflect on it much, the meeting had started again. "Dani Talbot?" Elizabeth Nelson was saying. "Are you here? Your father wants a word with you."

Dani clutched her mother's hand, suddenly overcome with fear. What was she doing here? She didn't believe in this kind of thing. This wasn't real. None of this was really happening. Her mouth was dry. She couldn't force a word between her lips.

"Dani!" a familiar voice exclaimed. "Dani, I'm so glad to see you."

"Daddy?" Her father stood two yards away, in the outside aisle.

"I wasn't sure you'd come, but I told you I'd be back, remember?"

Dani did remember. Before he had walked toward the bus.

"I know I told you that it was impossible to communicate with the souls of the departed while I was alive." He chuckled. "I guess you can see that I was wrong."

"Daddy, how?" Dani began, but Jack cut her off.

"Look, sweetheart, I haven't got much time. I have to warn you. Those people you were with, Shon's people, they're coming after you. You know that, don't you? Sooner or later they're going to find out where you are. But I have the edge now. I can see what they're doing and warn you. Do you understand what I'm saying? I can protect you now, like I should have when I was alive." His face filled suddenly with remorse.

"I did so many things wrong while I was alive. Now I want to make it up to you. You need a break, someone to take care of you. Thank God you have your mother to help you out, and I can protect you. Rest. Relax. And if they get too close, I'll warn you in time, and you can get away. I'll help you to always be one step ahead of them. I promise.

"I want you to take good care of my grandson." He smiled. "Yes, it's a boy. I'm so proud of you, honey. Now I have to go, but promise me you'll come back. And this time I want a promise I know you'll keep."

Dani faltered, "I-I promise. I'll come back."

"Good," Jack smiled. "Marilyn, what can I say? I miss you, and I love you. I'll see you soon."

He was gone as quickly as he had appeared, and Dani collapsed in her chair. She was vaguely aware of her mother's arms around her. Her whole body shook with sobs. Her father *loved* her. He was going to *protect* her. He admitted that he'd been wrong. She'd been *right*. Now they were going to start over.

And she was going to have a son.

Chapter Eight

Monday, November 29

She didn't come to him that morning.

Pope Xavier knew why, and he dreaded the following hours even more perhaps than he would have dreaded execution. He had spent the entire night in prayer, but nothing had happened that would have stayed the terrible judgment about to befall America. Tired and defeated, he rose from his knees and shuffled over to the television. He knew what he would see before he even turned it on.

America's favorite reporter, Greg Harrison, looking anxious but professional and obviously under a great deal of stress, spoke as scenes from professional as well as home videotapes played in the background, showing the massive earthquake that had decimated the West Coast of America. Even the professional footage was shaky.

"Not since the San Francisco earthquake and fire of April 18, 1906, which took nearly seven hundred lives and caused millions of dollars worth of damage in California from Eureka southward to Salinas and beyond, has there been anything like this phenomenon," Harrison said breathlessly. "We have reports of the earthquake being felt as far away as Oregon and Nevada. The 1906 quake reached an estimated 8.3 on the Richter Scale, but experts are still trying to get a specific reading on this morning's quake.

"I repeat, reports are now flooding in about an earthquake along the San Andreas Fault from San Juan Bautista north past Point Arena and offshore to Cape Mendocino. According to many apparent eyewitnesses, the west coast of California has dropped into the Pacific Ocean." He paused and shook his head. "We have no official report of the extent of the damage so far, but we will report further information as it becomes available. We now take you to Phillip Dwight, a scientist at Merck's Earthquake Research Facility, for more information on the earthquake."

The phone rang, but Pope Xavier ignored it.

Phillip Dwight looked as though he'd been up for hours. His fine, blond hair was plastered to his head on one side, his tie was crooked, and his glasses smudged. He stared nervously at the camera and cleared his throat continuously.

"Dr. Dwight, can you tell us how this happened?" the reporter asked him.

"Uh, yes, Greg, uh, first let me attempt to explain by giving you an, uh, idea, to some extent of what precisely causes an earthquake. You see, the earth's crust is fractured into a series of "plates" that have been moving, albeit very slowly, over earth's surface for millions of years now.

"Now, two of these moving plates were found in western California. The boundary between them was what we called the San Andreas Fault. The western plate is called the Pacific Plate, the eastern one the North American Plate. Now the San Andreas Fault is only the master fault in an intricate fault network that cuts through the rocks of the California coastal region. The whole San Andreas Fault system is, er, was, over eight hundred miles in length and extended at least ten miles into the earth."

Here Greg Harrison broke in. "Thank you, Dr. Dwight. We must pause for a station identification break. When we return, we hope to have some feedback from religious leaders on the possibility that this was caused by the Mother of God as was predicted by Pope Xavier, who is presently in Washington, D.C., for talks with the president of the United States and Gavin Larson, leader of the United Religious Coalition."

The phone rang again. This time Pope Xavier unplugged it. Within ten minutes there was a knock on his door.

"Your Excellency," gasped his personal assistant, "disastrous news. It is as the Holy Mother promised." The man wrung his hands. "They have all perished. And now I am beseeched by requests for your presence, from the president, from Mr. Larson's office, from the people at the television stations. Please, Your Eminence, what shall I tell them?"

"Tell them," Pope Xavier said, "tell them I shall be available momentarily." Then he closed the door gently on the distraught man and knelt to his prayers before readying himself for the demands of the day ahead.

* * *

The funeral hadn't been postponed, but it was poorly attended, even by Jack's friends and colleagues. Everyone was simply too worried about the disaster in California and its terrible consequences. By the time the funeral began, most of the nation firmly believed that the reason for the tragedy was just as Pope Xavier said. Scientists had been unable to offer any valid explanations why the Pacific Plate had simply sheered off and dropped into the sea . . . except that Pope Xavier had said that it would.

Mara was frightened. She was more frightened than she ever had been. She had called Randy that morning just to hear his voice and receive some measure of assurance that the entire world had not spun off its axis. "Can't you come out here?" she begged, knowing even as she asked the question that it sounded pathetic and needy, but she was past caring. She just wanted him there.

"I wish I could, honestly I do," Randy replied, and he sounded sincere. "It's just that I'm looking for Brian Willis, and I think something awful has happened to him."

Not knowing exactly what to say, Mara allowed a lengthy silence to follow. But she also sensed that Randy was just as disappointed as she was.

"Mara, Brian's got a family, and they don't have any idea what has happened to him. I just wouldn't feel good about not following up on this."

Mara vaguely remembered the man from the bombing incident. He'd had something to do with Gavin Larson and the United Religious Coalition, but she wasn't sure exactly what. "I understand." She tried to keep the disappointment from her voice. "But when you find him, will you come?"

"I'll be there as soon as I can, I promise," he said.

Mara took a deep breath and slowly exhaled in an attempt to calm herself. She thought she had been handling the stress reasonably well, but suddenly her stomach was doing flip-flops. She was frustrated and scared. She could barely comprehend all that had happened to her when she thought back over the past few weeks. She did know for a fact that she was tired of running scared. Tired of worrying about Dani. And now worried about Randy too. *Express your feelings,* her inner voice said. *You trust Randy, you trust him.*

"Randy, I'm scared," she whispered.

"I know, Mara. I know how you feel. I'm scared too. Really scared."

"What if we're not safe here? What if people become so angry at Remnant Believers that they become vigilantes and come here? What if they turn us in to the government? There are so many What-ifs that I'm afraid to think of them all. And what if you get arrested? I may never see you again. Randy, I worry about you."

"First of all, Mara, you have to trust in God. We have to know that God is in control."

"But the pope was right! California was devastated just as he said it was going to be! And he's blamed it all on the Remnant ahead of time."

Unexpectedly, she heard Randy's soft laugh on the line. Mildly frustrated, she said, "What are you laughing about? I don't see anything amusing."

"Mara . . . I think . . . well, I uh . . ."

"Well? What, that I worry too much. In case you don't know it, mister, that is what makes me a good doctor. I like to think ahead. It kind of makes me a worrier too."

"No, Mara, that's not what I was going to say at all," Randy said gently, his voice sounding more tender and sentimental than she had ever heard it. *Oh!* she thought, *is he going to tell me he loves me?* But then it was back to somber reality of disasters and persecution, wars and pestilence.

"Mara? I know this won't ease your mind about everything, probably not about much of anything, but I don't think the FBI will bother you, at least for a while. Remember that recording you accidentally made of FBI Director Kent Aldridge in my hospital room?"

"Yes," Mara said.

"I made sure Aldridge got a copy of it. I just sent him some very specific demands stating that I wanted you and anyone with you protected as well as myself, Lynn, and Alice Nolan. If he can't see that that happens, then another copy of the tape goes to the Attorney General and to the media."

Despite Randy's confident tone of voice, Mara frowned and worried some more. "But how much do you really think that protects any of us?"

"I don't know, Mara, I really don't. Maybe not much. But

it's something. It's all I've got. The rest is up to God."

"Please be careful, Randy," Mara said. Hesitating, she closed her eyes. "Will you pray with me? I know I'd feel a lot better if we prayed." She needed God—she needed Him to keep her sane. She needed Him to keep those she loved safe.

"Sure, Mara."

Now at Jack's funeral, Mara's worries returned. *But Randy promised,* Mara reminded herself. *He promised he'd come as soon as he found Brian Willis. Just find him quickly,* she urged silently.

Beside her, Dani looked a little pale. She was clasped in the arms of her mother, Marilyn, whom Mara didn't know well. The woman seemed to resent her presence. She was aloof and condescending when Mara spoke to her. She was dressed like a Mafia wife in mourning, in a tight, short black suit and ridiculously high heels. She had on a hat that resembled the one Jacquelyn Kennedy wore to the president's funeral, complete with an elaborate veil of black netting.

Dan Reiss had been requested to have the funeral service, and he was now talking about death and the promise of heaven. By now, Mara had read enough of the Bible and talked to Pastor Reiss enough that she understood that Jack wasn't *in* heaven. He was "sleeping" until Jesus came back. That comforted her immensely.

She'd always been terrified thinking that the dead were up there somewhere, looking down on all the horrible things that happened to their loved ones. She was sure the anguish they would feel would far outweigh the beauty and perfection of heaven. How could anyone be happy knowing that pain and sin went on for those you loved? It was nice to know that whatever happened from here on out would not torture Jack, because he would know nothing about it.

She leaned over slightly and gazed at Jack in the casket. He looked so peaceful. Dani had pointed out to her that the lines of pain that had been etched around his eyes and mouth since the accident were gone. To her, he seemed, finally, at rest. Marilyn was smirking at something Pastor Reiss was saying, and Mara surmised that she didn't put much stock in his view of death and heaven.

Dani looked perplexed, but Mara knew that Dani's thoughts about death and heaven were biblical and agreed with her own. No doubt about it, the girl was going to have some major adjusting to do. But at least now she could do it without the Freedom Society breathing down her neck. With her mother present and taking a healthy interest in Dani, Mara felt as though her obligations there were over, but still she was hesitant to leave.

She had so many questions. Little by little, Pastor Reiss was answering them, and she could feel that she was on the verge of a spiritual breakthrough. After the service on Sabbath, she'd gone for a walk and talked extensively to God, in a way she had never felt comfortable doing before because she'd been taught to approach Him through intermediaries. Now she was talking to Him on a one-to-one basis, and it was exhilarating.

No, she wasn't ready to leave just yet. But she was also anxious about Randy. They had talked on the phone almost every day since she'd arrived, and she'd even written him one very long letter telling him about some of the discoveries she'd made. If he could come to Idaho, then everything in her life would be as perfect as it could get for the time being. With absolutely everything in the future being so incredibly uncertain, it was about all you could ask for.

The service was over, and the pallbearers, all members of the police force Jack had served, took up positions to carry the casket out to the waiting hearse for the trip to Dry Creek Cemetery. Pastor Reiss offered her a ride to the grave site in his car, and she followed him out to the parking lot. Dani was riding with her mother, and Mara felt almost relieved.

"Has she talked to you?" Pastor Reiss asked as they followed the procession of cars.

It was bitterly cold, but there was no snow on the ground. Mara had been fascinated by how flat everything seemed compared to the green mountains of Vermont and the nearby Adirondack Mountains of New York. Pastor Reiss jokingly told her that the mountains were only a couple hours away and they were *big*. "Dani?" she asked, corralling her thoughts with great effort.

"Has she told you what her plans were?" Pastor Reiss elaborated. "You know, after the funeral. Is she going to live with her mother, or will she be staying on?"

Mara shook her head. "No, she hasn't talked about going to live with her mother. As far as I know, she's planning to stay with us."

Pastor Reiss sighed with relief. "I'm glad," he confessed. "Her mother scares the daylights out of me."

Mara choked on a laugh. "You?" she asked with a grin.

He smiled in return. "Not really for me," he said. "For Dani. I think her mother's into spiritualism or the New Age movement or something. I fear for Dani even associating with her."

"Yeah," Mara mused. "I get a strange feeling from her too."

Pastor Dan went on. "The best thing we can do is to support Dani and let her know that she isn't alone. She's going to need a lot of help to get through the next few months. If we can show her that God loves her and isn't the ogre she makes Him out to be, then maybe she can even learn to trust Him again." He drummed his thumbs on the steering wheel and stared moodily out at the road. "That's my sincere prayer."

"Amen," Mara agreed.

* * *

Kent Aldridge climbed into his limousine and was driven to the White House, where Secret Service agents escorted him to an emergency meeting in the situation room. Thomas Stolberg, the director of FEMA, was there, as were several advisors to the president on matters of national emergency. Eyes bloodshot and his complexion nearly white from fatigue and worry, Stolberg looked as if he hadn't slept in the past two days. When Aldridge was admitted, Stolberg was explaining to President Thurgood that the devastation was so massive his agency did not have the assets or personnel to make even a little difference.

Aldridge quietly came in and sat down.

"State and local emergency agencies were immediately overwhelmed," Stolberg was saying to President Thurgood. "FEMA's volunteer network in California and neighboring states was already alerted, and they went into immediate action. I had also put the Agency on standby after the pope's warning, but the enormity of the earthquake rendered us helpless immediately."

"Let me understand something, here," Aldridge interrupted. "You're telling us that you believed there would be an earthquake because the pope predicted it?"

"Yes, Kent, I put FEMA's volunteer network, as well as the military Reservists, on alert just as soon as the pope issued his statement. Although it appears the disaster was worse than anyone could have imagined, and certainly far worse than the nation's ability to react to effectively, I made the right decision. Despite the horrendous devastation and loss of life, thousands of lives were saved because we were prepared for *something.*"

"That's ludicrous. It was a coincidence. Nothing more."

"I take it you are not a religious man," Stolberg said.

"No," he answered. "I wasn't, and I'm still not." Feeling suddenly uncomfortable, Aldridge noticed that nearly everyone was staring at him. *Am I the only one who believes this was a coincidence?* he thought. *Or am I the only one in this administration who doesn't believe in a god?*

After Stolberg analyzed the extent of the devastation and FEMA's lack of resources to deal with it, President Thurgood ordered the Secretary of Defense to activate all military personnel who could be spared from national security to assist FEMA. The governor of California had already activated the state's National Guard and requested help from surrounding states.

When the meeting adjourned, Aldridge received a request from President Thurgood to a meeting in his private office. Shortly, Thurgood approached, and the two men walked together.

"How many people did you lose in California, Kent?"

"At this time it's impossible to say. The primary concern of most of my agents has been their families."

"I understand. Whatever help the government can give, those poor people need. The immediate responsibilities of your agents should be to assist the police in keeping order."

"Yes, sir," Director Aldridge said.

A Secret Service agent opened the door to Thurgood's private office. Gavin Larson was waiting.

Aldridge tried to ingore the intense feelings of dislike Gavin stirred within him and concentrate on the nice, warm beach somewhere where he would begin spending the several million dollars Gavin owed him. But it wasn't likely he'd be able to squeeze anything out of Larson if he didn't find Dani Talbot before Larson's men did. He walked over and sat down on the couch, watching President Thurgood and Gavin.

* * *

Unable to sleep for the cold, Brian draped his one blanket over his shoulders and hugged his knees for warmth. He found himself continually praying now, not because there was nothing else to do but because it helped. He could actually feel the presence of God. Thus it was that he spent a lot of time thinking about the apostle Paul, for he seemed to be sharing a similar situation.

Hearing footsteps ascending the stairs, he watched the door. A moment later, Dietrich entered with one of the guards. Without speaking, Dietrich tossed Brian gray coveralls and a used pair of sneakers. "Put those on quickly," he ordered.

Eager to have something to wear, Brian hurriedly put on the coveralls and sneakers.

"Come with me."

"Where?"

"Just do what I tell you," Dietrich snapped, his eyes cool and his features even more severe than usual.

Brian didn't doubt Dietrich would kill him if he thought he could do so. But after the angel had interfered before, Dietrich was reluctant to try. This made Brian wonder if Dietrich could sense the presence of the angel or if at some point later, after rationalizing his encounter with the angel, he would try again.

They handcuffed Brian like a criminal and took him out of the warehouse to a car, where he was pushed into the back seat—no blindfold this time—and driven to a internment camp of sorts. Nine-foot chain-link fences with spiked poles and rolls of razor wire on top surrounded low, hastily erected buildings with tin roofs and plywood walls. Men and women milled like pathetic cattle in the courtyard. Even though the temperature was near freezing, they wore nothing but thin garments that resembled Brian's. Some had coats that had seen far better days. Their heads were shaved, and they reminded him of the black-and-white pictures he'd seen of concentration camps during the Holocaust.

"What is this place?"

"For you, it's a prison. For those who are sick with this disease, it's turning out to be their last stop before dying."

Brian was led into a building and processed just as if he were a convict serving a prison sentence. During the whole process, he managed to keep silent, though inside he was seething with anger. He had noticed that several of the "guards" who weren't wearing yellow Racal suits wore broken barbwire tattoos on their wrists. *The Freedom Society seems to be any-where that someone needs a militant force,* he thought. Now that he was being moved to a different place, he began to entertain the possibility of escape again. He would have to wait and see what his chances would be like.

Finally, he was led into a small sterile room with two chairs and a table. *An interrogation room,* he thought. He didn't like the feeling he got when the door was shut. Less than five minutes later, Gavin Larson opened the door and walked in.

"Brian."

Seeing Gavin instantly brought a flash of anger and confusion. Jumping to his feet, Brian slapped the table aside and took a raging step toward Gavin before regaining a sense of control. As it was, two men appeared behind Gavin and would have prevented him from getting his hands on Larson. "Why have you done this to me?"

Gavin's eyes narrowed, but he didn't speak until after he had convinced his guards it was safe to leave them alone. Once the door was closed, Gavin said, "Sit down, Brian."

Brian remained standing. "Maybe they shouldn't have left me alone with you, Gavin. I'm not in the most reasonable frame of mind right now."

"I understand that. But I know you. I'm not worried."

The two men stared at each other for some time before Gavin put his hands behind his back and began walking around the room. Brian watched him carefully, his mind playing through a dozen different reasons for Gavin's presence.

"Gavin, what have you told my family?"

"Very little. Your wife must think by now you have run off."

Brian felt the life drain out of his body as he imagined what Ann and the kids were going through. He considered what another man might want to do to Gavin under the same circumstances. With Gavin in such close proximity, why, it wouldn't be difficult to imagine doing him serious harm, maybe even kill him. At the moment, it didn't seem to matter. *It would be justified, wouldn't it?* Brian snorted softly and shook his head. He still couldn't believe what was happening. He grabbed the table lying on its side against the wall and set it back up and then sat down. "Tell me what you want, Gavin."

"All right," Gavin began, "I want you to recant your Remnant beliefs. I don't think this is someplace you'll want to stay for very long. You won't have to stay here at all if you simply admit the foolishness of the Remnant Believers."

Brian's hands lay folded on the table as he watched Gavin talk. *What do you say to such a simple offer, Brian? Take it.* But suddenly, he was in no mood to be a good sport, shake hands, and put it off as some ridiculous mistake. "What about the horror and misery you've put me and my family through? Do you expect me to forgive and forget all of that?"

"It's the Christian thing to do, isn't it?" Gavin smiled wryly, as if he'd practiced that line for days.

"It amuses me that in your mind your actions seem completely justified. You and the word 'Christianity' can't be talked about in the same breath without tossing credibility out the window, so let's not be so sickeningly hypocritical."

Gavin's lips pinched. Clearly he didn't like criticism, especially from somebody he thought should be grateful to him. Brian thought he recognized Gavin digging in to play hardball. *Oh, Ann,* Brian thought, *you'd think I'm letting my pride interfere with good sense. Take the offer, you'd say. Sorry, Ann, Matt, Hannah.*

"You don't know what you're dealing with here, Brian. You never realized who I would become. Your high ideals. Your Christian love. Your eye on the future, dreaming of a nation full of the sickening sweet flavor of Christianity. You've always lived in such a fantasy world, caught up in an illusion I created." Gavin leaned back and chuckled.

For several moments they sat in silence, until, Brian guessed, Gavin must have thought his point had struck home.

"Listen, Brian, you've got nothing. If you can't see that right now, then you're more stupid than I thought. I'm where I intended to be. I'm sure you are not where you intended to be. It's time to throw in with the good guys. You can have your family back. You can have your life back. It's as simple as that."

"I'm sorry, Gavin. Nothing is ever that simple. I've found that to be especially true with you."

"Oh, you underestimate me, Brian. OK, you win. Keep your piddling little beliefs if they mean that much to you. All you have to do is act as if you've seen the light. You can have your life back. But there is one other thing I would like you to do. I want you to give a statement that thoroughly implicates FBI Director Kent Aldridge as the engineer of the Fairfield assassination."

"Aldridge wouldn't take the fall without bringing you along with him. If you used my testimony against Aldridge, the next thing Aldridge will do is offer the Federal prosecutors deals for *your* head."

"One would think so, yes," Gavin said.

"I don't see how it could be worth anything to you."

"It may not get him convicted, but it would remove him from office. Even if all an investigation did was buy me time, that's enough."

"Oh what tangled webs we weave . . . "

Gavin's smile disappeared.

"No, Gavin, I won't help you. And I won't even pretend to give up my faith."

"Fake it."

"Like you?"

Gavin shrugged, as if to say it worked well enough for him. Brian replied by shaking his head. "Financially, I can make it worth your while, Brian. I told the president that you were much too strong-willed to give up your Remnant Beliefs. But I'm not asking you to do that. Just pretend. That's all I ask."

Gavin stared at Brian for a long time. Although their eyes were locked, however, Brian could sense no warmth. It was as if

Gavin's humanity had been totally leeched from his soul.

"And just how would I spend my fortune in hell, Gavin?"

"Listen, Brian." Gavin leaned forward. "Think of your family too. I mean, look at yourself. You're confined here, your wife has no idea what's happened to you. She's going through torture, and you want to sit here and play cute. If all Remnant Believers are this weak, they'll be easier to break than I imagined."

Gavin's face was less than three feet away when Brian's hand flashed across the table and grabbed the knot in his tie, twisting until his fist began doing mortal damage to Gavin's trachea. Gavin's eyes bulged. He dearly wanted to scream for help but couldn't expel a sound. Even if he could have, he wisely would have passed.

"Let's get a few things straight, Gavin. Real Christians and wimps are not synonymous, and that's going to be your biggest mistake. Second, I figure the only thing I have left to lose, I mean *really* lose, is my relationship with God. I'm certainly not going to give that up because you ask nicely, threaten, or even try to kill me. You've already tried to have me killed, and God protected me. If you think I would consider for even one second trading the God of the universe in on your say so, you're stupider than I was when I got caught up in your United Religious Coalition." When he stopped talking, the silence was instantly palpable, and he wondered for a moment if the angels were clapping. It really felt good to get all that out of his system, to reaffirm his convictions and know that he really knew in whom he believed. And it helped mask his heartbreak over being separated from his family a little too. It wouldn't last for long, though.

Then he became vaguely aware that Gavin's face may not have lost its color because he felt particularly threatened. It was more likely Gavin wasn't getting any air. He let go, and Gavin nearly toppled from his chair before he got enough oxygen to his brain.

"You'll pay for that!" Gavin gasped.

Brian pursed his lips and shrugged. "More than I already have? At least I have my dignity. I will not deny my God, Gavin. Not for any price."

* * *

Outside the prison camp, Gavin huddled with Dietrich. "I want Brian Willis to die. Is that clear, Dietrich?"

"I wish I could. You know I've tried, but . . . " Dietrich had to let that thought trail off, because to acknowledge that a Supernatural being was protecting Brian Willis was not much of a leap from admitting that he could be right about his beliefs. So Dietrich shrugged, and Gavin understood the unspoken thought. "If he can't be killed, I can be sure his life isn't happy," Dietrich said.

"Yeah, you do that. I also want Dani Talbot found, and I want you to keep track of Aldridge's activities where that girl is concerned. I wasn't able to get Brian to agree to testify against the director, so what it is really going to come down to is whoever has the girl wins."

"Let me go get her as soon as I find out where she is," Dietrich said.

"Just find out where she is, and then we'll wait as long as Aldridge cares to wait. I want her child, Dietrich. You know how important it will be to me. Ultimately, the child is worth more to me than having Aldridge out of the way.

Section III

After the devastation of the California earthquake, where millions of people lost their lives, Remnant Believers were openly blamed for the catastrophe. Most Believers lost their jobs within a few days of the earthquake. Many applied for unemployment but discovered they would never see a check. Nearly all Believers were harassed, and many of those who had not been fired from their jobs were pressured to quit.

Even Remnant Believers who had long studied end-time events were surprised at the immediate moratorium on buying or selling imposed against them. Within a few days it became impossible for any known Remnant Believer to purchase even the most basic goods and services. Remnant Believers returned home from grocery stores empty-handed and extremely distressed. Often, they went directly to their pantries and freezers to inventory their supply of food.

With most all of his church membership out of work, families continually dropped by Pastor Reiss's house for spiritual encouragement. Some needed help with food, and Reiss gave what he thought he could spare and sometimes even more, always in faith that God would provide. It was a faith-building exercise, because Reiss's little community of Believers never had anything to spare, it seemed. Yet each time they shared their own meager supply, there always seemed to be enough to get them through the next day and the next.

Dan also felt it released his own worry and tension when he forced himself to trust completely in God.

During the following months, Pastor Reiss had insisted a few more families stay with him. They were families who had lost their homes, were caring for several small children, and had been disowned by their relatives. To have one's family disown you was easily the most disheartening result of the time of trouble for the people in Reiss's growing community. He could not bear to let them feel that God's family had disowned them too, and he welcomed them with open arms.

Between December and March, disasters happened regularly. Tornadoes erupted in Florida, while ice storms raged over the northeastern United States. Even the Northwest, which was usually quite free of catastrophic natural disasters, developed unseasonably warm weather after several huge crippling snowstorms, resulting in the worst flooding ever recorded in the region.

Chapter Nine

Monday, March 3

"I'm going to have to find a job that pays me something," Randy told Alice as he contemplated the cool spring weather and thought how unnaturally depressing it was. Alice and Lynn were seated at the kitchen table finishing breakfast.

"You have certainly done more than your share with your savings. Please don't worry about money, Randy. God has been very good to us."

"If anyone should be finding work, it should be me," Lynn jumped in. "I haven't contributed a dime."

"No, listen, both of you. There's no sense in us worrying about the money. Lynn, you worry about those people you are giving Bible studies to. Randy, you worry about your friend Brian and his family. I know the responsibility you feel. His disappearance has to be resolved, for your sake as well as his."

Randy gave Alice as much of a smile as he could muster and returned to staring out the window. Across the street from Alice's apartment building sat a Ford sedan with two FBI agents inside. Every day since he had left the hospital, he had been watched, and not very inconspicuously. And not only had they been watching *him*, but they had tailed Lynn and Alice too. With all the harassment Remnant Believers had received since the devastating California earthquake, he was surprised the FBI had not arrested the three of them and sent them to one of the camps the government had established specifically for Remnant Believers.

"Why don't they do something?" Randy muttered under his breath.

"What do you mean?" Lynn asked.

"The FBI. They've watched us for months."

"It's just harassment, Randy. Kent Aldridge doesn't dare do anything because he's afraid of that tape going to the Attorney General. Don't pay any attention to them. Just have faith that God will protect us."

Frustrated, Randy whipped around. "That's awful easy to say, isn't it?" he snapped. "But is God really going to protect us? Is He really?" Randy put his hands out and shrugged dramatically. "What's He done so far?"

Both Alice and Lynn set their utensils down and stared, surprised by Randy's sudden outburst. Lynn cleared her throat, and Randy realized the maturity, and the faith, she had acquired in the past three months. "I understand how you feel, Randy." She got up and wrapped her arms around her brother's neck, hugging him tightly. "Think about the fact that you and I are here together." she whispered. "Think about the fact that we have both come to love God. He is with us. Look at how He has protected you from Kent Aldridge. Look at how we are healthy and haven't gotten that virus. God is with us every step of the way."

Randy took a deep breath. "Maybe you're right, Lynn." He sighed. "I'm sorry for getting upset."

"You have certainly been under a lot of pressure trying to find Brian."

Randy nodded and sat down. "I don't know how much longer I can keep it up. In normal times, it would be a piece of cake compared to the kind of detective work I have to do now. Without the use of the FBI's resources, I've been confined to tracking down people who knew Brian or who might have seen him last. The person who would most likely have the answers is Gavin Larson, but I cannot get an appointment with him. The worst thing is that I have to go to the city morgues every day to see if Brian might have been one of the hundreds of people dying from this virus."

* * *

Amy Cooper tried to block out the coughs, groans, and cries of pain that surrounded her. The plywood sleeping platform that she rested on was crowded with the bodies of ten other women. Simply turning over was a major problem that involved everyone on the bunk. There used to be straw on the bunk, but the woman had taken it and shoved it into the cracks of the barracks to ward off the bitter temperature outside. Everyone slept in whatever wardrobe they possessed and huddled together for warmth, but trying to rest on the wooden platform was like sleeping on cement.

This was Camp Rehabilitation. At least, that's what it was called. Some called it by worse, and much more appropriate, names. It was, in nearly every detail, the same as concentration camps she'd read about of the Holocaust. The only difference she could see was that they were not required to work. Not yet. And no one was being gassed. Instead, they were being slowly tortured and starved to death.

"Converts" to the religion of the government were allowed to leave. In fact, they were even fattened up, given a makeover, and presented to television camera crews set up for the very purpose of interviewing them. Some days, when it was really bad, there were as many as ten or twenty converts. Other days there were none.

Amy had been in the Thurgood Rehabilitation and Detention Center since she had been released from the Slammer, the first person directly exposed to the Cartier virus able to walk out under her own steam. Gavin Larson had been waiting there for her. There had been no Slammer cake for her with 36 candles, representing the number of days she'd been stuck in there. Just Gavin's condescending face.

"Anything you'd like to tell me, Amy?" Larson had asked smoothly as he steered her down the hallway to where some heavyset types were standing by the doors to the outside. She'd licked her lips, desperate for a whiff of fresh air, just one lungful.

"About what?" she'd asked, playing ignorant.

"Come on, Amy, don't insult my intelligence. You have a marvelous career here just waiting for you to pick up where you left off. I know that you are aware that the only people in the country now testing negative for the Cartier's virus or its antibodies are Remnant Believers. Your blood test was negative. You don't have the virus, and you aren't a carrier. So . . ."

"So," Amy supplied. "That makes me a Remnant Believer."

"You catch on quickly," he said approvingly. "But consider my position, Amy. President Thurgood and I are running this country, and things are going our way. After that little tragedy in California, the citizens of America—or, more precisely, of the world—seem more than willing to do whatever we ask of them. They want to clean up their acts and get right with God. They have given us the ultimate authority over heaven and earth, if you will. In exchange, we promised them a scapegoat. And we didn't have to look far to find one."

"Remnant Believers."

"Of course. Remnant Believers. There are, naturally, a few other groups, but they are the main ones. Now, my concern is this. I can't have you on my staff if you are a Remnant Believer. It just wouldn't look right. You understand? But I hate to lose you as well. You are an incredibly gifted scientist. So I am prepared to forgive your little—how shall we say—lapse? If you in turn are prepared to renounce the Remnant Believers and all that they stand for. Do that Amy, and you can walk out that door a free woman with a great career ahead of you." He shook his finger under her nose. "Uh-uh, now I can see what you're thinking, but not to worry. While you were vacationing in the Slammer, one of our brilliant scientists developed a vaccine and a form of a cure for Cartier's virus. It keeps the virus in check. Not a true cure, but I am hoping that with this new breakthrough, you will be able to help us with that. Now, what do you say? Do we have a deal?"

Amy had bitten her tongue to keep from accepting. "I'm sorry, no," she'd said firmly instead.

"*Tsk, tsk,*" Gavin clucked his tongue like a mother reprimanding a naughty child. "I was afraid you'd say that." Suddenly he dropped all pretense of kindness. "You'll let me know, won't you, when you change your mind? And you *will* change your mind. I'll be waiting."

Amy shivered and clutched her arms tighter around her torso. She hadn't changed her mind yet, but she'd been sorely tempted to. On days when many women filed up to the guards' office and agreed to accept the government's religion, part of her yearned to join them. But a strong voice inside her spoke the truth and gave her strength. She had every reason to believe that she would die right here, in this stinking place, for her faith. And she was determined that she would not renounce it. No matter what the cost.

A rough barking voice cut into her thoughts.

"Cooper, Amy. Grant, Leslie. Worman, Kim. Eden, Nancy. Line up. You've been elected infirmary duty until further notice." The guard, a burly woman in a bright orange Racal spacesuit, shoved them roughly in line as they took their places bleary-eyed and exhausted. "We've had some converts today," the guard gloated, her voice sounding hollow from inside the suit. "Seems the infirmary help decided to renounce their stupid religious beliefs rather than stick around here up to their armpits in blood. So we've got *lots* of work to do. Are you ready to go take care of some sickies? No? Too bad. Move it!"

They trudged outside into the main courtyard of the compound. Directly across from them were the men's barracks. To the left was the infirmary. To the right was a large auditorium where they ate their scanty, mostly rotten, meals. The guard herded them roughly to the left. A light mist fell on them, and the air felt cold, but there was a promise of spring in the air. The woman behind Amy sobbed quietly.

The scene that met them inside the infirmary was more than even Amy had imagined. The entire infirmary was larger than the women's barracks. Each patient had their own cot. Some of the patients, Amy noticed immediately, were dead, pools of blood beneath their cots, their bodies contorted and disproportional as if they had exploded before dying. Some of the patients had lost their sanity, retreating into themselves and staring blankly out at the world. Others simply lay on their cots awaiting their fate with a quiet air of resentful resignation.

"Don't just stand there, clean up," the guard barked, shoving her automatic weapon into the small of Amy's back and causing her to stagger into a nearby cot containing the body of a young boy. Arms flailing, she managed to grab onto the bed before her momentum carried her onto his quickly decaying corpse.

Amy pushed herself away from the bed, trying not to gag. Doing an autopsy on the cadaver of a Cartier's victim while protected behind a spacesuit in a controlled environment was a world away from handling the bodies with no protection at all. The smell alone was enough to sicken the most stalwart. Amy motioned for one of the women in the group to help her as she began to wrap up the body of the boy. Although she tried to hold her breath, it wasn't much use, and before they had completed the job, both of them had vomited onto the floor, creating another mess to be cleaned up.

"Here, let me get that," a man's voice said.

Amy lifted her eyes to his face, hoping as she always did that it would be Ray. Her heart skidded to a stop for an instant and then chugged on in disappointment. Not Ray. "Thank you," she whispered.

"I'm happy to do it," he replied. "They tell me I'm fortunate. I had an accident as a kid and lost a lot of my sense of smell. I was never thankful for it until now. What's your name?"

"Amy Cooper," she replied. "What's yours?"

"Willis, Brian Willis."

"How long have you been in the infirmary, Brian?" Amy asked as she prepared to wrap up the next body. The woman who was working with her stepped aside to assist a patient, and Brian took her place.

"A week now," he said. "It just seems to get worse every day. The guards are only interested in how fast we keep things cleaned up in here because they have to undergo federal inspections once a week. Sometimes that's hard to do because of the sheer numbers of the dead. My goal is to help those who are still living, and it's a real challenge, let me tell you, because if the guards catch you, it's solitary confinement for a week. They don't feed you in solitary either, not that the chow is much to brag about on a good day, as you know.

"My only buddy got sent to solitary yesterday for sharing his faith with a man who was about to die. The man accepted Jesus just before he died, so I'm sure my friend isn't even noticing right now the condition of his cell or the fact that his stomach is even emptier than usual."

Amy smiled. "No, he probably isn't," she agreed. "He has food the guards know nothing about."

Brian eyed her keenly. "So, you are one of the Remnant then?"

"Yes," Amy admitted. "I'm a Remnant Believer."

"I'm so glad," Brain said. "These people really need us. We're their last chance, and I'm afraid I haven't done as much as I could to help. But we need to work together keeping an eye out for the guards so we don't get caught. Are you with me?"

"Yes. I'm with you. And may God be with us both."

* * *

"Our surveillance is continuing . . . without detection,"Agent Janet Roddrick said, lacing her voice with a hint of displeasure. Watching Dani Talbot had quickly become the most boring assignment she'd ever been on. She had made her supervisors aware of this, and in turn, they had informed Aldridge of her restlessness over not getting any arrests under her belt while most Bureau agents were racking up dozens of arrests a day. She wanted action.

"Good." Director Aldridge smiled. "Have you noticed any peculiar activity? Anyone else seem interested in this group of people?"

"No one. We have investigated everyone who is staying with Reiss, the pastor who owns the land. None of them have been in trouble with the law, well . . . until now. Now they are breaking Sunday worship and buying-and-selling laws. We've been tracing a couple of black-market rings that supply some necessities to these Remnant Believers, just for the fun of it." Roddrick smiled. "What's next?"

"Just keep watching. It's important we learn everything about them we can."

Roddrick stared at Aldridge.

"Is there anything else?"

"If I may speak candidly, sir. Why are we watching these people? Aren't there better things to do with the agents assigned to this case than to watch people who should have been arrested weeks ago?"

"Just follow orders, Agent Roddrick. Is that clear?"

Aldridge got a reluctant nod; then he dismissed Roddrick.

Monday, March 3

He knew she had a two o'clock flight back to Boise. Maybe it *was* time he sent the agents in to arrest the Believers and take Dani Talbot into custody again. Maybe it was that time. As Agent Roddrick made her way to the door, Aldridge stood and said, "How close is the girl to delivering her baby?"

Roddrick looked thoughtful for a moment. "I'd say any day now. We've done a considerable amount of background investigation to learn exactly when she might have gotten pregnant. I might be a few weeks off, but not over two weeks. I'm sure of it."

"Thank you, agent. That's excellent work. Let me know exactly when she has the child, and then you can make your raid."

Agent Roddrick smiled. "Yes, sir." She left with considerably more bounce to her step, Director Aldridge noticed. *She's certainly thinking about the feather in her cap for bagging all those Remnant Believers.*

Since the California earthquake, the Bureau's focus had changed somewhat. Most of the FBI's 12,000 agents were reassigned to making cases against Remnant Believers, searching them out, and making arrests. Although many agents had left the Bureau—surprisingly, quite a few Remnant Believers themselves—those who stayed seemed to really enjoy their work, much like Agent Roddrick. She was an excellent example of the gung-ho spirit among the agents who had suddenly developed a zeal for making as many arrests as possible. It was a contest of sorts, and the payoff could come in the form of a promotion.

Part of the enthusiasm probably stemmed from the satisfaction of immediate results. You investigated religious affiliation, talked to a few friends and neighbors of the suspects, and then you're breaking down doors to make an arrest.

Aldridge shook his head. People certainly seemed to have lost their heads. He just had to be sure and keep his, and everything would work out fine. Once he had Dani Talbot *and* her newborn child in his custody, he could write his own ticket. Now that he knew how badly Gavin wanted that kid, larger amounts of money were reasonable.

As soon as the door closed behind Agent Roddrick, Aldridge's phone rang.

"Sir, the president."

Aldridge smiled. *Secrets*, he mused. He kind of liked this game. He would miss it, of course, when he had his millions in blackmail money and had nothing to do but take in the sun on a tropical beach somewhere. A cliché dream, of course, but a nice one.

"Yes, Mr. President." For a second, he wondered why Thurgood was calling him himself. Secret meeting, perhaps?

"Get over here right away. We have some important news the pope says you should hear."

Oh, right. Now Aldridge understood the reason for the call. Not that it made any difference. One didn't turn down a presidential request. Frankly, that pope gave the president the jitters, and everyone knew it.

"Kent." President Thurgood's voice suddenly sounded troubled and ominous. "Kent, I think you will want to hear this."

* * *

Mara unloaded both her carts onto the conveyor belt and waited impatiently as the clerk scanned everything. She knew that the total in her UBC account was getting low. The old farmhouse was nearly bursting at the seams. It seemed that every new day brought someone new looking for a safe haven.

"Card, please," the clerk said mechanically, holding his hand out for her UBC card. Mara fumbled in her purse for the card while he waited. "You *do* have a card, don't you?" he asked irritably.

"Yes, I have a card," Mara replied, trying not to snap back

at him. "I wouldn't be here if I didn't, now would I?"

He shrugged. "Dunno. I've had quite a few Remnant Believers try to sneak through hoping I wouldn't ask for their card. Tried to pay me in cash. Even offered me bribes. But I never took them. The manager threw them right out of the store," he finished proudly, as he took her card and swiped it in the machine before handing it back.

Mara squirmed uneasily. It was entirely possible some of those people were at Dan Reiss's house at that very moment. Every day more people arrived with frighteningly similar stories. None of them had even the most basic ability to obtain food for their families. One family arrived with sixty-eight jars of home-canned tomatoes. It was all they had left. An elderly man showed up with a pickup truck full of last year's potatoes. What didn't come from the hand of the Lord came from Mara's UBC.

But lately she'd begun to wonder if that was right.

She was living with these people. And worshiping with these people. And studying with these people. And when she thought about it, she was shocked to find that she totally agreed with these people. She was a Remnant Believer. Granted, she hadn't told Pastor Reiss this—not that she figured he'd be very surprised—and she wasn't baptized yet. But in her heart, she was a Remnant Believer. And the question was . . . if she was a Remnant Believer, wasn't it time to start suffering like one?

She could think of two possible answers to that question. She felt that she was ready to begin to suffer along with every other Remnant Believer, but where did that leave the people who were depending on her UBC card for food?

"Don't you think I can take care of them?" a strong voice chided. Mara started and looked wildly around, expecting to see whoever had spoken, but no one was standing near her. The clerk gave her a mildly concerned look before ripping the receipt off the register and handing it to her.

"Thanks," she mumbled, and leaned against the handlebar

of the cart, pushing it and pulling the one behind quickly toward the entrance of the store.

"Don't you trust me to take care of My followers?" the voice asked again.

Mara gasped, and an old couple getting out of their car looked at her oddly. "Lord?" she whispered. "Is that You?"

"Do you trust Me, Mara?"

"Yes, Lord, I trust You," she replied firmly.

"Then trust Me all the way. With everything. I will take care of My people."

"Yes, Lord," she said again. "I believe You."

Quickly she transferred the groceries from the carts to the trunk and back seats of Dan's car. A feeling of confidence and gratitude welled up inside her, and she felt as though she would burst with the pressure of it. She couldn't wait to get home and tell the others about her experience.

As she pulled into the driveway of the dilapidated old farmhouse, she was shocked to see Dan on the porch in his stocking feet, with no coat on, scanning the road anxiously. When he saw her, he jumped up and down, waving his arms. Mara skidded to a stop at the foot of the porch and felt her heart leap into her throat. *They've found us here,* she thought. Instantly her peace was shattered.

"What? What is it?" she demanded, as she pushed the car door open and nearly fell out.

"Mara, it's Dani. I think it's time," Dan said breathlessly.

"Is that all?" she said in relief. "I thought there was something wrong!"

Dan danced down to the bottom of the stairs and grabbed her arm as she attempted to open the trunk. "There *is* something wrong," he insisted. "Could you come in the house please before I catch a death of a cold? Leave the groceries. Someone else can get them."

Mara allowed Dan to drag her up the stairs and into the house. "What? What is it? What could be so wrong? I examined

Dani this morning, and she looked great. We knew the baby could come any day. This is a first labor. It's going to take a long time."

As they rounded the corner and began to climb the old wooden stairs with its faded paint and buckled wainscoting, they were nearly forced back by the intensity of a scream. "Dani?" Mara asked in amazement.

"Dani," Dan confirmed. "She's been screaming like that for the last hour. Something has to be wrong with her."

Mara chuckled. "Not nervous, are we, Pastor? Don't you remember? To the woman he said, 'I will greatly increase your pains in childbearing; with pain you will give birth to children.' Babies have been born since the dawn of time. Dani will be OK. You just stay out here and boil water or something."

Dan halted at Dani's door, and Mara gently closed it against his worried face. "Really?" his voice asked with muffled urgency. "You really want me to boil water?"

"Just relax," Mara called back. She turned to find Dani lying flat on her back in bed. "Hey, there, Dani. How is it going?"

"Not good," Dani grunted. Her fingers, as she clutched the sheets, were nearly as white as the cotton.

Mara approached the bed and hooked her arm under Dani's elbow. "Let's get you up here, huh? You should be walking around, not lying in bed. This is counterproductive. We've got to get you moving."

"Moving? Are you crazy?" Dani shrieked. "I can't move! I'm having a baby!"

"And it's going to take twice as long if you don't move around," Mara insisted. "Gravity is your friend, Dani. Come on. Get up," she coaxed.

Dani swung her legs around the edge of the bed and began to get up when a contraction hit. Her shriek made Mara's ears ring as she supported the girl and reassured her through the contraction. "Breathe. That's a girl. Relax. Deep breaths. Let it go. Let it go." At the end, Dani was nearly sobbing.

"It's OK," Mara soothed. "Let's walk around for a little bit, and then I'll examine you and see if we can try the shower. OK? The warm water should make you feel better. But we don't want to do it too early, or it could stop your labor."

* * *

Upon his arrival, Director Aldridge was escorted immediately to the Oval Office where President Thurgood, Pope Xavier, and—as was so irritatingly predictable—Gavin Larson, were waiting. It appeared as though Thurgood couldn't make a decision without Larson. President Thurgood probably wasn't making his own decisions anyway, now that Aldridge thought about it. Thinking about how soon he would have Gavin Larson over a barrel, he flashed a charming smile and shook hands all around.

"What is so crucial that I have to be *here* to find out about it?"

"Actually, there are two reasons you should be here, Kent," Thurgood said as he turned to a cart and poured tea into three cups. "Oh, would you care for some tea?"

Aldridge shook his head. "No, thank you, Mr. President."

Thurgood picked up two cups and delivered one to Xavier, who was starting to look quite comfortable in the White House. Between Gavin Larson and the pope, Aldridge wondered if Thurgood actually made any decisions on his own. After watching him serve tea, he decided he pretty much knew the answer.

Careful with his tea, Gavin leaned forward on the couch across from the pope and studied Aldridge, as if he were expecting something. He smiled, one of those kinds of smiles someone gives who knows he's won a major lucrative deal, like he's had the inside track all along. Aldridge felt superlatively uncomfortable all of a sudden among these three powerful men.

He was definitely the outsider. He knew that; he always had, hadn't he? So what was the big deal? He controlled the resources of the Federal Bureau of Investigation, and he didn't want much—just a few hundred million dollars now, hard-earned extortion money, and he would be content.

"Kent," Gavin said. "Xavier here has some interesting news."

"Yes?" Aldridge raised his eyebrows. "You've discovered another atheist in our midst? I'd hate to think I'm the only one here with enough guts not to believe in a god."

"Kent, you can be rather stupid, can't you?" Gavin said. "I'm certainly not going to miss you."

"What do you mean, not going to miss me?"

"I mean miss you as in you no longer being around to be a source of irritation or a threat. At one time you were indispensable, but all that has changed now. The Coalition no longer has a need for you, and I've been trying to decide how to get rid of you."

"Yes, I knew my usefulness would be short-lived, but I've made arrangements that should anything happen to me, plenty of evidence will find its way into the hands of the Justice Department to indict you on murder and a variety of racketeering charges."

"Yes, so I would have guessed. But it appears I no longer have those worries." Gavin appeared to have forgotten everyone else in the room. He was gloating. Aldridge had the distinct impression he was about to get blindsided, and Gavin wasn't hiding the thrill of getting the better of him very well, either. He glanced around the room, but everyone seemed content to let Gavin proceed.

"So, what is this about?" Aldridge asked, and then he fixed Gavin with a warning glare. It was a warning that spoken aloud would have gone something like, "Don't forget that I can take you down, too, Gavin, whatever you're planning."

Gavin smiled smugly and turned to the pope. "Please, Your Excellency, will you tell Director Aldridge what was revealed to you."

Xavier looked gravely at Aldridge, pursed his lips, and then glanced at the carpet. *Clearly he isn't enjoying this as much as Gavin is*, Aldridge thought.

"The Holy Mother has given me another vision," Xavier said. "It concerns you."

Aldridge let out a disgusted breath and actually felt some of the tension leave his body. Gavin had given the impression of more concrete worries. "I've been called here to listen to more spiritual mumbo-jumbo? I thought I made it clear that I didn't believe in a higher being. That's not to say I'd discourage anyone else of his belief, so I'd also very much like to be left alone to believe as I please without having somebody's holy mother or god rammed down my throat. Is that too much to ask?" By the time he had finished, his voice was an octave higher and much louder.

"I think not!" Xavier replied a bit more sharply than apparently anyone had ever expected from His Excellency. "But I think you must be aware of your lack of reverence when speaking of spiritual matters. Your ignorance may be the reason for your impending death."

"My death?" Aldridge said incredulously. "Have you been playing with your crystal ball again?" He laughed until he realized he was alone. "What are you talking about?"

"The Holy Mother has told me you will soon be very sick. This terrible disease will infect and kill you."

"I told you, I don't believe in this stuff."

"I am sorry, my son."

Aldridge let out an unconvincing laugh. "I won't get sick."

President Thurgood finally entered the conversation. "I didn't have to tell you this news, Kent. I could have let whatever happens come to pass. But I know when I was dying I appreciated the chance to get my affairs in order. This disease is unpredictable. Sometimes it attacks the body's organs aggressively and kills within a few days. Sometimes it takes longer, much longer. You may only wish you were dead in that case. But I thought you deserved to know. If you choose not to believe Xavier, that is your choice."

Unsure how to react, Aldridge said, "Is that all?" He wanted to get out and think about this rationally. He didn't believe in supernatural powers, so that made all of this totally irrelevant. Nothing was going to happen to him.

Yet Gavin was not about to let it rest. "Kent, just this morning the Supreme Court unanimously agreed to allow the arrests of all Remnant Believers in the interest of protecting lives of the citizens of the United States. Last week, Xavier learned that two Supreme Court Justices were going to contract the disease. When that happened, the Court realized there was only one decision it could make. This disease will only disappear when all Remnant Believers join the Coalition."

"This was the second reason for calling me here? Because the Supreme Court declared open season on Remnant Believers?"

"Actually, no," President Thurgood said. "What you should have taken note of, Kent, was that Xavier said two justices were going to contract this disease. And, of course, they did."

* * *

Randy parked Alice's car and looked at Lynn. "Maybe you should let me go into the camp alone."

"Tell me, would it make any difference whether I'm in there with you or out here?"

"Maybe, maybe not. But I've been exposed so much that if I were susceptible to the disease, I would have gotten it by now. I don't think I am. I don't know why, but as many deceased people as I've been around looking for Brian, I should have been by now."

Lynn smiled. "If that's your logic, then Alice and I should have gotten sick before now too. We've been around lots of sick people. That's when the virus is most contagious, anyway. We're Believers, right? Believers in the one true God? Maybe one day one or both of us will come down with this horrible disease, but if we do, we know our Father in heaven. I have faith in Him and my love for Him."

Glancing at the Thurgood Rehabilitation and Detention Center through the car window, Randy nodded. "OK, we'll go together. But I want you to stick close to me. There is another reason I fear for you, and it's the fact that you and I are not sick." He got out of the car and opened the door for Lynn. Hand in hand they walked toward the gates of the compound. Through the high, electrified fence they could see hundreds of ramshackle makeshift buildings. "The majority of the people in these compounds are not sick. They're all professed Remnant Believers."

"What are you telling me?"

"Just that we run a great risk of being incarcerated just as the thousands of people who are already being held. The government has established a theory that Remnant Believers are responsible for this disease, because they are not contracting it."

"I know, and it's a stupid idea."

"I know it is. But the idea is easy to sell right now. People are frustrated, and if they're looking for someone to blame, Remnant Believers are an easy target. Remnant Believers are the only people who are not keeping the Sunday laws, and Pope Xavier specifically stated that total acceptance of Mary's requests was the only possible solution."

"When the Sunday law was passed, it made Remnant Believers outlaws. It made us outlaws, Randy." Lynn walked closer to Randy.

"I know, Sis. We have to be careful. We just have to be really careful. A few Believers at a time are being arrested and put in these concentration camps to take care of the sick. I'm surprised the government hasn't moved more quickly since the Supreme Court rendered its decision," Randy said as they arrived at the gate and sensed Lynn become tense. He tried to keep calm himself, but it wasn't happening. He felt as if he were walking into the lions' den. Worse yet, he was taking Lynn along with him.

A guard dressed in military fatigues stepped forward carrying a rifle. "Sir. Ma'am," he said, giving them an unfriendly look. "What is your business here?"

"We've come to visit a man whom I believe has been incarcerated here."

"The name, please." The guard adjusted a small headset mike in front of his mouth.

"His name is Brian Willis."

"Visitors for a Willis, Brian," the guard repeated into the mike. Seconds later, he nodded. "Understood. You two come with me."

Randy and Lynn were led up to the gate as several more guards appeared, the sudden crowding making Randy tense. Glancing at Lynn, he thought she looked awfully cool and unworried.

One of the guards pushed a buzzer at the gate, and a few seconds later, a motor began hauling the gate panels apart. Randy was fascinated by the fact that there were two high-security fences, razor wire strung heavily on the inside of the outer fence, and dogs patrolling the no-man's land in between. It was on par with any maximum-security prison, yet the living quarters the people in this facility were housed in were primitive at best. The whole compound was makeshift, except for the fences. This included the main office and center of operations, which were nothing more than modular units.

Randy and Lynn were escorted to the center of operations and let inside. When asked to sign in, both Randy and Lynn stepped forward.

"Only one visitor at a time." A guard halted Lynn with a raised hand. Although his expression was stoical, his eyes did not conceal that he was attracted to Lynn. "I don't think it would be a good idea for you to get close to any of the prisoners, Miss."

"Why? Is Brian Willis sick?"

"Whether he's sick or not doesn't matter. He may be carrying the virus."

"I trust God to protect me. I'm not afraid of the disease."

"I don't know why not. Everyone else is."

Lynn smiled warmly. "Not everyone. I don't imagine there are many Remnant Believers who are afraid of what will happen to them."

Randy cringed listening to Lynn bringing up the Remnant and talking so freely about God to the guard. She had to realize they had walked right into the lions' mouth, and they couldn't afford to attract attention. Touching her arm, he tried draw her aside and caution her. But when she looked at him, all he could see was total conviction. In no way could he convince her to trade witnessing for her personal safety. Dropping his hand, he stepped back and thought about Lynn's conviction to tell as many people as possible about God, His love, His truthfulness, and the approaching end of the world. She went about it without fear.

The guard, a nice-looking, clean-cut young man of nineteen or twenty, seemed to be sincerely interested as Lynn drew him into conversation. It was like watching a small miracle at work, and he realized how very strong Lynn's faith and convictions had become in just a few short months. She certainly had more courage than he did.

Randy glanced at his watch. *How long is this going to take?* Then, as if in answer, the door at the end of the hall leading to the compound grounds opened, emitting three men, two in Racal suits and a third in gray prison coveralls, his hands cuffed. Randy barely recognized the gaunt, unshaven prisoner who was deposited in a room near the end of the hall by the outside door.

One of the Racal suits came down the hall, and Lynn's conversation halted with the guard.

"Prisoner's here," the Racal suit said, "Let's hurry it up. I want to get out of this suit and go home."

The guard nodded and glanced at Randy and Lynn. "Only one visitor." It was clear who he wished that one visitor to be.

"I don't mind waiting out here, Randy," Lynn said.

"All right." It would have sounded ridiculous to tell her to be careful, but the look he gave her translated his thoughts clearly.

"I'm fine," Lynn assured him.

The guard walked Randy down the hall behind the Racal suit. The two guards in suits stationed themselves near the door and let Randy into an extremely small, completely bare, room, probably no bigger than six by eight feet. Brian was looking outside through a small window with heavy mesh wire screwed over it.

Randy waited until the door closed. "Brian."

Brian Willis turned slowly. "Yes?"

"I'm sorry I'm so late finding you," Randy said as their eyes met.

Brian froze, staring in disbelief through the sunken shells of his eye sockets. "Randy?"

Walking over, Randy grasped Brian's hand and hugged him. "Yes, it's me. I'm sorry. What has happened to you? You look like death."

"I'm tired. Extremely tired. I have never fully understood what has happened to me, and no one has given a legal reason for confining me."

"Who knows you're here besides me?"

"No one that I can think of who would be willing or able to help. Gavin is the one who put me here." Brian leaned tiredly against the wall. "Do you mind if we sit?" He slid down the wall and rested his arms on his knees. Randy sat down with his back to the opposite wall.

"What happened after I let you out of the car and you alerted the police?"

Brian closed his eyes, replaying the events that led up to

the president's death and his abduction. "I hurried to Gavin's motor home and found him inside preparing to speak. But he had me detained by a man from the Freedom Society. The Freedom Society is like his own personal military, Randy. When he needs to coerce people, kidnap them, as he did with me, or even kill them as he did with Stan Shultz, he can do so with the Freedom Society."

"You've been held against your will since that Friday?" Randy asked.

Brian nodded. "Immediately following the explosions, handcuffs were slapped on, a pillowcase put over my head, and I was driven out of the area to an abandoned warehouse."

Randy stared into Brian's eyes for a long moment. "Brian, I spoke to your family."

"Oh, God, thank You." Brian raised his eyes heavenward. "Are they all right?"

Randy nodded. Brian's shoulders seemed to cave in as he dropped his head and sobbed. Randy came over and placed a hand on his shoulder. "I'll tell them you're alive. I'll tell Ann where you are."

Brain nodded and raised his head. "Can you get me out of here?"

"I don't know. The rules of law and justice in this country don't seem to apply anymore. At least not in a way that protects Remnant Believers. The White House seems to be able to do anything it wants to do."

Embarrassed, Brian took a few moments to compose himself and dry his face. "I can assure you that my rights have been completely discarded, as were the rights of hundreds of others in this place. What has happened to the Supreme Court? Violations of rights, complete disregard for the Constitution, and nothing has been done to rectify it. Surely the Court has ruled that what the country is doing to its citizens is unconstitutional."

"Brian, I know its ridiculous that things are so mixed up,

but this disease is scaring everyone, not to mention the disasters that have taken millions of lives all over the world. The world seems out of control, and people are so scared they are completely willing to believe and do anything to appease God if that will return things to some semblance of peace and orderliness. People are just not thinking straight."

"I can imagine how Gavin Larson has been taking advantage of the chaos," Brian said.

"That's exactly right. Larson and Thurgood. And their job is made that much easier and credible with the spiritual advice of the pope who has stepped forward claiming he has the answers to saving the world."

"No one is willing to listen to reason?"

Randy shook his head. "It's a nightmare. What's reasonable? And furthermore, who dares to go against Pope Xavier's guidance? Tens of millions of people are joining the United Religious Coalition and embracing Sunday worship."

With noticeable resolve returning to his eyes, Brian looked at Randy. "There are a few people who openly oppose the pope and the United Religious Coalition. There are hundreds of them here. Remnant Believers. Besides the sick and dying, they're the only other group of people here in this hole."

"I know. And they are being blamed for the worsening disasters," Randy said.

"Is there anything you can do? You're an FBI agent."

"Ex-FBI. I'm probably on everyone's black list, and frankly, I find it amazing that nothing mysterious has happened to me yet." It just had to be that much of the reason he was able to walk around freely was because of the tape Mara had recorded of Kent Aldridge in the hospital. "I'm afraid that what is happening in this country is much bigger and has far too much momentum for me to be able to do anything about it. But I'll try to come up with something.

Brian nodded. "Thanks. I'm really not so much worried about myself as I am about my family. I'm afraid for them. So far here, I've been able to avoid too much pressure to change my convictions. Many others have been coerced into renouncing the Sabbath as *the* day of worship."

"And why do you think you haven't been challenged?"

"I think partially because I had not declared myself to be a Remnant Believer to get in here. The others are here because for one reason or another—their friends, neighbors, and bosses turned them in. They felt that by openly challenging the claims of the United Religious Coalition and the pronouncements of the pope, the Believers were undermining the serious efforts of the government and the Coalition to appease God."

Randy licked his lips, thinking seriously. "I'm afraid I'm not going to like where you're heading with this, Brian. Do you know what you'll be setting yourself up for?"

Brian nodded.

"And what about your family?"

"Ann will understand. My children . . ." Brian paused long enough that Randy became aware of the supreme effort he was making not to break down. "My children are the most precious part of my life. I—I can't bear the thought of—of never seeing them again." Brain sniffed. "I love God, Randy. I don't blame Him for my situation. I don't necessarily understand why I am here, but I trust Him completely. I believe that in a short time I will have to stand up for Him in a way that will require my complete love and faithfulness. As I have thought about this, I've come to accept that I may never see my children again on this earth. I've got to make more of a stand here than I have been. What I've done so far has been done largely in secret, but that must change. Too many people are losing their faith. I met several people here with amazing convictions for the Lord and keeping His commandments. I think the least I can do is help others with their faith, even if I have to walk through the whole camp singing at the top of my lungs about God. Besides, I have a feeling God is giving me no choice."

"But—"

Brian raised a hand. "If I had wanted to, I could have chosen Gavin Larson's path. I could be in the White House right at this moment helping to lead this crazy religious revolution. At any time, all I had to do was admit that I was wrong, and I would have been released and welcomed into the fold like a lost sheep. Even now, I could do this. I would probably never be totally free of suspicion and would probably pay years of atonement in some form or another. Of course, I would never be completely trusted again. But I would be free. And Gavin could use me, even now."

"So why not accept a deal from Gavin? See what it gets you, and then get away to your family. Flee the country."

Brian snorted and shook his head. "And go where? Is the rest of the world any different, any better? The United States has some kind of control in every part of the world. Now, with the pope leading out in the United States, Catholics all over the world are probably enchanted at the idea that the pope has such authority. It wasn't hard before for the world to chastise the United States for anything and everything. It takes no great imagination to picture what is going on now as disasters eat up the world's populations, crops, and resources and the pope on American soil claiming it all stops with religious reformation."

As Randy listened to Brian, he found himself amazed at his faith and focus. If he were in Brian's place, he imagined he would have bit on the first bait Gavin tossed him. But not Brian. Not this man who had once been so influential in the United Religious Coalition. What made a person able to give up his life, and in Brian's case, seeing his family again, for his beliefs?

"I can see what you're thinking, Randy," Brian said with a slight but warm smile.

"What am I thinking?"

"Let me just say that it's maybe not so much religion or belief or even 'Christianity' but a *relationship*—a relationship with my Savior, Jesus Christ, that gives me the strength to become so firmly entrenched in obedience to God."

"And where, my friend, is it going to get you?" Randy asked to be sure Brian was in charge of all his faculties, that he indeed understood what might be ahead should he pursue his current path.

"It gets me eternity to become better acquainted with Jesus."

"You sound so positive."

"I think I have to." A bank of silence ensued with both men aware they probably had little time left. With so much to talk about and try to understand, how difficult it was to arrive at a place to start. But then, as Randy felt sure Brian was aware, what could be done to help him? There was certainly no legal reason for him to be held against his will. In the shambles of the current legal system, due process was a fantasy, especially considering that Brian was in the same situation as thousands, possibly hundreds of thousands of others.

And then the expected moment arrived. Swinging the door open, one of the guards stuck his Racal-suited head inside and declared the meeting finished. The guards and their cowering use of the Racal suits annoyed Randy in a way he didn't understand. Helping Brian to his feet, Randy shook his hand once more, but Brian wouldn't let go.

"I need a favor," he whispered frantically.

Immediately Randy turned to the guard, and rather than ask for permission to have a few more minutes of privacy, ordered it as if he were still backed by the FBI. The Racal suit actually faded through the crack in the door and latched it shut.

"Whatever I can do," Randy assured Brian.

"Move my family. Take them someplace safe. I don't want them to suffer for my actions, and I'm afraid it isn't above Gavin to go after my family."

Randy nodded. "I'll do that."

"You know better than I the best way to go about it, but keep it in the back of your head that Gavin might have them watched. The phones may be tapped."

Now, his patience sufficiently used up, the guard swung the door open, slamming it against the wall. "That's all!" he snapped. "It's time to go!"

"All right, I'm through," Brian said, swinging his eyes off Randy, to the floor, then raising them humbly toward the guard. "Let's go."

The guards took Brian by the arms and quickly led him outside. One waited in the hall to lead Randy back to where Lynn was waiting. "You'll need to sign out the same as you signed in," he said.

Randy glanced back down the corridor, but Brian and his guards were gone. A heavy weight sank in the pit of his stomach. He didn't know why except that he wondered whether or not he would ever see Brian again and felt he probably wouldn't. He couldn't explain his intuition except that it came from being an agent for several years. Brian planned to speak more openly about God, criticize the United Religious Coalition, and surely that would upset people. Surely it would make Gavin angry.

One thing Randy knew for sure: If Gavin got upset at Brian, then he better have Brian's family someplace safe.

Signing out and leaving proved no more difficult than signing in to see Brian Willis. Yet Randy felt extremely uneasy. Why on earth had Lynn and he not been bothered? It seemed just as easy for them to walk around freely as it did anyone else who wasn't a Remnant Believer. He fussed over this on the way back to Alice Nolan's apartment.

"What's bothering you, Randy?" Lynn asked as they entered the apartment and were assaulted with the smell of spaghetti sauce and freshly baked bread.

Randy hung his coat in the closet and reached for Lynn's. "I'm troubled by the fact that we have been left alone. No police have harassed us as they have other Believers. We walked in and out of the detention compound without a fuss. I thought surely the fact you were talking to that guard so openly about Jesus would cause us some sort of problems."

"You worry too much."

"You think so?"

Lynn nodded. "I do."

Alice came from the kitchen wearing an expression of concern. "How is Brian?"

"He's not in good shape. He's managed to lose thirty or more pounds. Much of it has to be from worry, but I'm sure he's probably giving away most of the food he gets." Randy sniffed the air and wondered how he could eat supper with that thought running through his head. "He asked me to move his family someplace safe, where Gavin Larson can't touch them."

"Why would Larson want to harm *them?* They're innocent people, and Brian is a just man."

"I know, Alice, but these are not times of reason, and although I can't imagine why Gavin Larson would want to harm Brian's family, he's concerned and that means I'll do what I can to make sure they're safe. For Brian."

"You'll be leaving?" Lynn asked, reaching out for her brother's arm. "You'll have to go to Chicago, won't you? That's where they live."

"I will. I'll leave tomorrow, if possible."

As good as the food was, Randy was able to eat very little. After supper, he cleaned up the kitchen while Alice and Lynn studied at the table. He listened to their discussion and the texts as they read. After wiping off the countertops and putting water on the stove to heat, he made reservations with the airline that offered him the best rates for a one-way flight to Chicago. Once he found Brian's family and discussed the options with his wife, Randy would make the decision where to go from there. In the back of his mind, he toyed with the idea of going to Boise, Idaho, where he could see Mara. Bringing the Willis family back to Washington D.C. was out of the question.

Monday, March 3

Randy made tea for three and sat down.

* * *

Dan Reiss made his way into the kitchen of the old farm-house, but he was not soothed by the aroma of soup being cooked by several of the women currently residing in the house. Children scurried underfoot, and Dan was at a loss to understand how the women got anything done, but they always managed. Naomi Burnside dropped a gigantic ball of dough onto one of the floured wooden countertops.

"You're looking a little green around the gills, Pastor," she remarked dryly. "Bet you're wishing you went with the other men into the mountains to check on the relocation place."

Dan ran his fingers through his hair, making it stand up on end. He grinned weakly. "I am feeling like a fish out of water," he admitted. "I'm at a total loss for something to do."

"Why don't you call Dani's mother?" Naomi suggested. "Women usually like to have their mothers around when they have a baby. But you might want to check with her first. Sometimes that's the last thing they want too. Depends on the woman. And the mother."

"That sounds like a good idea," Dan agreed. He trotted back up the stairs and met Mara and Dani pacing slowly up and down the hallway. "How is it going?"

Dani glowered at him, so he appealed to Mara, who nodded and gave him a surreptitious smile. "We're doing fine."

"Speak for yourself," Dani growled.

"Um, Dani, would you like me to call your mother for you? Would you like her to come?" Dan asked.

Dani looked up and brushed wet strands of hair from her face. "I-I don't know. I'm not sure. Maybe. But not now." She clutched her abdomen and let out a scream, hanging onto Mara as a contraction gripped her. Dan felt his legs go shaky.

"OK, you let me know when, and I'll call her," he said, fleeing back down the stairs to the safety of the kitchen. He desperately wished he'd gone with the group of men and boys who had taken horses on a trip up into the mountains to scout out a place they could go to if the persecution became too bad. He felt so useless in the face of the current situation.

"Pastor Reiss?" a gentle voice asked. Dan looked up to see Cody's mother, Jenna, standing beside him. "Maybe you'd like to pray with some of us . . . for Dani. I know that when I had Cody, I really appreciated it when I knew that the people from my church were praying for me. I just went up and told Dani that some of us would be praying for her. Would you like to join us?"

Dan felt chastised for his lack of faith. Jenna had only been baptized less than a year and yet she'd taken the initiative to start a prayer group. "Lord," Dan muttered under his breath as he followed Jenna into the sitting room where some of the women and children had gathered, "please forgive my lack of faith. I know You're in charge. Thanks for reminding me."

Chapter Ten

Tuesday, March 4

Dietrich had been watching Kent Aldridge since yesterday. When he gave his report, Gavin appeared pleased as well as somewhat awed.

"You're sure of what you saw?"

"Yes. He definitely appears to be getting sick, just as you suggested." Dietrich's eyes narrowed. "So how did you know?"

"The pope himself warned Aldridge that he would become ill." Gavin shrugged. "This all came right after Aldridge professed his unbelief in a supernatural being."

Dietrich whistled. He had often thought of himself as having the ability to control people's lives. If he chose to, he could end a life in the time and manner of his choosing. Because of his skill, he could do such things with a reasonable certainty that he would not be caught or even suspected. Suddenly, after hearing that Aldridge was sick with the virus because Pope Xavier had forewarned it, he felt much smaller and vulnerable than a man of his profession should ever feel. An unfamiliar sensation swam in the pit of his stomach as a vague feeling of uneasiness swept over him.

"Well, *you* look a little pale around the gills," Gavin said.

Dietrich snorted.

"You are feeling well yourself, aren't you?"

"Yes, yes, I'm feeling fine," Dietrich lied. He studied Gavin's expression. *Could I be underestimating the availability of power to this man?* Considering his encounter with the "angel" who had stood between him and Brian Willis, he began to really see the spiritual powers at work. So, he didn't feel fine. He felt powerless.

"Tell me about the girl," Gavin said. "Have you discovered where she is."

"Yes. She is on a farm near Boise, Idaho."

"The baby should arrive any time," Gavin said. He narrowed his eyes at Dietrich. "I'm not at all happy you have failed me so much lately. Remember, this child is much too important to me for you to fail again."

Dietrich nodded with a grimace. What could be done? He actually detested Gavin, and he hated the idea that the pope could *cause* or even predict a person would be sick. Killing someone using supernatural powers, something he had never really believed in until now, seemed a cowardly way to operate. A killer, a hired gun he might be, but it seemed far more professional and respectful than coercion or killing with religion.

But he worked for hire, and he'd been hired by Larson. He considered what he had learned about the doctor.

The doctor hadn't been at all hesitant in using her UBC card, Dietrich had learned from his female contact at the Trust National Bank. Apparently she was eating a lot these days. Either that or she was feeding a lot of people—quite likely Remnant Believer people—because her grocery bills were topping $300 a week. She was buying these groceries in Boise, Idaho, which was spitting distance from the town where Dani was from. It didn't take a rocket scientist to assume the two might still be together.

"She is quite possibly harboring a load of Remnant Believers," Dietrich reasoned.

"So do you think you can go in, arrest them all, and take the child?" Gavin asked, his eyes narrow and his face drawn. The sudden rise to power might have been great for his ego, but it had aged him overnight.

"What's to prevent me?" Dietrich said irritably. "What *do* you want to do with it?"

Gavin laughed scornfully. "I guess that's my business, now isn't it? You just get that kid. I'll take it from there. How long is this going to take, anyway?"

Dietrich shrugged. "I don't know. It all depends on whether or not she's had the thing yet. Our records show the estimated conception date and projected delivery date, but I don't think they let the babies in on that sort of thing. It could be early, late, who knows. What I do know is that it shouldn't be more than a few weeks off either way, unless something goes wrong."

Gavin settled down and studied a large, fire opal paperweight on his desktop. "You can be sure Aldridge is keeping track. He knows I want that child. He may not know exactly why, but he knows how badly. But soon it won't matter." He looked up. "How soon can you make changes in your travel arrangements to get to Chicago?"

"At the most, a day," Dietrich said. He started toward the door, then paused and turned around. "I'd still like to know why you want the child."

Gavin closed his eyes for a moment. Then he nodded and picked up the paperweight and motioned for Dietrich to come back. "See this paperweight? I want you to concentrate on what you see inside." He paused for a few moments while Dietrich stared at it. "Don't you see a world, vastly different than this one yet recognizably the same?"

Dietrich shrugged and nodded. Gavin smiled.

7—M.H.

"There is a central government with great wealth and power. This government has inconceivable powers: the power to heal, the power to bestow eternal youth, even the power to raise people from the dead and to create."

"Yes, I think I see it now," Dietrich said. The paperweight twinkled in the natural sunlight glancing on it from the window. Fire seemed to shoot from inside it.

"Thrilling, isn't it?" Gavin's smiled broadened. "It's the power that we should have had all along." Suddenly, he covered the paperweight with his hand and returned it to the desk. Dietrich blinked.

"But *how* does the child fit?"

"The child is simply a token of my allegiance to the one who has imparted me with this vision. I was given the vision so that I might ready as many people as possible to follow the one whom I serve. Once I have the child, I can prove my complete loyalty."

"Who are you doing this all for? The Christian God?" Dietrich asked.

Gavin folded his hands under his chin. "Molech. The ancient God of the Israelites."

"That's all you're going to tell me?"

"For now."

Dietrich blew out a disgusted breath as he turned to leave.

"You didn't see a thing in that paperweight, did you, Dietrich?"

"Not hardly." Dietrich slammed the door behind him.

"You will, when Molech wants you to see."

* * *

Dani gritted her teeth and glared at Mara.

"Push!"

"I am pushing," she screamed. "I've been pushing for hours. Something is wrong. Can't you operate? Get this baby out!"

Mara's reassuring touch on her knee annoyed her. A steel band gripped her abdomen and searing pain shot through her. She leaned heavily against Jenna, who had come upstairs to help. She was behind Dani, supporting her beneath the arms as Dani squatted beside the bed. Although they'd been in that wearying position for what seemed like hours, Jenna had not complained. Every now and then, she leaned over and whispered encouragement into Dani's ear, assuring her that she was doing a good job and it would soon be over.

But it felt like it would never be over. Rather than getting better, the pain had only gotten worse, and there seemed to be no end in sight. Her hips ached with the strain of squatting, her abdomen was on fire, and each new contraction felt as though it was squeezing the life out of her.

"Every time you push, the baby advances down the birth canal," Mara repeated. "You're halfway there already. When the next contraction comes, push hard."

Dani panted and felt defeat wash over her. Halfway there. Only halfway. She couldn't endure this pain for another minute. "I can't," she sobbed gently. "I can't do this anymore."

"You have to."

Dani groaned as a fresh contraction gripped her, and she felt her body work to expel the baby. Summoning strength she didn't know she had, she concentrated on pushing. Veins in her forehead felt as though they would burst open with her effort. With a stubborn determination she thought she'd lost, she hung on until the contraction spent itself then she sagged against Jenna.

"That was good," Mara praised. "I think with the next contraction I'll be able to see the head. I can feel it now."

Immediately Dani's mood lifted. "You can?" Throughout her labor Mara and Jenna had assured her that her baby would soon be here, as if that was something Dani could identify with, but she couldn't. If they would just make the baby disappear, she'd gladly forfeit it in exchange for relief from the pain. But now that it was almost a reality, she felt her flagging spirits revive. The baby was finally coming!

"Here, feel for yourself," Mara said, taking Dani's hand and guiding her fingers into the birth canal where she could feel the firm head of her baby. "If you push really hard, you'll be able to birth the head with the next contraction."

But it took three more contractions before the head finally emerged. "Pant," Mara instructed as she suctioned the baby.

"I can't," Dani wailed. "I need to push."

"Pant," Jenna said firmly. "Don't push. Not yet. She's got to get the shoulders out one at a time so you don't tear. Pant, there, that's it." She panted as an example in Dani's ear and Dani struggled vainly to follow her lead.

"OK, now a gentle push with the next contraction. That's it. Now push!"

Dani pushed with relief and felt the baby slip from her body. In the next instant, Mara was smiling broadly as she held the baby, covered in the fluids of birth. "It's a boy," she exclaimed.

Dani sagged against Jenna. "I know," she murmured. She ignored Mara's puzzled look. "Can I see him?"

"Just a minute. Come on baby, breathe for me," she gently rubbed the baby's back and his color improved. He squirmed and began to cry. "Here you go, Mama." Jenna eased Dani onto the floor where she sat as Mara laid the baby in her arms. "Now just relax a few minutes. The afterbirth will be coming soon. Let me know when you feel the urge to push again."

"What?" Dani looked up with some alarm.

"Don't worry. It's all downhill from here. You'll hardly notice it."

The baby squirmed and wailed in her arms, and she turned her attention to him. He wasn't very red like Mara said he'd be. Instead, he was kind of pale. His head was round as a bowling ball, perfectly shaped.

"He's hardly got any molding at all," Mara said, watching her study the baby.

"You mean his head?"

"Yes, see how nice and round it is? Have you thought of a name?"

Dani felt tears well in her eyes, and her throat constricted. "His name is Jack Daniel Talbot, after my dad and Pastor Reiss."

Mara smiled gently and squeezed her arm. "I'm sure your father would have been very happy to know that."

Dani nodded. "He is."

Mara's eyebrows knit themselves into puzzlement. "What do you mean, he is?"

Dani clamped her lips together. She'd said too much. But Mara let the comment pass and busied herself with examining the afterbirth which Dani expelled. After she was cleaned up, Jenna and Mara helped Dani onto the bed where she attempted to nurse little Jack for the first time. "He seems to know what he's supposed to do," she said anxiously, as the tiny baby clamped down on her nipple and began to suck vigorously.

"Yep, he's a natural," Mara agreed. "A little barracuda."

Dani smiled and tried to relax, but her mind was racing. Instead of feeling tired after her long ordeal, she felt pumped, wired, ready to take on the world. And then she remembered something that made her blood run cold. She looked down at Jack's sweet face and was filled with a nameless terror. No, maybe not so nameless after all. Her terror had a name, and it was Dietrich.

* * *

He was spending more and more time in the "other world" where things were beautiful, and he was young and vibrant. The Holy Mother brought him there for their visits because she couldn't stand the horror of his world. After each visit, when he was forced to return to it himself, he agreed with her wholeheartedly. At first it hadn't been so bad, rather like having an extremely pleasant dream and waking up. A bit disappointing, but thrilling nevertheless. The tingle of excitement stayed with him for hours and surged through him whenever he thought about the visit.

Now, however, he was like a man withdrawing from a drug like heroin or cocaine. Coming back from the visit wasn't like waking from a pleasant dream but like entering a nightmare of astronomic proportions. There was no tingle of excitement thinking back on the visits, only a gut-wrenching yearning to return. He spent the hours between visits fitful and restless, like a man waiting for lab results from a tumor biopsy.

When the Holy Mother called, he returned to her with a leap of the heart and a feeling of relief that made him giddy with joy. She often told him how pleased she was by the expediency with which her desires had been carried out since the West Coast earthquake disaster. In recent days, she had alluded to something exciting that was about to happen. Today, he hoped he might find out.

When she called him, he found her pensive and a little sad. She was in a semi-reclining position against a mound of satin-covered pillows. She smiled faintly and motioned him to an ornate silver chair with a cotton-soft cushion that he sank into with a sigh of absolute contentment. "Hello, my little father. How are you this afternoon?"

"Mother, I am with you. Life does not get any better than this."

"No," she replied slowly, gazing at him with beautiful blue eyes filled with sorrow and yet, somehow, brimming with excitement. "Life will never get any better than this. But I will tell you a secret. This old life will soon pass away."

Xavier sat up in his chair, keen with interest. "Mother, what do you mean?" He saw his reflection, mirrored in her irises. When visiting her he was young again, his hair black and glossy as a raven's wing, his face without wrinkle. His features strong and handsome.

Tuesday, March 4

"How would you like to be with me forever, little father?"

"Mother, you know that I would. It is my most cherished hope."

"I will tell you something, but I am not ready to share this with the world yet. Can you promise me that you will yet guard it as a secret?" When he nodded, she appeared satisfied and continued. "My Son has informed me of the date when He will return to claim His faithful. Shall I tell you?"

He nodded vigorously, holding his breath in anticipation.

"So eager, my child," she chided with an indulgent smile. "The date my Son has chosen to return is April 28. On that day, those who hope to go with Him into paradise must be ready to receive Him. Do you think it is possible for you to convince the world, His bride, to be prepared to receive her Bridegroom?"

Rapture filled his body in a warm flood. "Oh, Mother! What wonderful news. Yes, I can convince them of anything when that prize awaits me. I will use whatever means necessary."

Mary smiled with satisfaction and reclined against the pillows that supported her. "I know that I can depend on you," she murmured.

* * *

The light seared her eyes and seemed to send sparks shooting around the room. She was so tired. She'd been up for forty-eight hours working in the infirmary. But instead of bringing her back to the barracks, the guards had brought her here and grilled her for what had already seemed like days but had probably been about twelve hours.

They came in and out of the room, but a guard stayed all the time, hitting her in the back of the head if she closed her eyes or nodded off. When they came in, they smiled and bobbed their heads, grinning at her through the face masks of the Racal suits. Their muffled voices were dreamlike, and she found herself wondering if maybe this wasn't just a nightmare.

Midnight Hour

"So, Colonel Cooper, have you thought about our proposal?" It was the one called Major Thule. She was a big woman who leaned across the desk, her manner as gracious as it was false. Listening to her, Amy would have thought Major Thule had her best interests at heart. It was almost believable. But when she stubbornly shook her head and received a walloping thump across the back of the head that made her see stars, she knew differently.

"Come, Colonel," Major Thule's voice was sarcastic now. "You can't expect me to believe that this God you hold so dear is going to save you. If He can help you, then why doesn't He? It's because He has no power." She leaned across the desk again, her bloodshot eyes inches from Amy's. "I, on the other hand, have the power to make this all stop." She snapped her gloved fingers. The sound was muted, but it jolted Amy like a lightning bolt. "Just like that. I could make it all stop. You could be on the outside, have a nice hot bath, and be at home with your husband in a matter of hours. I've already called him. He's waiting for you. All you have to do is sign this written recantation. Will you do it?"

Amy shook her head, cringing away from the guard who struck her again.

"A pity," Major Thule said. "We'll just let you think about it some more, shall we?"

And she was gone again. Amy was thirsty, and she licked her cracked lips. The guard noticed and sauntered over to the cooler, took out an ice-cold soda, and drank it in front of her. Amy averted her eyes, but the guard's sadistic laugh echoed in her ears.

To block her out, Amy let her thoughts wander. She wondered how Brian was doing. She hadn't seen him in nearly a week. For a while they'd been on the same shifts, and then suddenly he was gone, and there was another man in his place. She'd tried to get to know the man, but he was scared and wouldn't talk to her. All she was able to find out was that his name was Ed, and he'd been incarcerated for four weeks. It was all he would tell her.

Suddenly Amy heard the door behind her open, and she was hauled up roughly by her arms. "Come on, Colonel," Major Thule's voice boomed. "We've got your quarters ready. I thought you might appreciate some time alone in which to contemplate our attractive offer."

Amy staggered against the guards as they yanked her down a corridor. As they headed outside, she opened her mouth and took great gulps of the sweet air. Their gloved fingers dug into the soft flesh beneath her arms as they pulled her, nearly supporting her full weight. As they crossed the courtyard, the realization of where she was heading penetrated Amy's dull senses.

The prisoners called it the Snake Pit. It was a large hole dug in the ground, covered by a crude iron gate of bars. More than half of the prisoners who entered the Snake Pit did not come out alive. The ones who did died of terrible suffering shortly after being removed. It was infested with rats, snakes, and black-widow spiders. Although they didn't know for sure, most of the prisoners speculated that the prison actually employed people to bring in fresh stock expressly for the Snake Pit.

Terror filled Amy as she saw the iron gate lying on the ground. A light mist fell on her face, and she let her feet drag on the ground, forcing the guards to carry her the last hundred yards. Major Thule seemed pleased by this.

"Are you sure you don't wish to reconsider?" she asked in her most persuasive voice. "Fresh sheets and a warm bed await you at home. I've already called your husband and told him to expect you. You wouldn't want to disappoint Ron, now would you?"

Amy's resolve, which had been slowly crumbling under the combination of sleeplessness, interrogation, and the threat of going into the Snake Pit, snapped into position. With one word, Major Thule had proved that she was lying, and Amy was jolted into reality. "My husband's name is Ray," she said slowly.

If Major Thule didn't know Ray's name, she couldn't have called him. Ray wasn't waiting for her. Chances were, Major Thule didn't even know where Ray was. Hopefully.

Frustration crossed Major Thule's face. "Ray," she snapped. "That's what I meant. Now which is it, Colonel? Home or the Snake Pit?"

Amy didn't reply, and Major Thule jerked her head toward the guards who pulled open the gate and shoved Amy into the pit. She fell with her arms outstretched, which broke her fall, but she sank into six inches of mud. Something moved by her right side, and she felt a sharp pain in her calf. She clambered to her feet and staggered to one corner.

The entire pit was dark, and she couldn't see so much as her hand in front of her face. The corner gave her leverage. She backed into it slowly, feeling with her hands tentatively in the darkness. "God," she prayed softly, "I know You're here, even in this awful place. Please protect me the way you did Daniel in the lions' den. Send Your angels to shut the mouths of the snakes."

She felt another sharp pain in her calf. Reaching down quickly, she found a snake, its fangs sunk into her leg. Panicking, she ripped it away and stomped it into the mud. She'd been bitten. All the snakes in the Snake Pit were deadly.

Lo, I am with you always. Remember my servant, Paul.

Amy shuddered from exhaustion and fright. Paul—he'd been bitten by a viper and had suffered no ill effects. Maybe that was how God would protect her too. She sank slowly onto her heels. Whatever was going to happen, it was in God's hands. Worrying about it would not change one thing. She huddled into as tight a ball as she could and closed her eyes. Sleep overtook her quickly.

Amy remembered waking over and over throughout the night to fight off rats and snakes, but when morning paled the sky, she was alive and able to stand on shaky legs. There was to be no reprieve, however. The guards, disappointed to find her still alive, marched her back to the infirmary, where she worked another sixteen hours before being allowed to return to her barracks and fall deeply asleep crammed in with the others.

* * *

"Are you sure that's where they took her?"

"Yes. Positive," Ed said.

Brian closed his eyes and prayed. "God, please protect Amy Cooper. Give her peace." He heard Ed praying too. When he opened his eyes, Ed was staring at him.

"You know, she's a real Christian. A good doctor too." Ed gestured futilely. "This country's so messed up. It's been that way for the past couple of months, but I tell you, this really brings it home—when they throw the best doctor we got in the Snake Pit just cause she won't give up her Remnant beliefs."

"You like her." It was dead time, about half an hour before the lights went out and everyone was supposed to be in place for the night or risk getting shot. Although he had seen him around a few times, Brian had never met Ed Vicars. He always seemed to shy away from people . . . until now.

Ed smiled from one side of his mouth. He looked at Brian, but he was seeing a distant something, the past, Brian thought.

"Yeah, I guess I do. Couldn't help it. She was always tryin' to get me to talk. Nice woman, you know, but talk? Boy, she'd talk your ear off if you let her. Always thought she was goin' to get me into trouble." Ed quieted down for a few minutes. "She don't know it, but she helped me keep my faith."

"You wish you would have told her."

Ed's eyes narrowed. "You're good. You know what everyone is thinkin'?"

"No, no," Brian laughed. "I certainly don't."

Ed nodded once and smiled. "Shhuurre. Anyway, you're a preacher, aren't you?"

"No."

"Funny, that's what Amy said about you. Said you were one of the most godly people she's ever met. Said you led a lot of folk to God, and while you were here, you'd helped a lot keep their faith. Amy was always asking someone about you to see if you were all right. That's why I thought I'd come and find you and tell you what they did to her."

"I'm glad you did, Ed."

Ed's eyes closed, and he smiled. "So am I. I'm going to miss her. She reminded me of my daughter."

Chapter Eleven

Thursday, March 6

Dan Reiss sat at the old desk in his study, his fingers laced together, his forehead resting lightly against them. On the desktop in front of him was a list Jenna had compiled of their current food supplies. There were now twenty people, including the children, living in the ramshackle old house, and even with Jenna's uncanny ability to stretch one potato to feed four people, they still wouldn't have enough food to last them for the next two weeks. And yet, somehow food always came just when it looked as though they were going to run out.

"How are you going to provide for us this time, Father?" Dan murmured. And he was sure in his heart that God would provide. Somehow. Fortunately they had Mara's and Dani's UBC cards that helped take the edge off grocery hunting. But it really wasn't the food that he was thinking about at the moment. It was the news. Or rather, an accumulation of news reports.

Things were steadily getting worse. Until now, their suffering had been mostly in finding enough food, but God always provided for them. They had shelter, heat, and loving Christian companionship. There were many Remnant Believers who had suffered much worse than they had. Some had sacrificed everything, even their lives.

The American public was becoming frightened. Fed by media coverage reporting the proclamations of Pope Xavier, and wholly endorsed by Gavin Larson and President Thurgood, people felt justified in persecuting the Remnant Believers because the United Religious Coalition claimed they were responsible for the horrors that now assailed the country on every front. Disaster followed disaster in such quick succession that CNN struggled to keep up in reporting each new one.

National panic had reached a frenzied pitch, and Dan knew it was only a matter of time before they were discovered in their snug hideaway. For days now, he'd felt as though the Holy Spirit was urging him to head into the mountains. The arrival of Dani's baby had delayed their departure somewhat, but the urging grew stronger each day, and Dan knew that it would not be wise to ignore it longer.

He also had a sneaking fear that they were not as safe as it appeared. What if they were even now being watched until someone felt it was the right moment to sweep in and arrest all of them? But if so, what had kept it from happening before now? *Ahh, it's just paranoia, Dan*, he told himself.

Tonight, he decided, tonight he would call a meeting and tell the others that it was time to think about leaving their haven. A potential site had already been located, and they had some horses. A few members had owned them before coming to the farmhouse and had brought them along. They were a little on the skinny side, but they appeared healthy. The horses would make adequate pack animals, and some of the smaller children could ride into the mountains.

His thoughts were interrupted by a knock on the door. "Pastor Reiss?" It was Mara.

"Mara, come on in."

"I hope I'm not disturbing you . . ." She glanced around the room and seemed relieved to find him alone. "I was wondering if I could talk to you for a minute."

Dan sat back and turned his attention to her. "Certainly. What can I do for you?"

Mara found a seat on a rickety wooden chair that was leaning up against one wall. "It's about my UBC card," she said. "I know that everyone really relies on it, and I've been very happy to help, but I've been thinking, and I can't in good conscience continue to use it."

"I see," Dan said, but before he could continue, she cut him off quickly, her words coming so fast they slurred together.

"The reason I can't use it is that it would be hypocritical of me. None of you can use your UBC cards because of what you believe. Well, I believe the same things that you do, so I shouldn't be able to use mine either."

"Do you mean," Dan asked slowly, excitement making his voice shake, "that you would like to be a Remnant Believer?"

"I already am," Mara replied. "I mean, in my heart. And I'm ready to do anything that I have to to make it official."

"You understand what you're committing yourself to? I realize it can't be the easiest of decisions in light of what's going on in the world. Becoming a Christian has always meant sacrifices, but in our times it could mean the sacrifice of your life . . . tomorrow. Are you prepared for that?"

Mara nodded solemnly. "As much as anyone can be. Pastor Reiss, you have no idea how long I've waited to make this decision. I would have made it sooner, only I was too busy being a doctor, giving myself to medicine. Since Dani came into my life, everything has gone haywire. I've been shot at and nearly killed, I've left my home and everything that I know. I've even fallen in love. But, through it all, maybe *because* of it all, I got to know Jesus and to rely on Him for . . . *everything*. More than anyone, you've shown me what life can be like when you let

Him lead you. And I believe He's leading me to make a stand for Him as a Remnant Believer. I'm ready to do that." Mara sat back, a serene look on her face.

Dan swallowed against the lump in his throat and tried to speak past it. "Mara, words can't describe how thrilled I am. You know that I would be happy to baptize you whenever, wherever, but I must tell you there is one small complication. Nothing the Lord can't work out, mind you," he assured her hastily.

He leaned back in his chair and regarded her solemnly. "I'm going to tell the others later, but I might as well tell you now. It's time to move."

Mara looked at him blankly. "Move? All these people? Where?"

"To the mountains. The Holy Spirit has been urging me strongly to flee up into the mountains. As you know, the situation here has been precarious for some time. We've received threats, and there has been some vandalism. Nothing serious but it won't be long now. Satan is being given full reign with those who have not committed their lives to Christ. We've only seen the tip of the iceberg.

"The only reason I've waited this long is because of Dani's baby. I was hoping for some additional time, a grace period, before we had to move. I want the baby to be old enough to travel, but, also, I am worried that if we move too soon, Dani will decide not to come with us. But I'm afraid the decision can't be put off any longer. Dani will soon have to make her choice.

"Which brings me to you. There isn't a suitable place nearby in which to baptize you. My church has been confiscated by the government, and a beach is much too public. However, on our way into the mountains, we are certain to pass streams that would accommodate a baptism. My suggestion is that you enter the Remnant Believer church on a profession of faith, and at the earliest possible moment, I will baptize you. How does that sound?"

Mara smiled wistfully. "A mountain stream? That's kind of romantic."

Dan stood up, offered his hand to Mara with a smile, and pulled her up out of her chair. "I'm sorry. I know it'll be pretty chilly, but it's the best I can do outside of a bathtub. Now let's go tell the others."

Dani was the only one not present when the rest of the house assembled in the living room for the meeting. Mara had little Jack cradled in her arms and when asked, she informed Pastor Reiss that Dani had gone out with her mother to one of their "meetings" again. Dan felt a clutch of fear in the pit of his stomach. He wasn't completely sure what Marilyn's meetings consisted of, but he surmised enough to make him suspicious.

He pushed aside these dark thoughts and concentrated on the task ahead of him. The adults looked sober and nervous. The children were wide-eyed and a little fearful, the younger ones clinging to their mothers. He tried to picture them sitting at the feet of Jesus soon, and the thought made him smile. Instantly, the entire room relaxed.

"My friends," he began. "These are trying, but miraculous, times we are living in. . . ."

* * *

Mara was rocking little Jack when she heard Dani slip in the side door. Outside all was dark, and the spring peepers chirped loudly. Dani tiptoed across the kitchen floor, and an old board creaked. As she rounded the corner and began to head up the stairs, she glanced in the living room and saw Mara there with the baby in the dim light. She redirected her steps and instead came in to sit on the couch beside Mara.

"Has he been asleep for long?" she asked in a whisper.

"No, he just drifted off about ten minutes ago," Mara replied. She searched Dani's face. It seemed tense. There were lines of worry drawn around her mouth and eyes that shouldn't have been chiseled into the face of a seventeen-year-old. But, then, Dani's life wasn't that of an ordinary seventeen year-old. Still, something else lurked in the depths of her eyes as well.

Fear.

It struck Mara suddenly that Dani was afraid, very afraid. She felt her own heart, which had been beating peacefully only a moment before, speed up like the hoofbeats of a seasoned thoroughbred coming out of the starting gate. She sat up quickly, heedless of Jack, who gave a disgruntled cry of protest before falling back to sleep. "Something's wrong." It wasn't a question. "What is it? Is it Dietrich?"

Dani's voice was guarded. "What makes you say that?"

"You, the look on your face. You may as well advertise."

Dani turned away, averting her eyes and shifting on the couch so she could avoid looking at Mara directly. "I don't know what you're talking about."

"You do too," Mara hissed. "Dani, you can't keep running away. You're got to face your life. Dietrich is one big bad dude, I'll grant you that. But, God is so much more powerful than Dietrich. Give your life to Him, and then you'll never have to worry about Dietrich again ever."

Dani snorted. "Oh, sure, that's easy for you to say. And what if he shows up on the doorstep tomorrow or the next day and takes Jack? Huh? Then what? Where will God be then?"

Mara felt a flicker of light penetrate her mind, then, like a candle snuffed out in a strong wind, it was gone. Mentally she groped around in the darkness trying to find it again. "Jack? Why on earth would Dietrich want Jack? What would a killer want with a baby?"

Dani clamped her mouth shut so tight that a line of whiteness appeared around her lips. She flew out of the chair and raced toward the door. "Dani!" Mara's voice raised in warning, and Jack flailed a tiny fist. "Come back here."

Dani stopped at the door, her back rigid, her shoulders squared. For an instant Mara thought she'd walk through the door and either leave the house or race up to her room. But instead, she turned around and retraced her steps carefully back to Mara. She sat down slowly, deliberately, on the couch. Her eyes raised to Mara's, and Mara felt a shiver of fear course through her at the look of abject despair in Dani's eyes.

"OK, you want to know? I'll tell you. You've been wondering this ever since that night in the hotel. After all you went through with me, I suppose if anyone has a right to know, it's you." Dani took a deep breath, and Mara found herself dreading what she was going to hear next. Dani held out her arm and pointed to the tattoo on her wrist.

"See that?" Mara nodded dumbly and Dani continued. "I got that when I became a member of the Freedom Society. In order to get one of these, you have to prove your loyalty to the Freedom Society. You've got to do something sacrificial. For Shon, it was killing Stan Shultz. That proved that he loved the Freedom Society more than life itself. For me it was having Shon's baby and giving it back to the Freedom Society."

Dani paused to let these words sink in.

"Shon's baby, my baby—Jack—belongs to the Freedom Society. It is my debt to them. I never even thought about what that meant until Jack grew inside me and started kicking me and moving around. Even then I'm not sure I really understood what I was giving up until I held him. Then I knew!" Dani dropped her face into her hands and her shoulders shook. Before Mara could reach out to put a comforting hand on her shoulder, she looked up again, her eyes blazing with a fierce, protective anger.

"I will not give him up," she stated flatly. "My father says that Dietrich is coming and that he wants to take Jack and that they're going to sacrifice him in some kind of spiritual ceremony. Well, I won't let it happen. No one is going to take my son! Do you hear? No one!" Dani was shouting, and Mara struggled to calm her down and settle the baby who startled violently and threatened to wake up.

"Wait, slow down, you're talking crazy. How did your father know about Dietrich? He never even met him."

Dani wiped her eyes viciously and stared at Mara as though her brains had fallen out. "My father didn't know Dietrich, not when he was alive. But he knows him now."

"Knows him now?" Mara echoed dumbly. "How can he know him now? You told me yourself that he wasn't in heaven and he wasn't in hell. He was just sleeping. And now I believe that too. So, if your father didn't know Dietrich *before* he died, then he can't know him now."

"Yeah, well, that's what I thought too. But I was wrong," Dani snapped irritably. "I know. I've seen him."

"Seen him? Where?"

"At the meetings," Dani explained impatiently. "My mother's meetings. Dad comes to every one. He tells me where Dietrich is and what he's doing. Tonight Dad said that Dietrich is getting ready to take Jack. And he told me about Gavin Larson's plan to sacrifice Jack once Dietrich takes him away from me. I won't let that happen."

Tears threatened to overtake Dani again, and Mara fought to come up with something rational to say. She knew, *knew* beyond a shadow of a doubt, that Dani had not spoken with her father. And she knew that under normal circumstances, Dani herself would never believe that she had spoken with her father. But the stress she'd been under, the grief of losing her father, and her fear of the Freedom Society had combined to create the ideal situation for Satan to manipulate her mind and present her with something she would ordinarily refute without a second thought.

"Dani, listen to me. You told me, you've *always* told me, that you know what the Bible says." Dani nodded. "But you said that you don't believe what the Bible says. And yet, you've lectured me many times. Do you know that I believed you? Oh, not all the time, I always looked it up to see if you were right. And Dani, you were always right. That's why I decided to become a Remnant Believer."

Dani gasped and looked up sharply. "You? Why?"

"Because they're right. And you know, Dani, you showed me that. You may say that you don't believe in the Bible, but I think that deep down you do. You're just afraid to admit it. I'm not sure why. Maybe it helps to put distance between you and your father if you spurn something that meant so much to him. Or maybe it gave you a picture of God that you didn't want to accept. All I know is that in the Bible it says that the dead don't know anything. *You* showed me the verse! So I can be positive that you aren't talking with your father. You're talking with Satan."

"That's ridiculous," Dani scoffed. "Why would Satan give Dietrich away? He's in league with the devil if anyone ever was."

Mara shrugged. "I don't know, but you can be sure of one thing. He has a very good reason. Maybe he's hoping to discourage you or frighten you so that you won't consider running with Jack. Maybe he's hoping you'll give up and give in and make his job that much easier. Or maybe, and here's what I think, he knows that being here with people who love and trust in the only true God makes you that much less vulnerable. Satan is afraid of the Dans, the Jennas, the Rays, and the Maras. He's afraid of you, too, I think, because he knows that deep inside you know the truth."

"I am discouraged. Maybe he's already won."

"I certainly don't think that is true. What I do think is that he's working extra hard on you because he knows you really do love God and you're just confused and hurt and have been angry for so long that it's impossible for you to see how much God loves you. I think Satan hopes that if he works hard enough, you'll give up on God once and for all."

Dani's eyes flashed. "Well, if that's what he thinks, he's got another thought coming," she said forcefully.

"Does that mean that you believe me?" Mara asked carefully.

Dani didn't answer for a moment. When she did, she appeared to be considering each word. "It's been in the back of my mind that there was a possibility that it wasn't my father. You're right about one thing. I didn't just tell you about those things in the Bible. I really did believe them. Maybe it would be more truthful to say that I believed them, I just didn't want to accept them.

"But this thing with my dad. I just don't know. It's hard for me to believe that it's really not him. I mean, if you could see him now, you'd understand why. He's so different. When he was alive, we *never* got along. Now we couldn't be closer. I think part of me was just hanging on for that reason. It felt so nice to have the kind of relationship with my dad that I always wanted. Even if it was a fraud, I didn't want it to end."

Dani sighed and stood up. She held out her arms for Jack, and Mara placed the baby carefully into them. "What will you do now?"

"Truthfully? I don't know."

* * *

During his flight to Chicago, Randy calculated that he had twenty-one hundred dollars left in his UBC account. *Twenty-one hundred!* He was nearly broke. It certainly wasn't enough money to fly four people to Idaho. Although the problem had crossed his mind, he hadn't devoted much thought to it because he knew his approximate financial status. He simply figured he would have to rely on the Willis's to supply their own airfare.

The instant the seat-belt indicators flashed off, Randy unbuckled himself, grabbed his only luggage—a sturdy sports bag—and took his place in the aisle. He was determined to get out of the airport as quickly as possible, but he also wanted to disembark with the majority of passengers and disappear among the crowd of family and friends who were waiting for loved ones.

He was among the thickest wave of passengers that poured into the concourse. He dodged a couple who ran to greet their daughter. A wife and two children hugged a man in a business suit, which reminded Randy of Brian and his family. Would Brian ever get to hug his children again?

A few years had passed since the last time he was at O'Hare. He checked an airport map, noted the concourses he must traverse to get to a taxi, and hurried along. Keeping his eyes moving, he was alert for anyone who might be watching him, but he also shied away from as many people as possible and kept eye contact to a minimum.

Suddenly, he slowed. His trained senses had picked up on something that caused him to react defensively, although initially he wasn't completely aware of the problem. *Randy, you're way too paranoid,* he told himself.

Then an instant later, he recognized the trouble.

Dietrich!

Thirty yards away, Dietrich stood in front of a McDonald's. Randy recognized him and immediately cut a diagonal path to the opposite side of the concourse. What was Dietrich doing here? For a moment, Randy considered that Dietrich was after *him.* But that made no sense. Dietrich had had plenty of opportunity during the past few months to repay him for betraying the Freedom Society, if indeed that's what he was here for.

Suddenly, Randy knew Dietrich was not here for him. Dietrich was in Chicago for the same reason he was—to find Brian Willis's family. And for what reason? This is what Brian had feared and why he had asked for Randy's help in taking his family to safety. Gavin was putting even more pressure on Brian, Randy imagined.

Coincidence aside, Randy appreciated the gravity of the situation. It now meant that he had to move fast and get the Willis family out of Chicago. And it meant that his mission had become extremely critical if he was to protect them from danger.

Randy suppressed the urge to look back as he walked. A hundred yards beyond Dietrich, he went down an escalator and crossed underneath the tarmac on the underground automated walkway, thrilled that the tunnel was dimly lighted. When he emerged at the main terminal, he stepped out of the flow of humanity and chanced a look behind him as he dropped the paper he'd been carrying into a trash receptacle. Dietrich could not be seen, and yet that made him more anxious than ever. He finally did something that had yet to come naturally. He prayed for God to guide him as he worked to get the Willis family to safety. He prayed quickly but fervently for protection, and he asked God to bless him, Lynn, Mara, and Alice, the people whom he had developed a special closeness to that he hadn't had with anyone for several years.

Praying gave him a sense of peace, and he wondered why he didn't think of it sooner and do it more often. He smiled a little, thinking how far he had come in his relationship with God, how near to God he felt, and how unconcerned he felt knowing that he had put things into God's hands. He thought of Lynn and how things were going back in Washington, and he felt a touch of anxiety and sickness, wondering if he might never see her again. He decided quickly that it was a thought he had to put out of his mind and leave with God. He couldn't be everywhere at once, he couldn't protect everyone, not even himself, really. It was all up to God.

Randy walked quickly out of the airport where taxis waited to pick up fares, waved for the next cab, and stepped out briskly to open the door and jump in. But the door handle flipped up quickly, and he lost his grip. Bending down, he looked through the window at the driver.

"What's up?" He motioned at the door lock.

Oddly enough, the driver leaned over and seemed to be inspecting him. Then he hit the automatic door locks and let Randy in.

"Sure, and we can't be too careful," the driver explained in a thick Irish brogue. He glanced in the rearview mirror as he pulled away from the curb. "It's every cabbie that's having a policy 'bout letting the sick ones ride is all." He shrugged. " 'Course t'would be putting us out of business if we were only taking the healthy ones. So, now and again we break our own rules and let on the folks as aren't too bad. Yourself, now, you don't look sick a'tall. Sure, and that's unusual 'round these parts."

"What's unusual?"

"Why, that you aren't sick, man. Have you not noticed that most folks have been stricken with this sickness?"

Actually, Randy had noticed, and he had sensed the animosity. He also noticed that the driver looked a little under the weather and decided it would be best if they got off the subject. He gave the driver his destination address and closed his eyes for a few minutes.

* * *

"Hey there! Watch what you're doing. Let me help you with that." Amy jerked fully awake with a feeling of panic. Her arms loaded with fresh linens, she was heading toward the window on the third floor of the infirmary. Her mind was so sleep deprived that she'd thought she was heading out the door. Brian Willis grabbed her by the elbow, took the linens out of her arms, and steered her out into the hallway.

The third floor of the infirmary was reserved for guards and high-ranking officers only. Because of this, it was outfitted like a hospital rather than a M.A.S.H. unit like the floor for prisoners. To be assigned to this floor was like getting a promotion, and neither Brian nor Amy could understand why they'd been assigned here. Let alone together. They were suspicious that the guards knew of their growing friendship, because in

the preceding weeks they'd never been scheduled to work together.

"You've got to be more careful," Brian was saying. "I can't
have you walking out a window. Then where would I be?"

Amy laughed feebly. "Oh, somehow I think you'd manage
just fine without me. But it would be a sad end. And after all
I've been through too." She winced and ruefully rubbed her
left forearm, which had been bitten five times by one of the
snakes in the Snake Pit. In her three trips to the Snake Pit,
she'd been bitten a grand total of thirty-five times, mostly by
snakes. Although they had left ugly red welts that alternately
itched and stung, not one bite had even made her sick.

The guards had finally given up throwing her in the Snake
Pit, out of pure disgust. That and the fact that her escapades
in the Snake Pit were becoming fuel for encouragement among
the other prisoners. They couldn't have that. So they devised
other, crueler forms of torture instead. But Amy was beginning to think that sleep deprivation was the hardest one to
live with.

"Are you going to be OK now?" Brian whispered as they
neared the nurses' station. Amy nodded, and he passed the
linens back to her and put some distance between them so the
guards wouldn't know he'd been helping her. Amy clutched at
the stack of bed sheets, wrapping her spindly arms around
them. They felt as heavy as a ton of bricks. She nearly staggered beneath the weight as a dizzy spell overcame her, and
Brian grabbed her and steadied her. "You're sure."

"I think so." Then she held his gaze for a long moment and
said, "Brian, I'm so happy I met you. I don't know if I could
have survived without your encouragement and the prayers I
know you have offered for me."

Brian smiled, and tears suddenly flooded his eyes. "I feel
the same way about you." He reached up to wipe the tears from
his eyes. Then he took a deep breath and shook it off.

"Are you all right?" She realized there was something going on inside him. Doubt? Fear? Or just plain exhaustion? She knew those feelings, and maybe she was a bit beyond them, she thought, to the point where she could walk out a window in a state of near catatonia. "Brian, are you going to be all right?" she asked again.

Brian nodded and smiled. "Yes. I'm really not depressed or sad or anything. In fact, just the opposite. I feel more at peace than I have ever felt in my life. I think. Strange, isn't it?"

Amy's face looked puzzled.

"I take it you were not expecting me to answer that way."

"Well, no, not exactly. I was expecting you to feel as tired and hopeless as I feel."

"I do. I know, I know, I'm not making sense. But think about it. You've been to the Snake Pit how many times? Three?" Amy nodded. "And God has protected you each time. The story about Daniel in the lions' den gave me goose bumps when I read it as a kid, and that happened a long, long time ago. But right now, you're a modern day Daniel. And look at me. I'm still here, even though people have tried to kill me. I've seen an angel protect me from death. But most comforting of all is the fact that I feel God's presence with me." He wrapped his arms around her in a quick embrace. Then he turned around and walked away.

* * *

The trip to Willis's home turned out to be a thirty-minute drive, during which time Randy tried to work out what he was going to say to Brian's wife, Ann. It had to be to the point and effective.

As the driver took him past several clean and well-manicured lawns of upper-class suburbia, Randy thought how difficult it was to believe the world was in such turmoil and that every source of news blared horrible disasters. In recent months, millions had died in earthquakes, not only on the West Coast but on every continent, and yet right here, things looked peaceful, at least on the outside. But he noticed that despite the pleasant weather, he had seen very few people outside.

"The streets are kind of bare."

The driver nodded. "That they are. Likely you'll find nearly every fourth or fifth house deserted, if you want to know the truth of the matter. Moved away they have or gone to stay in one of those centers. Sure, and most will die in there."

"You seem rather ambivalent."

The driver shrugged. "Shocked, more likely. It was my brother I lost, along with his family, in the great California earthquake. Folks are dying left and right. Never was a believer in God, was I, 'til the world turned upside down. Now, I'm of a mind that if there isn't a God up there, well, there should be. Sure, and lots of folks are thinking it's God Himself causing us all this misery on account of His being angry with us. And yourself? What does yourself think?"

Randy cleared his throat. *"Umm,* I believe in God, but I don't think He's a vengeful God. I think of Him as a loving God." Randy let that sink in a little before continuing. "I think all the misery, all the world catastrophes and crisis, all the dying, all of it is simply the world of evil. I believe God is slowly withdrawing His protection of the earth, and the more He does, the more the devil is allowed to destroy."

"And why would this 'loving' God be allowing so much misery? Sure, and that makes no sense a'tall."

Randy leaned forward as he noticed they were slowing down. "Because the time has come to end the struggle between God and sin. I think—no, I know—that as the end draws near, those people who know and *love* God, and by doing so want to obey Him, will become sealed. And then the hell of evil that He has protected this world from will be allowed to fall in its full fury on the earth."

"So, it's a time of reckoning that's arrived, is that it? The beginning of Armageddon? That's a mite hard to swallow, man."

"Oh, you bet," Randy replied solemnly.

That earned him a narrow look from the driver, and Randy wasn't sure if it meant confusion or something more akin to anger or hatred. He considered backing off, not throwing all this heavy end-of-the-world stuff out there where it might cause him more trouble than he could deal with, but he felt impressed to continue.

"You seem undecided," he said.

The driver mulled this over for a moment while he hunted house numbers. Finally he shrugged and said, "You could say that. It was six weeks before President Fairfield was killed, Lord preserve us, that I sent in a card for free Bible studies. I got it out of a religious magazine. A few weeks later a parson came a visitin'. A really nice man, he was, and a Remnant Believer. It was once a week we studied together. Just when I was thinkin' it was the truth he was having, then the government clamped down on the Remnant Church. Me? I took to me heels. A coward, I was." He pulled over abruptly. "This is the place you're wanting." He turned to look at Randy. "Myself, it's undecided I am and surely wishing I knew a lot more about God than I do."

Randy looked the driver squarely in the eyes. "Are you telling me you don't feel you can make a decision for God as your Savior without more study?"

The driver scratched his head in puzzlement. "And how is it you're knowing about this personal Savior stuff? Sure, and that's what I remember from those Bible studies. Aye, and maybe that's the case. The parson was asking me every night, he was, if I was wanting to make a commitment to God. Sure, and I put him off. Myself, it's a certain fact that I'm not good enough nor learned enough."

"Sounds like the idea of God's grace was hard to accept. Believe me, I know the feeling. My sister helped me understand grace, because the whole concept of God's unconditional love escaped me. What I finally had to do was say, hey, accept that God loves you, Randy, and wants to have a genuine relationship with you."

"For sure and certain?"

"Yes. And don't forget, there's no sitting on the fence. Trust me, there's a war going on between God and the devil, and the final conflict is being played out right now, right here on this earth. Unfortunately, if you don't choose God, you've automatically chosen the devil. It's something scary to think about, but I'll tell you what, it's not that hard to imagine. What makes it worse is the fact that the devil has disguised himself so well that even people who profess Christianity are playing right into the devil's trap. Look around. If you're not a member of the United Religious Coalition, you're under suspicion or being persecuted. Remnant Believers are being blamed for all the disasters and problems in the world."

The driver nodded. "Aye, and it's plain you're one of them, you are. A Remnant Believer?"

This had been an issue with Randy. He considered himself a Remnant Believer, although he hadn't been baptized yet. He wanted to be, though. But so far it seemed circumstances had gotten in the way. At any rate, it was something he wanted to do to profess his commitment to God and acceptance of Jesus' dying on the cross to save him. He knew the commitment was still there even if he hadn't had the opportunity to get wet yet. "Yes, I am a Believer." With that, he got out of the taxi. "I'd appreciate it if you waited. I hope this doesn't take too long." The driver nodded, but Randy wondered if he would actually stay or not, maybe he would find his bag sitting on the sidewalk when he returned.

At the door to Brian's home, Randy took a deep breath and rang the doorbell. He didn't have long to rehearse what he was going to say, because a little boy pulled the door wide open. But as quick as a flash, his mother stepped into the door frame and reminded him never to open the door, especially when she wasn't right there.

"Yes, may I help you?"

Thursday, March 6

"My name is Randy Burton, Mrs. Willis. I've talked to you over the phone. Told you where Brian was not long ago?"

"Oh, oh yes." A mixture of concern and curiosity came over her face like sunset shadows on a mountainside. She moved back and asked Randy to come in. When he was seated across from her, he on the couch and she in a recliner, she said, "I'm sorry I didn't connect the name, but I didn't expect to see you on my doorstep. Did Brian ask you to come?"

"Why, yes, he did, actually." Randy was a bit surprised she didn't seem more concerned about Brian. Ann Willis stared at him for a few uncomfortable minutes without saying anything.

"I wish Brian would have the decency to give up his crazy crusade and come home," she finally said coolly. "I've used up all our savings and have spent the past week looking for a job. I don't know what I'm going to do with my children should I find work, anyway. So, why did Brian want you to come?"

Randy couldn't believe what he was hearing. He thought it must be some kind of coping mechanism. Denial, maybe. "Brian has been terribly concerned about you and Matthew and Hannah. He's afraid Gavin Larson might try to use his family against him, and he's afraid for your safety. He wanted me to take you somewhere safe."

Ann let out a laugh, totally incongruous to the gravity of the situation. When she stopped, she stared at Randy again and then shook her head in disbelief. "Why don't you go back and tell Brian that if he wants to make sure we're safe, he can just drop all his silly Remnant beliefs and come home. Doesn't he realize that all the trouble he's caused himself and the misery he's caused his family is all his fault?"

"Mrs. Willis," Randy said as calmly as he could, "I'm not sure you understand. Brian is not on a silly, worthless crusade. He can't just give up and come home because it seems too difficult. This is about staying right with God. It's about eternal life. Brian knows that. You can't expect him to give up what he knows to be right."

"I can expect him to take care of his family," Ann replied quickly.

Randy looked Ann squarely in the eyes, but she wouldn't hold his gaze. She glanced down at the floor, then across the room, then at her two children who stood quiet as mice in the entrance to the kitchen. He hadn't noticed them watching him until now. They were both very cute children, neither favoring one parent over the other in their features, he had noticed.

Randy's thoughts flashed on Dietrich. He'd been watching the time, and between his conversation with the taxi driver and stalling out here with Brian's wife, he knew he was pushing his luck. "Listen, Mrs. Willis, I came to take you and your children someplace safe. The sooner we leave the better. I believe a killer, Gavin Larson's right-hand man, has come here to do just what Brian feared, use you and the children to get to him."

Ann seemed to mull something over. "Do you suppose it's possible I could get to see Brian then? If I went with this man you believe is a killer?"

Randy couldn't keep his jaw from dropping. "Are you serious? What is the matter with you? Brian is afraid for you, and he has every right to be. Gavin is determined to get what he wants, and right now I'm willing to bet he wants Brian's complete capitulation. And you're talking about willingly doing whatever he says. Where is your loyalty to God and to Brian?"

"I'm only thinking about what is practical, Mr. Burton. I only want my husband back and for him to quit this nonsense. Surely those Remnant beliefs he's attached himself to aren't *that* important."

It occurred to Randy at just that instant that Ann must have spoken to Gavin and they had arrived at some sort of arrangement. She was probably innocent to Gavin's motives, but the fact was crystal clear in Randy's mind all of a sudden that she was determined to get what she wanted.

"Mrs. Willis, they *are* that important. Surely you have read the Bible and understand the significance of what is happening now. Those very same prophecies spoken of in Daniel and Revelation are coming to pass. Your husband is a brave man, but more than that, he is a godly man. He will not give up his God for Gavin, for freedom, or even for you. I pray he never knows how willing you are to betray him."

Abruptly, Randy stood up, through with the conversation. He'd observed enough people to know that when they sounded as fervent as Ann Willis sounded now, they were not going to change. At least not at this stage in the crisis. Also, he knew he couldn't spare whatever remaining time he had in fruitless conversation. If Dietrich wasn't in Chicago to force Brian's family to Washington, D.C., he was there to escort them, and Ann seemed entirely willing to do whatever Gavin wanted. She would go willingly.

But now he had a far more forbidding problem. How on earth could he take the children? He certainly didn't like thinking of himself as a kidnapper, but he knew there was no way Ann would let them come with him.

Still, for Brian, he had to try something. He glanced at Matthew and Hannah. "Your father wanted me to take the two of you someplace safe. I can't take you without your mother's consent, but I would like to know what you, Matthew, and you, Hannah, want to do."

Ann gasped, causing a distinct moment of silence before she burst out yelling at Randy. "You have no right to do that! Children, do not answer this man!" She jumped up, strode over, and hit Randy on the right shoulder with the heel of her hand. "Get out of my house! Now!"

Reluctantly, Randy headed for the door then paused before opening it. He turned back to Brian's children. Matthew, being the oldest and apparently speaking for his sister as well as himself, stepped forward.

"We want to do whatever our daddy wants, Mister. I've been reading my Bible, and I know my daddy is right in being a

Remnant Believer. I want to be a Remnant Believer too."

"Your daddy's not here, Matthew," Ann reminded him, "so you'll just have to mind me. Besides, you're too young to make decisions like that."

"I think they should speak for themselves," Randy said.

"Mr. Burton, you either leave, or I will call the police. They are only children. They cannot make this kind of decision on their own."

"At any other time under any other circumstances, I would agree with you, Mrs. Willis. But these are decidedly spiritual times. If your children understand the choices they are making, they must be allowed to do so."

"But they don't. Now get out!"

Randy raised his hands defensively. "All right. I hope you understand the consequences of what you are doing. Somehow, I'm afraid you don't."

"Don't lecture me about religion, Mr. Burton. After all, being one of those Remnant Believers yourself, you really should be paying for the misery you're causing the rest of us." Ann stepped up and flung the door open. "Now get out!"

Randy decided he didn't have a choice. He was going to have to leave the children. He glared down at Ann before walking out.

Before he had completely passed through the doorway, he and Gunnar Dietrich locked eyes. Dietrich was striding up the sidewalk. He reached inside a light jacket and pulled out a pistol, and Randy launched himself backward into the house before Ann could shut him out. Besides anger, Ann Willis's face registered confusion.

Randy grabbed her by the arm and pulled her down as his eyes darted around the room for the children. Where had he seen them last? *In the kitchen doorway*, he thought. Flipping the front door lock, he sprinted to the kitchen. They weren't there! He saw the stairway and climbed it in three giant steps as he heard Dietrich banging on the front door. As soon as Ann got her wits about her, he knew she would open the door for Dietrich.

Now he was in the upstairs hallway, throwing open doors and calling for Matthew. Both children were in the second door on his left. Too late he realized that he'd scared them.

"Kids, if you want to go with me, I'll take you!"

Alarms wailed in Randy's head. *If I take them, I'll be wanted for kidnapping.* Even as he told the kids he'd take them, he knew he couldn't. And he realized that he didn't have the time as Ann Willis's bansheelike screaming curdled his blood. Suddenly he realized she was shouting his location to Dietrich.

"He's upstairs! That way! Kill him!"

Then, hearing Dietrich running up the stairs, Randy ran through what he assumed was the Willis's bedroom after spotting curtains that hung to the floor and hoping they were covering doors that led to a balcony. If not, he was going to have to exit through them regardless. Covering the room in four strides, he flung back the curtains. *Good,* he thought, and unlatched the sliding glass door.

Outside there was a small problem—no stairs—but he didn't have time to move cautiously. He boosted himself onto the railing, swung his feet over, and jumped all in one nearly fluid movement. Landing slightly off balance, he tucked his right shoulder in and rolled, his momentum bringing him back to his feet in a crouching position. His eyes went directly to the balcony to see if Dietrich was already there and ready to shoot him dead. At first all he saw was Matthew, who had chased after him. But as he pushed off running, the corner of his eye caught the image of Dietrich rushing to the railing. Rounding the corner of the house, he heard the distinctive sound of a slug bury itself into the siding and Dietrich screaming at everyone to get out of his way.

Randy hopped a fence and sprinted for the street and the taxicab he prayed was still there. It would be a deathblow to him if the driver decided he'd heard enough of Randy's preaching and took off.

But as he came around the front of the house, he was surprised to find the driver had gotten out of his cab and was cautiously headed toward the front door. Seeing Randy, his eyes flashed open like headlights, and he stiffened in his tracks.

"In the car!" Randy yelled desperately. "Hurry!"

"Wh . . . Uh . . . " the driver sputtered as Randy grabbed his arm and turned him around.

"Move unless you want to get shot!"

Properly motivated, the driver nearly overtook Randy in their desperate race to the vehicle. He yanked his door open and had the taxicab started by the time Randy slammed his own door shut. Randy glanced through the rear window as they sped away, but Dietrich had given up quickly and was returning inside with Ann Willis.

Turning back around, he fastened his seat belt with a heavy sigh.

"What was the cause of all that, then? As I waited, I saw a man arrive in another taxi and head for the house. It wasn't a moment later he pulled out a pistol and began to shoot."

"His name is Dietrich. He's a hired killer and was probably sent here to escort the family that lives in that house to Washington, D.C."

The driver shook his head as if trying to clear cobwebs. Since picking Randy up, there'd been nothing but a series of discussions about God, doomsday talk, and now he'd just witnessed a man try to kill his fare. Randy reached across and shook the man's hand.

"Thanks for sticking around. I owe you big time."

The driver glanced at him, still white-faced and barely in control of his shaking. "Sure, and I know that you do."

For ten minutes they made a sequence of turns that nearly left the driver himself confused. But he wanted to make sure he wasn't being followed, and Randy wasn't about to argue. Finally it occurred to him that he didn't even know the driver's name. He was just about to ask when the driver started talking.

"My name is Flynn O'Neill. This may sound odd to your ears, but myself, I'd like to know more about this God of yours, like you were telling me earlier."

Randy smiled and reached across to shake Flynn's hand again. "It's good to know you, Flynn. I'm Randy Burton. Sure, I'll tell you everything you want to know or everything I know. Whichever comes first. Remember, though, you picked me up from the airport. I don't have a place to stay yet, because . . . well, you saw what happened." He chose not to mention the confrontation he'd had with Ann Willis.

"If it's all right with you, you can stay at my place. It's off the clock I'm going, so I can take you there, and you can tell me more."

Randy shrugged and nodded. "Sure." When Flynn turned back to concentrate on driving, he mused at Flynn's sudden passionate interest in God and the beliefs they had discussed earlier. Had God led Randy to Flynn? Was there some sort of divine intervention at work here? Randy was sure that there was, and it helped to take the edge off his confrontation with Ann Willis. Then his thoughts drifted to Brian's children. How would they fare? What could he have done differently? And then he decided that God was watching over all and knew the hearts of every man, woman, and child. Something Alice had told him once began to nag at him. Unbuckling his seat belt, he reached back for his bag and pulled out his Bible.

At the time, they'd had their Bibles out. *Matthew*, he thought it was. That's where the texts she'd quoted to him were from, he was almost positive. He opened his Bible to Matthew 10 and read verses 29 and 30 and read about how God knows about the sparrows. He read on through verse 32, "Whoever acknowledges me before men, I will also acknowledge him before my Father in heaven."

It took them another ten or fifteen minutes to get to Flynn's apartment. It wasn't much of a building to look at, but then, neither was the neighborhood. Flynn seemed extremely excited about Randy coming along, and he started talking about his family, the city, and his neighborhood as if Randy were an old friend who needed some catching up. Randy smiled and kept his end of the conversation going as best he could. Flynn unlocked his apartment and swung the door open for Randy, patting him on the back and inviting him in.

Immediately Randy connected the pat on the back with the symptoms Flynn exhibited of the disease, and although he could honestly say he was OK with being touched, he felt it helped explain some of Flynn's intensely genial attitude. Although Flynn was a taxi driver, he was probably starved for sincere and honest companionship.

The apartment was small and sparse. It looked lived in but not messy. Flynn was a passionate Chicago Bulls fan, and the walls announced it with pennants, posters, and jerseys, as well as a variety of Bulls caps. Randy set his Bible on the table while Flynn went and poured them a couple of glasses of water.

He's certainly serious about this lesson study stuff, Randy thought. Flynn returned, put the glasses down, and got his own Bible that had been lying on a scarred coffee table.

"I'm ready," he said eagerly, his eyes shining with anticipation.

So this is how Lynn must feel when she's teaching people about God, Randy mused. He was beginning to feel really excited about this as he sat down.

Flynn was confused by the philosophies of the United Religious Coalition, which was running an intensely negative campaign against the Remnant Church. The Coalition preached a lot about the vengeance of God, and it certainly never mentioned His love. So, like nearly everyone else, Flynn thought the right thing to do was obey the Coalition. Randy began by telling Flynn that God loved him unconditionally and that if he accepted Jesus as his Savior, there was not a litany of works he had to do to be saved. But Randy also pointed out that becoming a Christian was not a spectator sport. It took more than just believing there was a God; it took commitment to God and trust in Him. Knowing God resulted in action was the best way Randy could explain it. Then he thought maybe he was getting ahead of himself.

"If you love God, you'll want to do what He says. You'll know what is right because you're willing to open your mind to listen to Him. It's a natural process. More natural than may seem possible."

"Are you trying to tell me that if I really know Jesus, it's natural that I'll be following Him? I won't be feeling I must *do* things to be saved or following a list of rules?"

"Right. As near as I can tell for myself, that's what's happened. I don't believe there are any exceptions to the Bible. I'm speaking here of anything the United Religious Coalition or the pope might preach. I've been studying the Bible carefully because it helps me understand God better. And the more I study, the more that makes sense to me. Consequently, I've found myself eager to keep His commandments."

"I've a wee problem with some of them," Flynn admitted ruefully. "Particularly the Sabbath day. It seems to me to be the main issue between the Remnant Believers and the rest of the world. Is it not like one of those things you must do to be saved?"

"It might seem like it if you only kept the Seventh day holy because you thought that by doing it God would save you. But I ran across a text that really struck me one night. It's in John 14:6. Jesus says He is 'the way and the truth and the life.' That text told me that Jesus is my Savior, my only Savior. Nothing I can do, and certainly nothing anyone else can do, will save me. So, I have made Jesus first."

Flynn stared at the text in his own Bible for several minutes and then looked up with tears in his eyes. "Is it too late for me to be knowing Jesus Christ like you do?"

Struck hard by the question, Randy reached over and squeezed Flynn's shoulder. "No, man, it's not too late. You're talking to a man who watched his sister go from complete despair to the strongest and most passionate Christian I have ever seen, all in just a few days. I think Jesus fills every part of your heart you let Him into. My sister got a glimpse of Jesus and made a big room in her heart for Him, and it really changed her." Randy thought of another text he really liked. He grinned when he thought about it, because it was kind of a good text for the underdogs of the world, the people who quietly build a personal relationship with Jesus. "I know how you're feeling, though. Have you ever heard this text? 'This is what the Lord says: "Let not the wise man boast of his wisdom or the strong man boast of his strength or the rich man boast of his riches, but let him who boasts boast about this: that he understands and knows me, that I am the Lord, who exercises kindness, justice and righteousness on earth, for in these I delight," declares the Lord.' That's found in Jeremiah 9:23, 24. Flynn, just let Jesus into your heart. Pray. Study. He will do the rest. I guarantee it."

"Is that a promise?"

"It's a promise." With that Randy closed his Bible and stood up. He felt restless all of a sudden. They had studied for three hours.

Flynn got up and stretched. "Sure, and you're welcome to stay here if you like."

As Randy took his glass into the kitchen and refilled it, he thought about Flynn's offer; he thought about his restlessness and concluded that he didn't like the idea of staying in Chicago any longer than he had to. Suddenly, he wanted more than ever to see Mara. He'd tried to get Ann to go with him, but that had failed. There was nothing left for him to do here, and after such a disappointment, he just wanted to be with Mara, to feel her touch and to talk to her and be comforted by her. He stood in the doorway to the kitchen and took a sip of water then said to Flynn, "How would you like to come with me to Boise, Idaho? I know a group of people there, solid Remnant Believers, who are preparing to take refuge in the mountains. You're certainly welcome to come."

He didn't expect an answer right away, and he didn't get it. Flynn asked for some time to think it over. Feeling exhausted, Randy lay down on Flynn's couch and quickly fell asleep. A few hours later, after darkness had set in, Flynn woke him with an answer.

"I'm grateful to you for the offer, I am. And I'd like to go with you." He held up a sports bag not unlike Randy's. "I'm packed, and we can take my car."

"That's a long drive. What is it? Fifteen hundred miles or more?"

"Near enough. A few hundred more, perhaps. I've mapped it out. It's the driving I'll be doing, and you can be telling me more about God if it pleases you."

"Sure you don't want to fly?" Randy asked, gathering his Bible and bag as Flynn headed to the door.

"Not myself, no sir. I've always hated it. If we take no breaks, we'll be there in less than two days."

Frankly, Randy was hoping to see Mara a lot sooner than that. "All right, Flynn. Let's go."

Chapter Twelve

Last Days

During Brian's work, he used every opportunity he could find to encourage people and talk about God. He knew he was watched, and he guessed his wardens knew what he was doing. Usually, he tried not to be so obvious, but it was inefficient to wait until he absolutely knew no one could see him. Talking to Amy for as long as he had had been an extremely lucky break.

So on this day, Brian kind of forgot his work routine and made contact with as many of the sick and imprisoned as he could until he was forced to quit. He didn't know why exactly. Maybe it was the looks of hopelessness he saw in every face. Maybe he was just too tired physically and mentally to continue on with the same routine day after day, knowing all the while that it wouldn't end until he was dead.

After leaving Amy Cooper, Brian got away with what he was doing for a good hour and a half before things started getting rough. He was encouraging a former Catholic man who used to be quite a successful stockbroker. Shortly after Christmas, the man did an about-face religionwise and decided that what the Remnant Believers were teaching was the truth. This while most folk were making a mass exodus to the coalition of religions whose signature doctrine seemed to be Sunday observance. Brian knew it went much deeper than that, but many people were finding Sunday observance a small concession toward order in an ever-worsening chaotic world. It didn't matter what people's motivations were. That fact was, if they decided to listen to man instead of the Word of God, then it didn't matter what their reasons were. God could not save them.

In their brief exchange of words, Brian prayed for the ex-stockbroker and his faith. He patted him on the shoulder and moved on . . . but not far.

A Racal-suited guard stepped in from seemingly out of nowhere and slugged him in the stomach. All the air left Brian in a *whoosh*. He tried to keep his balance, but an ironlike fist hit him just in front of his left ear, and he went down hard on his side. Immediately, he was dragged to his feet.

"You've been stirring up trouble," one of the guards said.

"No." Brian shook his head. "There's been no trouble." In fact, he knew things were often more peaceful when the people interred there were allowed to talk freely, to give encouragement, and to remind each other of God.

"We've heard some complaints that you've been giving Bible studies again."

Now, he was held up by the shoulders and pushed against a wall in one of the concrete-block corridors of the camp. His stomach was beyond merely hurting, and he felt on the brink of being sick. The bile rose in his throat, but he fought it down and said, "I doubt any of the prisoners were complaining. If there were complaints, they were from guards, and they were lies."

That earned him another thrust in the gut. His stomach contracted involuntarily, and whatever was left from breakfast spewed out of his mouth.

"Oh, great!" the second guard made a double-handed gesture at his boots. "Look at this!"

Brian got jammed up against the wall again, and his head hit the concrete hard enough to knock him unconscious. When he came to, he was alone and violently ill. He struggled to his knees, retched a couple of times, then braced against the wall for balance as he got his feet underneath him. Most of all, he wanted to get back to his pallet, but he knew he would not be allowed to rest. The guards would force him to work.

Considering that made him wonder why he had been left alone. Surely he was in severe trouble. After a few moments rest, he began moving. He got out of the building and was walking, or mostly staggering, across the compound when Ed Vicars suddenly appeared beside him.

"Here, let me help you. You look horrible." Ed ducked underneath Brian's right arm and hooked his left arm around Brian's waist.

"Thanks, Ed, but you've got to be careful. If they see you helping me, they'll probably do the same thing to you they did to me."

"Don't worry about me. It's time you started worrying about yourself. At the rate you're goin', you'll end up killing yourself before the month's out. Is that what you want? I mean, I appreciate you talkin' to me and givin' me Bible studies, but if you don't lay low for a while, they'll probably end up killin' you."

"Maybe you're right," Brian said.

"You bet I'm right."

Ed suddenly hesitated, took a few more steps, then paused and began to move in another direction.

"What's up?" Brian whispered.

"Guards. They're comin' our way."

"They're coming for me, Ed. Just let me down and walk away."

"I'm not doin' that. What kind of friend you think you got here, anyway?"

"An awfully good one, Ed. So, as a friend, I'm asking you to leave me. I don't want you getting mixed up in this."

"Ah, come on. I can handle myself. Besides, it's my turn to do you some favors."

"Fine. Have it your way." But inside, he was grateful for Ed's loyalty. In times like these, solid Christian friends were one of the best sources of strength.

A few seconds later, Ed and Brian were grabbed by the arms. Without Ed's support, Brian almost went down, but the two pairs of rough hands held him even though his legs lacked the strength keep him from falling. None of the five guards said anything as they hauled Brian and Ed to a building known to the two prisoners only by reputation. Brian glanced at Ed and saw surprise and fear in his eyes. He wished Ed had walked away when he had had the chance.

They were pushed through the steel door of the concrete-block building and left in what had once been a stockade or storage unit for the base. If it had once been used for storage, then the rooms would have been larger and fewer of them, Brian decided. But it was hard to be sure, because the whole base was a relic. And it really didn't matter, anyway.

Ed had been taken in ahead of him and shoved viciously into one of the rooms. Brian saw and heard him try to gain control before he hit the far wall, but his balance was off, and he fell on the floor and slid into the wall. Brian heard a loud *umph!* and then silence.

The guards laughed behind their Racal face masks while Brian wondered if he'd ever get up again if the same thing happened to him.

But oddly enough, he didn't receive the same brutal treatment as Ed Vicars. His guards let him in his small room directly across from Ed's and gave him what amounted to a nudge just to make sure he was inside before slamming the door. When he thought the guards were gone, he got back to the door and tried to get Ed's attention.

"Hey, Ed? Are you all right?"

No answer.

Brian took a deep breath and then rested, trying to get rid of some of the dizziness he felt. A few minutes later, he called again and banged some on his own steel door. If there were any guards pulling duty inside the building, Brian imagined he would have been told to knock it off by now.

"Hey, Ed!"

Finally he heard a weak voice that almost sounded like a whisper. "Here . . . Feel ter . . . ble."

Brian got out of Ed that he felt nauseous and thought he had a concussion, but he was pretty sure no bones were broken. Just a lot of bruises. Then Brian told him to rest. Night came, and they slept despite the cool floor and no blankets. Since he had first been kidnapped, Brian found himself increasingly amazed that he was in America. These were the kinds of conditions prisoners of war suffered in foreign countries, not honest, hard-working Christians in America. *This is the land of religious liberty,* he mused sometime around four in the morning. He knelt and prayed for two hours, during which the sun rose, although he was deprived of seeing it. He had a feeling about this day. Like every day since he last saw his family, it was bound to be filled with some sorrow and some spiritual growth.

Sometime around seven that morning, Brian judged, the main door of the building was opened. He listened carefully and heard what he thought were more than four pairs of feet. Then someone began fiddling with the lock on his door. Still very weak and knowing he wouldn't get any stronger without food, Brian scooted out of the way of the door but did not stand up.

"Brian?"

The voice was followed by Gavin Larson filling the doorway, along with two of the ubiquitous Racal-suited guards. Gavin glanced down. "Oh, there you are." Brian's condition garnered no sympathy.

Brian sighed. "What do you want now? I thought we were finished."

"I've come to give you one last opportunity. Will you take it?"

Brian couldn't tell if Gavin actually cared one way or the other. "No, of course I won't. I told you before," he said, his eyes flashing with disgust for the man he had once revered.

Gavin casually waved him off. "Of course, of course. I know you have. But things have changed, I believe, and I am prepared to act on those changes."

"And do what? What has changed?" Brian could sense that indeed something was different today. Despite all the adversity he had faced, the worst of it was about to happen. He eyed Gavin uneasily. "So what do you want this time?" There was very little room in the tiny cell. Little enough for one man, let alone Gavin and his entourage. Then Brian wondered who else was there, down the corridor, out of sight. "Where is Dietrich?"

"Oh, Dietrich is here," Gavin said, making a show of looking at his watch. "He just returned from Chicago."

"What was he doing? Did you send him there to hurt my family? It's your style to attack a man through his family."

"*Tsk, tsk,* Brian. Things could have been so much different, so much easier, if you had only cooperated."

Furious, Brian got his knees underneath him and attempted to stand, using the wall as support. Gavin coldly kicked him down, and Brian rolled onto his back in the middle of the floor. He stared up at Gavin with tears of terror for his family's safety. "Please! What did you do to my family, Gavin?" Yet in the back of his mind he knew Randy had gotten to Ann and the kids before Gavin tried to use them against him.

"I wish it were easy just to let it go. But you brought this on yourself." Gavin turned and gestured for someone down the hall.

Dietrich, Brian thought. *How will he try to kill me this time?* Knowing he was incapable of withstanding the endless onslaught of mental and physical torment, he closed his eyes and prayed for Divine strength.

"Brian? Is that you? Look at what they've done to you, my poor baby."

Shocked by the muffled but familiar voice, Brian was afraid to open his eyes. "Ann?" he asked tentatively. Gloved hands, but that gentle caress was familiar. He could hardly believe his wife was the woman kneeling on the floor beside him as he opened his eyes. "You're here." This was hardly a question, for he had expected her to be safe with Randy. The shock of seeing her in a Racal suit three thousand miles from where he had hoped she was stunned him.

Ann turned her face up toward Gavin. "Mr. Larson, I would like to speak to my husband alone now."

"Of course, ma'am," Gavin said congenially. He smiled and left, having the door closed behind him.

Ann looked her husband over carefully before speaking. When she finally opened her mouth, her tone was not quite pleasant. "Why are you letting them do this to you, Brian?"

"Why am I *letting* them? I'm not *letting* them do anything."

"You are too. Why not just tell Gavin what he wants to hear and come home with me? I know you, Brian. You're not a quitter. You'll stick to what you believe no matter what. Remember when we talked about you quitting the Coalition before you came to Washington? I thought that maybe at least part of you was doing it for me and not just because you disagreed with Gavin. Imagine how the kids and I feel knowing that we come after your beliefs."

"You know that's not how it is, Ann," Brian said softly, taking her hand. "You're not being fair. Being a strong, sincere Christian means putting God first. You know that. You grew up in a Christian home. I remember talking about God's place in marriage and family before we were married, and we were both of the same mind."

"Brian, I know. Don't throw that in my face. Don't you think this is taking it too far, though? I don't think God expects you to turn your back on your family over a few beliefs that most religious leaders agree are either incorrect or irrelevant."

Brian shook his head and let out a short, incredulous breath. "If these Remnant Beliefs are irrelevant, as you say, then why the persecution? Why are so many Remnant Believers being punished?"

Ann pulled her hand away. "Don't play mind games with me, Brian. If I am not important enough for you to say that you were wrong so I can have you back home, then stay here and rot, for all I care. But I'm not going to sit here in this horrid place and argue with you." She stared at Brian for a moment as if she expected him to change his mind, but he just sat there in desolation as tears began to course down his cheeks.

"I can't, Ann, I'm sorry." He didn't even think about it, afraid that if he did he might end up doing what she asked.

Ann unexpectedly slapped him across the face and jumped to her feet. "I hope you burn in hell!" Turning her back on him, she banged on the door. "Get me out of here!"

"Ann," Brian yelled. "What has gotten into you? I love you!"

Ann beat on the door and screamed louder, drowning him out.

The door swung open. Gavin stepped in and clutched Ann by the arms. "Well?"

"He won't change his mind."

"I'm sorry for you, Ann," Gavin said.

"I just want it over with," Ann snapped. "I should have admitted to myself a long time ago that he didn't love me." She cast pitiless eyes on Brian. "At least I know I tried."

Brian watched and listened to the exchange between Gavin and Ann and couldn't figure it out. Gavin gave her a comforting hug, as if they were old friends, and then as suddenly as she had come to Brian, Ann disappeared. A moment later, two guards entered, lifted him off the floor, and helped him walk out of the building behind Gavin. Brian frantically searched for Ann but never caught another glimpse of her. He did see Ed, however. Two guards in Racal suits were dragging him roughly behind Brian.

Brian looked around again and found it odd that other prisoners and many patients were also being herded outside. *Now what is happening?* He finally realized everyone was headed for the concrete wall that had been built about eight feet high and left just standing in isolation in the middle of the compound.

He was made to wait without explanation near the wall. Still very weak, he tried to sit on the ground, but every time he slumped downward, a guard jabbed him in the kidneys. It went on that way for fifteen or twenty minutes. In the interim, several thousand people were being assembled outside, more than he'd realized were in the camp. *I've touched so few lives with the message of Jesus' love and His soon return,* he thought, *so very few compared to how many are here.*

His eyes found Gavin Larson again, but he saw nothing of Ann, though he'd meticulously run his eyes over every foot of the camp within his line of vision. As he watched and waited, he tried to understand what was happening.

The second time he saw Gavin, the man was smiling as he watched three helicopters approach. The one in the middle was the Sikorsky VH-3D of Marine One, the president's helicopter.

It flew over the camp once. Flanking it were three attack helicopters, loaded with weaponry. All four aircraft did the one fly-over and then returned. However, only Marine One approached and landed within the compound and set down ever so gently, as if it were a bird settling on its eggs. The rotors slowly beat to a stop as well-armed Secret Service agents poured out. Brian noticed that all the guards seemed to stand a little straighter and act more alert. A few moments later, President Thurgood emerged, staying close to the helicopter. He'd just been ferried into the middle of a diseased-riddled camp. The unorthodox idea of risking exposure to the president made

Brian think something extremely significant was about to take place. And the next thing he saw confirmed it.

Just as he was about to look away, Brian saw Pope Xavier exit the helicopter. *Now, what on earth?* he thought. *Why is the pope here, and why is he with the president of the United States?*

He swung his eyes to Gavin Larson, and as if he could sense it, Gavin turned his head and looked straight into Brian's eyes, smiling widely yet at the same time void of all humanity. Gavin was a man who had completely rejected God, and it showed in the shallowness of his soul as it filled steadily with bitterness and hate. Brian wondered if Gavin realized he had chosen the wrong side but his pride and guilt kept him from repenting, because he had never come to know the true character of God. Or was the devil fooling him so completely that he sincerely believed he was doing the right thing? Brian guessed that sometime soon Gavin would see the truth about God, as would the universe. His eyes, which he chose to keep shut now, would be opened.

In that brief moment when their eyes locked, Brian felt a chill chase along his spine. Gavin gave him a slight nod, as if to say it was time. Brian glanced to his left and saw Ed staring at him, his ashen face conveying profound fear. Ed whispered, "What's happening?"

Brian shook his head.

Suddenly, they were grabbed by the arms and dragged quickly toward the concrete wall. Gavin followed, with his hands clasped behind his back. The guards stopped about three feet away from the wall and allowed Brian and Ed to get their feet underneath them before letting go.

"What are you doing, Gavin?" Brian asked, although in the back of his mind he thought he already knew.

Gavin smiled malevolently while making a grand, sweeping arc with his right hand. "Millions upon millions of people have died in the last six months for no other reason, it appears, than the stubbornness of those who call themselves the Remnant. This epidemic that now spans the globe infecting hundreds of thousands of people a day is a direct result of these 'Remnant' people."

"How have you come to that simple-minded conclusion, Gavin?"

Gavin's slow smile seemed to originate miles away as he looked a long time at Brian before speaking. "I never meant things to be this way, Brian," he replied vaguely. "Years ago, I had a vision of worldwide unity through religion. Granted, for centuries, the Catholic Church did the same thing, until the Reformation. But in this day and age where gay marriages are the norm and debate about abortion is nearly passé because the arguments have shifted to partial-birth abortions instead, many people who were aware of the trend felt as if the world was spiraling into self-destruction.

"When Donald Thurgood and I conceived of the United Religious Coalition, I perceived that many Christian denominations would embrace a unified religious organization in order to strengthen the United States instead of allow it to be weakened by liberalism. However, the popularity of the United Religious Coalition far surpassed our expectations. The major Protestant churches quickly agreed on some fundamental doctrines, and as simple as that, the Coalition was off and running. Most of what I have said you already know, Brian. But what you don't seem to grasp is that you have become part of the problem by rejecting those fundamental doctrines the coalition of churches has agreed upon."

Brian slowly shook his head. "The Coalition and everyone who is persecuting Remnant Believers is wrong, and you know it. You can condemn the Remnant. The pope can fool anyone who hasn't learned the truth. And the government of the United States can lead the persecution against Remnant Believers, but there will come a time when you will take a hard, honest look at yourself and realize you have been the biggest fool of all.

Gavin didn't even blink. "You utter the empty words of a

doomed man, I'm afraid, Brian. If there is anyone to blame for the condition of the world, it is people such as yourself who defy the compromises the rest of the religious world has deemed acceptable in order to be in one accord."

This last statement struck Brian as incongruous, at least more so than the rest of Gavin's rhetoric. "In 'one accord' to what end, Gavin?" He narrowed his eyes. "You are a student of the Bible. And doesn't it say in Revelation 13 that everyone will be forced to adhere to certain requirements? The compromises you defend so righteously have become nothing more than statutes. They are no more holy than laws against speeding, and yet you enforce them as if they were the keys to your salvation."

Gavin grinned wickedly. "More than the keys to eternal life, my friend. But keys to the right hand of God. I was called to lead the world through this crisis by eradicating all who dare defy the world church and a new world order. Once this nation has huddled together morally and religiously, how difficult do you think it will be to change the world? Not difficult at all, Brian, because it is already happening. Look out there. You see the pope. Do you know how many Catholics there are in the world?"

"Lest you actually be so gullible," Brian said, "remember that the devil is the great deceiver. His easiest conquests may be those who believe themselves to be without fault. And certainly it is no great trick to deceive masses of people who are not sure what they believe. If you and the pope are willing to join alliances, why shouldn't hundreds of millions of people who haven't taken the time to learn the truth about God follow you? It's the easiest thing in the world to go with the crowd. But just because all those people think you are speaking for God doesn't make it so. Are you sure it is God you are listening to, Gavin? Or is it the devil, and does he have you wrapped around his finger?" Brian watched the fury rise inside Gavin, watched it manifest itself like rising mercury in his face.

"Enough!" Gavin snapped. Gavin whipped around and

summoned the camp warden with a snap of his fingers. "Let's get this execution over with."

While Brian was still trying to digest what he just thought he heard, the thin, balding warden issued orders for the firing squad to fall in. Gavin was handed a two-way radio, and Brian watched him look across the compound as he spoke with the president. After a few moments, he glanced up and nodded, and immediately the whole compound came to life, like sharks in a feeding frenzy.

"Brian!" Ed yelled frantically. "They're gonna kill us!"

Ed seemed to comprehend the situation before Brian did. "Gavin! This won't work. You can't scare me into rejecting my Remnant Beliefs. God's laws stand as they were written! No power on earth or below can change them!"

"Guards! Shut that man up!"

Two guards stepped forward to gag Brian, but he held up his right hand and warned them off. With fire in his voice, he said, "You may kill me, but you will never silence me. Stand back!" The guards immediately stopped, looked quizzically, then fearfully at something no one else seemed to be able to see. *Angels?* Brian thought.

Things moved quickly during the next few moments. Guards fell back, and the news crews moved in as close as they were permitted. A few years ago it might have been considered the most crass form of sensationalism, but society had changed so drastically that it barely maintained order today.

Six men in Racal suits marched in front of them and were ordered by their commanding officer to halt; then came the order to right face.

The warden came up to Brian and Ed and asked if they wanted to be blindfolded, and both declined. He motioned for the guards Brian had warned away earlier to come and tie their hands behind their backs.

"I'd rather my hands weren't tied," Brian said. He glanced at Ed.

Ed cleared his throat. "Uh, me too."

The warden nodded. "I think that's fair. I don't think you'll go anywhere."

"Thank you."

"Brian," Ed said when the warden walked away, "I ain't got a family, but I was wonderin'. . . what about yours?"

Despite the things Ann had said to him, Brian's eyes misted over, not for himself, necessarily, because he was so shell-shocked, but for her and the path she had chosen. He could not see how it was possible that she had gotten so far away from God that she was willing to bow to the devil. "Ready!" The order sent a wave of deathly silence over the compound.

Are you going to protect me this time, too, Lord? Brian asked silently.

"Aim!"

Tears flowed freely from Brian's eyes, but he held his head up proudly. Ed followed suit. "I'll see you in heaven, Ed, my friend."

"Me too," Ed choked.

"Fire!"

* * *

Amy sat in the holding cell and stared at the backs of the two guards waiting to escort her into the packed courtroom. At first, when they'd told her that she was going to be put on trial for her beliefs, she was almost relieved. The prospect was terrifying, but at least it would get her out of the camp. Unfortunately, that wasn't how it worked. Each day, severe looking, uniformed guards came to collect her and escort her to the courtroom. At the end of the day they brought her right back.

She wasn't given any leniency, either. As soon as she returned, she was forced to work at least six hours before they let her crawl onto one of the filthy platforms. Out of necessity, she compressed her body into the smallest possible proportions so she could fit. They allowed her four or five hours of sleep before it started all over again.

Amy played with the chain linking her handcuffs. *Dear God*, she prayed silently, *please give me the words to say again today. You know I didn't have much time to learn about You before all this started. I'm just a baby Christian, Lord. I'm not a Bible scholar. Speak through me. Use me to tell these people about Yourself and Your love and Your plan for them. Help me to stay strong for You. Don't let me cave in under the pressure. Be my rock and my shield. Thank You. Amen.*

This was the fifth day of the trial. They'd been prompt about it. Somehow, they'd pulled the whole thing together and begun the day after Brian's execution. While Amy's brain was still reeling over his horrible death, she'd been plunged into this nightmare. Rather than stagger her, though, the whole experience had been somehow calming. As though only she could see that God was still in control. She could clearly see how Satan was manipulating the people around her, and yet she remained unafraid.

There would be death at the end of the trial. She was sure of it. They would not go through the bother of trying her without executing her as well. Of the outcome of the trial there could be no doubt. She was an example. She would be tried. She would be convicted. And she would be executed. In swift succession, she believed.

It was almost a relief, except that she'd come so far she couldn't help being sorry that she wouldn't be able to see the Lord coming as she had supposed she would. He had saved her from so many dangers so far, why not this one more? Surely it couldn't be much longer now?

Then she shuddered, suddenly cold. Maybe it was better this way. Maybe she was not able to be strong enough to make it through the final hours without a mediator as those who remained alive until He came would have to do. Perhaps that was why God was allowing this to happen. The other times He had saved her had been for a purpose. Hundreds in the barracks had become believers, and hundreds more had been strengthened in their faith. This had so outraged the guards that she was kept from the Snake Pit and other tortures because the only purpose served was to make the others stronger.

A faint smile touched her thin lips. She had only done what she thought right, and God had used her in His work. She felt humbled by this thought. If only she could do more! She just didn't see how that was possible in her present circumstances. She jingled the handcuffs anxiously, and a guard turned to give her a quizzical stare. His eyes were unreadable. He turned back around.

Ten minutes later, they were leading her through the jammed courtroom to sit at the table with her attorney, a slight, wiry woman who looked perpetually frazzled. Her face was set in a permanent grimace, and her small black eyes darted nervously, never resting and never looking directly at anyone. Amy was quite sure that even under the best of circumstances, the jury would never trust a word from her lips.

The prosecuting attorney, on the other hand, was a suave lieutenant, uniformed and polished like a brass medal. His manner of speaking was both engaging and charming, his voice low and even. The brown eyes in his tanned face lighted on each member of the jury separately when he spoke to them, compelling them to listen to him, persuading them to believe him. He was agonizingly sincere, mixing truth with subtle falsehoods until the two were very hard to distinguish.

Amy sat down slowly and surveyed the room. It was packed as it had been the previous four days. *"You'll be doing us a favor,"* Major Thule had gloated, holding the statement of recantation out between her gloved fingers enticingly. *"If you don't sign this, we'll try you and get more publicity for our cause than you can begin to imagine. Every television station in the country will follow this story, and when we win, it will break the backbone of the remnant movement. They'll be begging us to forgive them. And you'll be dead. But if you sign this form, right now, I'll see that you get clemency. It's possible that you will even at this late date be reinstated in your old position at Fort Detrick. You could be back to work whenever you choose. Of course, I expect you'd want to take a vacation first."*

She had paused to allow Amy to consider these things. Then, "you'll be needing a pen. Here take mine. Sign right there at the bottom, right beneath my signature." But Amy had refused to take the pen, and in the end Major Thule had cursed her heartily.

Amy's eyes searched for the Major, but she did not find her. She'd given her testimony yesterday, and Amy had been surprised to find that outside of her spacesuit she was very unassuming. Reserved and quiet, she had answered the prosecutor's questions in such a low voice that he'd been forced to ask her to repeat herself several times.

Amy wondered idly who today's witnesses would be. She leaned over to ask her attorney, but the woman just shrugged and averted her eyes, shuffling papers on her desk and avoiding the question. Amy sighed deeply and settled back in her chair to wait.

* * *

Mara was certainly glad that Jenna had been put in charge of organizing the move into the mountains. There were so many details to consider that Mara was sure if she'd had to do it, many of them would have been forgotten. But under Jenna's watchful eye, nothing escaped notice. She had even come up with a plausible way to get them all started on their journey.

"How," Dan had pondered one evening as the three of them sat around the kitchen table after most of the house had retired for the evening, "will we get all of these people and our supplies anywhere near the mountains without arousing sus picion? We can't even go at night because of the patrols. We'd be caught for sure. And we certainly can't all troupe together like a caravan. We'd be caught immediately."

Mara had no solution, but Jenna spoke up in her soft voice. "Why couldn't we do it over several days? We could move a few families out under the guise of a horseback riding trip. We'd load the trailers with food and gear along with the horses. A few would stay behind each time. If we didn't go every day no one would get suspicious. After all, some would return each time with the horses. It would just seem as though we were really getting into horseback riding."

Dan had nearly hugged Jenna in his enthusiasm for her plan. It was decided that two families would go out each time, but only one would return. The family that was left in the mountains would push further in, leaving behind markers to show where they'd gone. The last party through would remove all the markers so there would be no trace of their path. When they felt secure, the first party would camp until everyone had caught up together.

So far, the plan had worked splendidly. Two families had already departed, leaving three plus Dan, Mara, Dani and Jack, who comprised one "family" group. The only problem was that Mara wasn't sure Dani and Jack would be coming. Dan had spent the evenings talking with Dani. Mara, too, had tried to convince her that she should go with them. But at the moment, her mother seemed to have more sway with her.

While she was musing over these things, Mara studied the list of supplies that Jenna had printed out in her careful hand. They would all have to be packed in pack saddles and made ready to load onto the horses when they arrived at their destination. She sighed and tried to ignore the bustle around her. A knock on the door interrupted them all. Little James Worther probably took himself outside to watch them load the horses for the day's outing and then couldn't get the door open because the rusty knob was too high for him. He would knock until someone came and opened it for him.

"I'll get it," Mara announced, grimacing as she got up. She'd been sitting with one foot tucked up beneath her, and it had fallen asleep. She hobbled awkwardly to the door. The knock came again, louder. "Hold on, James," Mara shouted, yanking open the door.

Only it wasn't James.

Randy Burton stood on the doorstep looking anxious and excited and extremely wonderful. A slow grin spread across his face when he saw it was her. Forgetting her foot, she threw herself at him, nearly knocking him down. He staggered a few steps, his arms warm and delicious around her.

"When did you get here? Why didn't you tell me you were coming?" She peppered him with questions, but before he had time to answer any of them, she dragged him inside. All activity stopped, and conversations were cut off as wary eyes took in the new face. Mara felt a twinge of sadness that they had become such an untrusting group. She pushed the feeling aside.

"Everyone, this is my friend Randy Burton. He's from Washington, D.C., and he'll be going with us." She turned to Randy. "You will be going with us, won't you?" she asked with some concern. All at once she was frightened by Randy's silence. What if he'd changed his mind sometime between now and the last time they'd spoken? After all, that had been nearly a week ago. A lot could have happened.

Randy introduced Flynn O'Neil to the group and told a little of their story. Then Randy gripped Mara's hand. "It's really nice to meet all of you. Mara, could we go somewhere to talk?"

His voice was low and had a serious tone to it that made Mara's stomach knot up with foreboding. Whatever he wanted to talk to her about didn't sound good. She nodded but didn't trust herself to speak. Silently she led the way onto the old porch. She settled herself onto the loveseat, hoping Randy would sit beside her, but he stood, pacing nervously.

Mara swallowed hard. "Randy, what's wrong?" She heard

the quiver in her voice and despised herself for it. She sounded like a moonstruck adolescent.

Randy's long fingers ran through his hair. His face was thinner than when she'd seen him last and his frame sparser. There was a haggard look in his eyes that hadn't been there when she'd left him standing at the church in Washington as Alice had driven her and Dani away.

"Look, Mara, I don't know of any easy way to tell you this, and maybe you've already heard, so I'll just say it. Brian's dead. They executed him. I found his wife and kids, but they refused to come with me. I was on the way here when I heard it on the radio."

Mara kept her features still while she absorbed this information. Emotions crashed over her in waves, but she steeled herself against them. "I'm sorry about Brian," she said carefully, trying not to cry. "But I think I'm more sorry about his family. At least, we'll see Brian again soon, but it doesn't sound as if we'll be seeing his wife."

"It gets worse," Randy said dismally. "Amy is on trial. It sounds as if she's being railroaded. I think she's going to be executed next." He paused and studied her as if gauging how strong she was. "And we don't have much time, either. I ran into Dietrich in Chicago. I think he will be escorting Brian's family to Washington. It won't take him long to be here next. He will not have forgotten about Dani."

"No, he's after Dani's baby," Mara corrected him, her voice dull. All of a sudden it felt as though the Spirit of God had completely deserted her. She felt cold and very lonely. "Why is this happening?"

She wasn't really asking Randy, but he seemed to feel compelled to answer her. He came over and squatted on his heels, took her hands in his, and looked into her eyes. "I'm so sorry. I know this was a lot to dump on you all at once. But there just wasn't time to break it to you slowly."

Mara blinked back tears. "I suppose if I paid any attention

to the news, I would have known half of it," she said. "But we've been so busy getting everything ready to leave I haven't watched the news reports. Pastor Reiss has been keeping track of everything and telling us about it. But he never mentioned . . . how could he have known? They were just two names among scores of persecuted. He had no way of knowing I knew them."

Randy reached up and brushed his thumbs across her cheeks, wiping away tears that finally spilled down her cheeks. Then he pulled her into his arms and smoothed her hair as though she was a small child in need of comfort. "I'm sorry," he repeated over and over. "But think of it this way. It's almost over. This is the end. Soon there will be no more suffering, no more tears, no more sadness."

Mara shuddered. "Not if we make it, but Randy, what if we don't? What if He comes back and He *doesn't take us?* I think of that every day. What if I'm not strong enough to make it until the end? I mean, I've only been a Christian a short time. Oh, I know, I was brought up as a Christian, but I didn't really know what that meant. Not like now. What if I can't make it? What if I fall at the end and I'm lost for eternity?" Her voice was squelched in an anguished cry, but Randy shook her shoulders sternly.

"Now, you listen to me. Don't you think God is strong enough to keep us until He comes back? He's not going to let us falter. He won't, not even in the darkest hours, not even when we *feel* forsaken. What you're talking about, God has already told us would happen. We will know we aren't worth saving, not of ourselves. But God is covering for us. Trust Him. Have faith. He's coming back soon, and we're going with Him. Together," he finished fiercely.

Mara peeked up at him, taken aback by his sincerity. Randy had always been rather shy about stating his convictions. "How come you're so sure?" she asked. "Don't you ever wonder, you know, if it really stuck?"

Randy eyed her quizzically. "Wonder if what stuck?"

Mara shifted uncomfortably, slightly embarrassed. "You know, conversion. Being saved. What if it didn't stick, and so you don't get saved? I haven't been baptized yet. I made a profession of faith in front of everyone. But I have nightmares that Jesus comes back before I can get baptized and make it official."

Randy chuckled. "And you think that Jesus might exclude you on the basis of a technicality?"

Mara felt herself blush. "Well, yeah, I guess so." She grinned sheepishly. "I guess it is kind of silly, huh? But I just want to be righteous, you know? And I feel so unworthy."

"I don't think anyone who is righteous will feel that way. Because the way we become righteous is to draw closer and closer to Jesus, and when we do that, we can clearly see how despicable we really are. All the things that we thought were so terrific we can then see how selfish or wrong they really are. And we feel very unworthy. And we should." Randy stood up and drew Mara to her feet. "We *are* unworthy. If we weren't, then Jesus wouldn't have had to die for us in the first place.

"But He isn't going to let one of His children be snatched out of His hands. Particularly because of a technicality. It's what's in your heart that matters. There wasn't any way for the thief on the cross to be baptized, but that won't keep him out of the kingdom. Jesus knew that if he could have gotten down off that cross and lived the rest of his life, he would have been baptized."

Mara smiled and leaned against Randy, burying her face in the warm softness of his shirt. "I guess I never thought of it that way before." She felt Randy's arms tighten around her, and she sighed contentedly. "I'm so glad you're here," she breathed.

"Me too."

* * *

Dani sat through the now familiar calling of the spirits, but her mind wasn't on what was happening. Her heart didn't race as she anticipated the arrival of her father. In fact, she dreaded it. Ever since she'd talked with Mara about her father's presence being a manifestation of Satan, she had not enjoyed the visits at all. Her father had recognized something was amiss the very first time, but Dani, skilled liar that she was, put him off.

That was when her father had started talking to her about Mara and Pastor Reiss. "They're influencing you," he told her. "They're turning you against me. You really should leave there and go live with your mother. They'll destroy us, Dani."

But she'd denied his accusations and ignored his advice. It had been going on long enough. Tonight she was prepared to put an end to it. She was going to tell her father and everyone else present just what she thought was happening in the meetings and let the chips fall where they may.

But she was scared.

Possibly more scared than she had ever been in her life. For the last two nights she'd gone as far as studying her Bible to load up on ammunition to hurl at him. She wanted proof that he wasn't really who he claimed he was. However, in her search, she'd also noticed stories about demons, and they'd frightened her.

Do not let your hearts be troubled. Trust in God; trust also in me.

The voice came soft and low in her ear, and Dani started, looking around to see if anyone else had heard it. Beside her, her mother was staring with rapture at Miss Nelson. Several people in the audience were already in trances, communing with the spirits of those they wanted to talk to. Already many of the "dead" walked among them, reuniting with lost loved ones. Dani didn't see her father anywhere.

She felt a shiver of revulsion, and at that moment she realized that she had become one of *them*, a Remnant Believer. It amazed her that she hadn't known it before. But as she looked back, she could see how in the last week she had made her choice and she had decided for God. It had happened after a conversation with Randy Burton shortly after he'd come to stay at the farmhouse.

"Dani, you and I have never had a chance to talk, did you know that?" He had said one night as they sat on the porch of the farmhouse, and she had rocked Jack to sleep. Without waiting for an answer he had continued. "I didn't know your father, so I can't tell you if he was a great man or a horrible man. Despite what *you* may think of him, to me he was a great man. He gave his life for the children on that bus.

"You should have seen them, Dani. They were terrified. But more than buying them life, he bought them time. If they didn't already know God, they had more of a chance to get to know Him before it's too late. You know God, don't you, Dani?"

This time he had waited for her to answer, and she nodded sullenly. "Yes, I know God. And I don't like Him. He took everything from me."

"He did? Or you did?"

Dani's eyes had widened with surprise. A flash of anger swept over her like an electric shock. "What do you know about me?" she had demanded. "Nothing. You can't judge me."

"No," Randy had agreed. "I can't. But you can judge yourself. Did God hook you up with Shon? Or ask you to join the Freedom Society? Or kill your father? No. He didn't. In fact, He has miraculously preserved you despite your poor choices. That's not right, either. He hasn't simply preserved you, He's *blessed* you."

"Blessed me?" Dani had nearly choked on the words. "*Blessed* me!"

"When I became a new Christian," he had said, "I was thankful for whatever happened to me, good or bad. Do you know why? Because I found out that what I deserved was death. *Death*. Anything above death was a *blessing*. It's not always easy to think that way, I'll grant you. In fact, a lot of times, it took me awhile to learn to be thankful."

He had leaned forward until his face was inches from hers. He smelled good, and his eyes were compelling. Dani had found herself mesmerized by those eyes. "Don't you see, Dani? We all deserve to die, but instead, we get to go to heaven because Jesus died for us. He *gave up* everything so that we could *have* everything. Why would God, who gave up everything for you, turn around and beat you down so that you wouldn't take it?

"The truth is, Dani, that we reject God. He never rejects us."

There had been a long pause, and Randy leaned back in his chair. Dani remembered feeling as though she was going to cry again. It was so unfair. Everything he said was true. She knew it, knew it beyond a shadow of a doubt. But if she acknowledged that it was true, she would be defenseless. Her anger, her outrage, over the consequences of her decisions would be on her own head. She didn't think she was strong enough to bear that.

"We've all got choices to make, Dani," Randy had observed mildly. "God is always willing to help us make a good decision. But He will not shield us from the results of making poor decisions without Him."

"I know that!" Dani had yelled, finally unable to take any more of what he was saying. It was like a great verdict hanging over her head. A sentence of "guilty" proclaimed. The weight was oppressive. She felt as though she couldn't breathe. She was drowning under the weight of it.

Every bit had been her own fault. She could see clearly, as though someone were guiding her memory back to each decision, showing her how she selfishly chose what she thought was the best for herself without thought of anyone else, least of all, God. It all swam before her eyes while the dreaded word *GUILTY* rang in her ears, drowning out everything, even the sounds of her own sobs.

When she had come to her senses, Randy Burton was cradling her in his arms. He was whispering *shhhh* over and over.

She lifted her face away from the dampness of his shirt, which had absorbed all her tears. Randy didn't let go but searched her face with some concern.

"Dani, are you OK? You started screaming, but you were crying so hard it was difficult to tell what you were saying."

She hadn't told him that day. But that night she had talked to God. *Really* talked to Him. She'd poured out her heart, and she'd asked God to forgive her for what she had done. She'd begged for forgiveness. At the time, she hadn't thought of herself as a Remnant Believer. They were too *good*. But now, she realized that what made her a Remnant Believer was the fact that she didn't buy into Satan's lie. She believed in Jesus with her whole heart.

"I sense a dissension among us," Miss Nelson was saying. "There must be unity of mind and purpose. Unless there is unity, we cannot continue. Someone in this room does not believe. I feel a hostile aura. I must ask the dissident to please leave."

Dani had felt her face getting progressively redder at Miss Nelson's words. But when she was asked to leave, she angrily jumped to her feet. "So, that's how you can manage to keep tricking everyone? Just ask people who don't believe you to slink away? Well, I won't slink. These people have a right to know who they're dealing with."

"Dani, no," pleaded her mother, ashen and trembling at her elbow. She grabbed Dani's arm and tried to pull her back into her seat. "Dani, please, stop."

Dani ignored her pleas. "No, I won't stop." Out of the corner of her eye she saw a pair of burly men leave their posts at the door where they had been greeting newcomers and head up the aisle toward her. "You are all being fooled!" she screamed. "You're not talking with the spirits of people you love. You're talking with Satan, the prince of lies. Can't you see this woman is tricking you? There are no spirits of the dearly departed. It's all a lie. The people you love are sleeping in their graves. They won't know anything until Jesus comes back. They're dead! Dead! They don't know anything!"

"Dani!" Her mother went limp in her seat. Immediately, Jack stood beside his wife.

"Marilyn, Marilyn," he coaxed, rubbing her wrists. He turned angrily on his daughter, and Dani shivered at the inhuman light in his eyes. "This is all your fault. I told you to leave that Benneton woman and Pastor Reiss. I told you to go live with your mother. You've caused her nothing but heartache. What kind of a daughter are you?"

"I'm not afraid of you," Dani whispered. "You're not my father. You're a demon."

"You should be afraid of me," Jack hissed. "For your son's sake, if not for your own."

Dani took a step back into the aisle and bumped into one of the security men who grabbed her arm. She flailed at him with the free one, but it was soon captured by the other guard. As they began dragging her away, her mother revived. Her eyes began to focus groggily on Dani.

"Wait! Wait!" she shrieked. Staggering, she got up out of the chair and lunged after Dani. "Give her a chance. Dani, say you'll come home with me. Tell them that you'll renounce these strange beliefs. Do it for me, Dani. Please."

Dani shook her head firmly. "No, Mom, I can't, and I won't."

Marilyn's eyes filled with tears, and she groped for Jack's hand, which reached out to steady her. "If you won't come with me, then I am going to go to your father. I am happiest when I am with him, and I'm unbearably lonely when he's gone. I can't tell you how disappointed I am in you, Dani." Marilyn reached slender fingers into the jeweled bag that hung from her shoulder. She withdrew a pistol and placed her mouth around the barrel. One loud shot rang out. Dani's last conscious impression was of her mother slumping to the floor in slow motion and the look of utter triumph on her father's face.

When she woke up, she was propped up against her mother's

car. The parking lot was empty. Vomit reeked in her nostrils and covered the front of her clothes. She stood on shaky legs and managed to get in the car with one thought in her mind.

She had to get to Jack.

* * *

Agent Janet Roddrick's once fair skin and pretty face were a loathsome mixture of tough leather and pure hatred for everything under the scorching sun, but especially anything that had kept her in Idaho for the past several weeks watching this pathetic band of Remnant Believers. These were people she could crush in a matter of minutes—kill some, arrest a few. Actually, if she ever got orders to raid the farm, she planned to kill most of the people there.

Now, nearly an hour after seeing Dani Talbot leave the farmhouse, obviously no longer pregnant, Agent Roddrick trembled, her blood hot with rage. She'd sent one agent to tail Dani, and she had another on the phone trying, so far without success, to get her a direct line to Director Aldridge. She knew that since their last meeting, when he ordered her not to make any moves until he sanctioned it, he had contracted the disease. Just in the last couple of days, she had learned that he was near death. Yet he still held the position of director of the FBI, and he could still cause her a considerable amount of grief and ruin her career if she went against his orders.

This is just senseless, she thought as she peered through her spotting scope. They seemed not to worry about being raided at all. None of them carried weapons. When she'd first noticed the lack of weapons, she was sure it was some kind of trick and that they were really very well-armed. But the more she and the other agents she was in charge of watched, the more convinced she became that there wasn't a weapon on the place. Even if there *were* weapons, none of her agents had seen anyone training with them. And what good were weapons unless you were serious enough about using them to train heavily?

Agent Paul Miller, who had accompanied Roddrick while interviewing Randy Burton in the hospital and planted the bug, came up beside her with a pair of field glasses.

"Apparently Aldridge has been violently ill and unable to address our situation."

"Then he should be relieved of command *of* this situation," Agent Roddrick snapped.

"I say we go ahead and raid the place as soon after the girl returns as possible. You're the Agent in Charge. You're on the scene. You should be the one making the decisions anyway."

With biting sarcasm, Roddrick replied. "Yeah, and it's no reflection on your record if I take the blame for disobeying orders."

Agent Miller shrugged. "Either way." He was behind Agent Roddrick enough that she couldn't see him smile.

* * *

Amy fidgeted in her seat. The tension in the courtroom had reached a fevered pitch. It was as if everyone present except Amy knew what was coming next and was keenly anticipating it. She felt a deep foreboding enter her soul.

"Your honor, I would like to call my next witness," the prosecuting attorney said. "The government calls Ray Cooper to the stand."

Amy felt the numbness enter her and spread from her scalp to the soles of her feet. She stared in helpless horror as her husband shuffled toward the stand. Every effort had been made to give him an impression of normalcy, but Amy, who knew his every mood in intimate detail, recognized immediately that something was wrong.

Although makeup had been skillfully applied to his face, she could detect multiple bruises and swelling. He carried his left arm carefully, and the way he moved suggested that he had other injuries as well, perhaps some of them internal. His eyes were lifeless, and when they turned toward her, did not even register recognition.

"Mr. Cooper," the attorney began, "can you please state your full name for the record."

"Raymond Peter Cooper."

"Age and background?"

"41. I'm an editor for the *D.C. Times*."

"And will you please identify your wife for the court?"

Ray nodded and rested his eyes painfully on each face. They came to a stop at Amy and flickered momentarily. He raised one arm carefully to point in her direction. "That's my wife," he acknowledged.

"Mr. Cooper, is your wife a Remnant Believer?"

"Yes."

"Are you a Remnant Believer?"

"No." Amy's heart, which had been painfully scudding around in her chest, dropped like a stone.

"And, Mr. Cooper, did you agree to become a Remnant Believer yourself?"

"Yes."

"Please tell the jury why."

Ray took a slow deliberate breath. "My wife worked for USAMRIID. She had a high position there at Fort Detrick." He did not mention that he had begged her to get out of USAMRIID, Amy noticed. "I was real proud of her work there. She had the opportunity to help lots of people. But then when this virus broke out, she started asking herself a lot of questions. And we—uh, I mean, she—started talking a lot about God and what He had to do with this. That's when she started checking out churches.

"She met a woman named Alice Nolan, who got her involved in a church. I didn't know it was a Remnant Believer's church at first. When I found out, I was furious, of course. I begged Amy not to have anything to do with them. I knew there was something wrong with them even before they were being blamed for all the disasters. They're just plain weird."

The attorney interrupted him. "And yet, Mr. Cooper, you agreed to become a Remnant Believer yourself."

Ray nodded slowly. "Only because Amy threatened to leave me if I didn't. I didn't want to lose my wife. We'd been having problems for some time, and I thought maybe if I did this thing for her, then she wouldn't leave like she'd been threatening to."

"And did it work?"

Ray shook his head. "No, she left me for another man. His name was Brian Willis. They were together for some time before they were apprehended and put into the Thurgood Rehabilitation and Detention Center. Even in the camp, under dire circumstances, I've been told by the very guards at the camp that they continued to carry on their illicit affair until he was put to death six days ago. It is now common knowledge that Brian Willis was the leader of the Remnant cult. I think now that it was he who influenced Amy to join the cult in the first place."

Amy's attorney jumped to her feet. "Objection! That is not within the knowledge of the witness."

"Sustained," the judge said. "The witness's last remarks will be stricken from the record."

The prosecuting attorney smirked, happy that the suggestion of motive for the attraction had been planted in the minds of the jury. Amy felt outrage and a sense of injustice rising in her like mercury on a hot day. She wanted to leap to her feet to defend herself, but a soft voice in her ear quenched the fire raging in her breast and filled her with calm.

"If the world hates you, keep in mind that it hated me first. If you belonged to the world, it would love you as its own. As it is, you do not belong to the world, but I have chosen you out of the world. That is why the world hates you. Remember the words I spoke to you: 'No servant is greater than his master.'

If they persecuted me, they will persecute you also. If they obeyed my teaching, they will obey yours also. They will treat you this way because of my name, for they do not know the One who sent me."

Amy looked at Ray, and tears of compassion sprang up in her eyes. The last time she'd seen him had been on the day of her baptism. She hoped he knew her well enough to know that she would never betray him in the way they were claiming that she had. It was obvious they had worked him over good to get his testimony. She didn't blame him for his accusations, but she wished with all her heart that he had not given in to their demands.

"I forgive you, Ray," she whispered. Her attorney shot her a dirty look but said nothing. When asked if she wanted to cross-examine the witness, she declined. Amy felt as though she was being betrayed on all sides. The weight of her disappointment and their condemnation was almost more than she could bear. She felt as though she was being pressed into her seat by invisible mounds of wet sand.

"Thank you, Mr. Cooper," the prosecuting attorney was saying. Amy realized that she had missed some questions. As Ray slowly made his way past the table where she sat, he turned and spat at her. Amy sat stunned, but her attorney drew back with a gasp of horror and disgust.

"There is nothing so contemptuous as a faithless wife," he said harshly. "If you wanted to be with Brian Willis, Amy, you could have at least divorced me decently first."

"Bless those who persecute you," the Voice in her ear whispered. "bless and do not curse."

Escorts were in no hurry to remove him from the courtroom, waiting to see if his words could provoke Amy into a response that would further their cause. She said nothing, however; she simply hung her head. She did not look up again until she heard him shuffle away. She heard her own name called.

"The government calls Amy Cooper to the stand," the attorney was saying.

After the preliminaries were over, Amy could see in the prosecuting attorney's eyes that this was the moment he'd been waiting for. He could scarcely conceal his jubilation. She felt like a lab specimen strapped on a dissection table.

"Mrs. Cooper, are you a Remnant Believer?"

"Yes."

"Did you work at Fort Detrick?"

"Yes."

"Is that where you met Brian Willis?"

"Objection," Amy's attorney stated. "Irrelevant."

"Your Honor," the prosecutor said smoothly, "I am trying to establish a relationship between the accused and Mr. Willis."

"Sustained," the judge said sternly. "Rephrase the question."

He turned back to Amy. Annoyance tightened his forehead and made his eyes into small slits full of malice, which squinted at her malevolently. "Where did you meet Brian Willis?" he asked, apparently deciding not to beat around the bush.

"I met Brian Willis at the Thurgood Rehabilitation and Detention Center," Amy replied.

"Mrs. Cooper," his voice dripped with patience. "I'm sorry, but have you forgotten we have a sworn testimony by Gavin Larson confirming that you met with Mr. Willis several times in your capacity as an informer for the United Religious Coalition?"

A gasp rippled around the courtroom, and the judge made no move to stop the audience from voting. Amy felt her face get red with humiliation. He made her sound so sneaky. But had she met Brian in that capacity? She surely didn't remember, though she had met with several of Gavin's men or talked with them on the phone.

"Mrs. Cooper? Is that true?"

"I-uh-I don't know. I don't remember," Amy murmured finally.

"You don't remember? Or you choose not to tell the court?" the attorney stated triumphantly. "Isn't it true, Mrs. Cooper, that you met Brian Willis while you were an informant for Gavin Larson? Isn't it true that the two of you became attracted to each other and began your affair? Isn't it true that you carried on that affair even after being placed in the Thurgood Rehab/Detention Center?"

"Objection, Your Honor!" shrieked Amy's attorney as she leapt to her feet. The cords in her neck strained as she struggled to maintain her professionalism. "That question has been asked and answered."

"Sustained," the judge said laconically.

The attorney smirked. "The Prosecution would like to submit into evidence a videotape made by the guards at the Thurgood Center. It contains scenes, intimate scenes, between Amy Cooper and Brian Willis."

Amy remembered Brian's encouragement, his support, and his kindness, and she wanted to rail against the falseness of the charges, but she knew it would do no good. The jury would believe just what this man wanted them to believe. Even her attorney, it seemed, was powerless to stop him.

"Your Honor, I would also like to enter into evidence copies of hotel room receipts provided by Gavin Larson, booked in the name of Mr. and Mrs. Willis. And a statement from Mrs. Ann Willis stating that she was not the "Mrs." indicated in the occupancy." He handed the pile to a bailiff and then turned his attention once more to Amy. "Mrs. Cooper, I ask you once again; would you like to restate your relationship to Mr. Willis? And may I remind you that you are under oath."

Amy shook her head firmly. "I would not. Brian Willis was a wonderful friend, but we did not have an affair. I love my husband, and I have been faithful to him every moment of our marriage."

The attorney made a *tsk-tsk* sound under his breath. No one attempted to stop him from attempting to inflame the jury, and Amy felt like screaming. He went on. "In light of your duplicitous nature, that might be rather hard to swallow. Don't you agree?"

Last Days

"For some," Amy agreed, sitting up straighter and looking him in the eye. "It would all depend on how familiar they were with the truth."

"Ah, yes, the truth. That is certainly what we are after. And in our search for truth, justice and the American Way, Mrs. Cooper, could you please tell the court how long you were a spy for Mr. Larson and the United Religious Coalition?"

Amy's lawyer sat dejectedly and made no move to object, although there was no evidence to support the accusation. She appealed to the woman with her eyes but received no response. "I, uh, I wasn't a spy, exactly. I was working on the inside of Fort Detrick, relaying information to Gavin Larson."

"You were a spy." It wasn't a question. "For how long?"

Amy conceded the point. "For eight months."

"And is it true, Mrs. Cooper, that you informed Gavin Larson, before anyone else, that the vice president of the United States had succumbed to Cartier's virus? Was it not your duty, as a member of the military, if nothing else, to first inform the president of the United States?"

"Yes, it's true. I called Gavin Larson first. We were trying to prevent the spread of national panic, you see, and . . ."

The attorney cut her off. "And isn't it true that when you asked for a promotion and a raise and Gavin Larson refused you, you became a turncoat and joined the Remnant Believers to use the information you had gained as Gavin's spy to their benefit?"

"No!" Amy cried. She sought her attorney, "aren't you going to stop him? It's lies, all lies!"

"Order," the judge demanded. "Mrs. Cooper, if you cannot control yourself, I will have you removed from this courtroom."

"Mrs. Cooper," the attorney said indulgently. "You claim that I am lying. Yet, I find no other compelling reason for you to join the Remnant Believers other than your affair with Brian Willis and spite against your former benefactor, Gavin Larson. Please, Mrs. Cooper, if you would, indulge us with your version of the story."

Amy recognized her chance immediately. *Lord,* she thought, *tell me what to say.* "I am a Remnant Believer, I don't deny that. In fact, I'm proud of it. Even though you may kill me for it, I would not renounce my beliefs or the God who inspired them. It was through the Remnant Believers that I came to know who Jesus is and what He did for me on the cross. I found out the great price He paid so that I could have eternal life.

"It doesn't matter what you do to me today or tomorrow or any day in the future. My future is secure in my God, and it's eternal. Nothing you can say or do will prevent me from spending it with God, and that's all that matters to me. You say that I was a spy for Gavin Larson, and you're right. I'm not proud of it, but I was. Still, I felt that what I was doing was in the best interest of the people of the United States. In my position at Fort Detrick, I also had no choice. I asked for a transfer, but it was not granted. I was on the verge of terminating my employment when I was arrested.

"So, you want to know why I became a Remnant Believer? It was because I believe in God, not in Gavin Larson. You can't do anything to me that God doesn't approve of and though He slay me, yet will I trust Him."

"Enough!" the attorney spat. "I asked for an explanation, not a sermon. Your witness, Counselor."

Amy's attorney brushed a hand in the air in front of her face as though swatting a pesky fly. "No questions."

Amy made her way down from the witness stand. Even the hostile eyes of the jurors could not dispel the warm feeling of love that enveloped her. It truly didn't matter what happened to her. *Paul was right,* she decided, *to die is gain.* She looked forward to the end of the trial with a feeling that bordered on anticipation.

* * *

Dani drove to the house as if pursued by a legion of demons. Fortunately, no police officers were around to record or take note of her speed and write her a ticket. As she hit the dirt road that led to the farmhouse, her thoughts chased themselves in sick circles.

She would get back and take Jack and go . . .

Where would she go? She had nothing, no one. Not a friend in the world and a killer right behind her. Mother, father, both dead. In an instant, Dani knew what it was like to be totally alone. And in that moment, she couldn't bear the weight of it. Slowing the car, she pulled off the road a short distance from the house. The vehicle bounced slightly as it hit a rough patch and then rolled to a stop, partially concealed behind some shrubs.

An inhuman wail gushed out of Dani's mouth as she laid her head down on the steering wheel and gave full vent to her grief. She felt as though a gaping hole had been torn in her middle. Clumsily she pulled her knees up to her chest, hugging herself into a tight ball, trying to keep it all in. But there was no containing her grief.

It seemed like hours before it had spent itself, leaving Dani tired and dazed, sitting in the car, rocking gently. She stared sightlessly out of the window as the afternoon sun blazed. She was vaguely aware that although the weather broadcasts were announcing raging heat, she didn't really notice it. The interior of the car felt almost cool. Across the road in a meadow a deer wandered along the fringe of woods. It didn't seem to be affected by the reported tremendous heat, either. Another followed. Timidly they made their way among the shadows toward the road.

Dani heard a soft sound, a muffled *thud,* and the first deer dropped in its tracks. The second, startled, bounded back into the cover of the woods. A figure suddenly materialized in the meadow, seeming to come from nowhere. In the withered field where the hay had dried on its stalks, he made his way to the fallen animal and dragged it back, disappearing again, as if swallowed up by the earth. The whole episode had taken maybe thirty seconds.

Dani held her breath, panic rising in her chest. They were watching the farmhouse. They—someone. Who? The Freedom Society? No, they would have made a move much sooner, stormed the place, and taken what they wanted. Unless . . . unless they were waiting for her to return.

Suddenly she felt exposed, as though she stood naked in the road. They must see her, must know she was there, in her car. They had probably watched her display of emotion through long-range binoculars. But they had not molested her. They had not approached her or tried to take her. Why not?

She debated what to do. If she started the car now and drove on to the farmhouse, they would see her. If instead she sneaked out of the car and into the bushes on the side of the road, gaining entry to the house by the back way, they might not notice she had left. It would buy her some time.

She pulled the key from the ignition so the car would not ding when she opened the door. In case they were watching, she made as though to go to take a nap on the seat, lying down. Just when she thought her legs might go to sleep, she cracked the door on the far side and slithered to the ground. Hugging the earth, she crawled and slid into the ditch and then to the woods beyond.

* * *

Part of Aldridge's security detail looked on in horror as the dying FBI director heaved repeatedly into the bucket. The three agents perspired heavily inside their Racal suits. In fact, everything in the house was sterilized, and the whole structure had been covered with plastic. How they wished the director had gone to a hospital or some other facility designed for caring for the diseased.

They cast wide-eyed glances at each other. One of the agents was a twenty-six-year-old microbiologist named Tami Chin, who seriously regretted her desire to become an agent.

The other two—equally young men—shared similar thoughts about their predicament. All three knew they were spending their time sweating profusely at the director's side because everyone else had seniority over them. *A cruel world,* they thought, and they blamed it largely on the stubborn Remnant Believers, as did the rest of the world. That's what Gavin Larson, head of the United Religious Coalition, and the pope preached every day on every television and radio station. They claimed God was talking to them, and everyone believed it.

Finally, it appeared as though Aldridge was through choking up his guts. *Considering how much blood the man has vomited,* Tami thought, *it's a wonder he is still alive.*

"Give me that phone," Aldridge muttered hoarsely.

Surprised, the woman glanced down at the phone in her hand; it had been so long, she'd entirely forgotten about it. "Sorry, sir," she said, stepping forward and handing the phone to Aldridge.

"Get Agent Roddrick," Aldridge said, barely able to speak.

* * *

Out in the blazing heat, well past one hundred and thirty degrees for the wicked, twelve FBI agents broiled as they watched the farmhouse. Agents Miller and Roddrick were watching Dani Talbot's car when Roddrick finally got to speak to Director Aldridge.

"Sir, we know the girl has had the baby. She's just now returning to the farm. We should raid the place now. Now is the time."

"No," Aldridge wheezed.

"No? But . . . you can't be serious!"

"I've been a fool," Aldridge said slowly. "I believe in the God of the Remnant Believers now. Leave them alone."

Roddrick squeezed the phone until she heard the plastic begin to protest. Pure hatred glowed in her eyes. *All this time wasted on a wild goose chase!* Suddenly, as if listening to

Aldridge babble about a god weren't shocking enough, Miller let out a gasp.

"What the devil!"

"What is it, Miller?" Roddrick snapped. "You're not going to believe this, but some idiot just shot a deer right in plain sight of the girl. She *must* have seen it."

Roddrick immediately thought that the heat had sent one of her agents over the deep end. But it couldn't be anyone on her team. They were all accounted for and preparing for a raid. "Who did it?"

"It's got to be the Freedom Society. Like Aldridge said, they're after the same thing he is. That girl and her baby."

Roddrick turned her attention back to Aldridge on the phone. "Mr. Aldridge," she said, "I consider you no longer fit to give orders. It seems I don't have any choice but to go ahead with the raid considering that there is every reason to believe Dietrich and several members of the Freedom Society are here to do the same thing. Regardless of your rather late decision to believe in a god and repent, I have to do my duty and arrest this group of Remnant Believers."

Roddrick held the phone, waiting for a response.

"Hello?" a female voice said faintly.

"Who is this? Where is Director Aldridge?"

"I am Agent Tami Chin from the director's security detail. I'm sorry to have to tell you this, but I think he just died."

* * *

Every shadow and noise became a danger, and she fought an overwhelming urge to panic and run blindly through the trees and brush to the house as fast as she could. Finally, she reached the back door and let herself in quickly and quietly.

She heard Mara's voice in the sitting room talking with someone, probably Pastor Reiss. She crept to the door and entered. Mara, looking up, seeing her pale face and glittering eyes, rose to her feet with a startled exclamation. "Dani! What is it? What's wrong?"

Pastor Reiss, to her left, also rose. Another man, sitting in the shadows, stood as well. Dani glanced at him and saw that it was Randy. A feeling of relief swept through her. "They're watching the house," she said. "I saw them. Men with guns, really sophisticated guns. They shot a deer."

"In front of the house?" Pastor Reiss was incredulous.

"Across the street, in the meadow, about a hundred yards down. I was right there, and I barely heard a sound. You would never have noticed unless you had been looking right at them."

"Are you OK?" Mara took her by the shoulders and gave her a little shake. Dani felt as though she was returning, mentally, from a faraway place. She felt like fainting. Her head spun.

"I'm OK. Where's Jack? Is he all right?"

"He's safe. In the nursery," Randy answered her.

"We have to leave. Right now."

They all stared at her.

"That's impossible," Pastor Reiss objected. "There are three groups yet to leave. Only half of our people have gotten out. We can't leave all in a group. They'd stop us for certain. What difference does it make if they're watching us? They aren't doing anything about it. We have to stick with the plan, or we'll all be arrested. It's the only hope we have."

"Then I have to go." Dani was amazed the idea hadn't occurred to her before. "It's probably Jack they're after anyway. Even if they come for you and I'm not here, maybe they'll let you all go. But I can't take that risk."

"You must trust God, Dani," Pastor Reiss urged. "Trust Him to take care of you and Jack. Can you think of anyone more able to do it?"

Dani felt her eyes swim immediately with tears. It was true she felt inadequate to protect Jack. But to trust God . . . A voice that she had followed for too long spoke in her ear. *Hasn't God taken away everything you hold dear already? First Shon, then your father, now your mother. Certainly Jack is next. God is punishing you for your mistakes. It's God you have to save Jack from!*

These thoughts swirled around in her head, and panic at the thought of the men stationed outside overwhelmed her. She felt the room begin to swim, and then everything was black. Strong arms carried her, and there was a low murmur of voices. And then everything faded, and she rested in merciful peace.

* * *

When Dani woke up, Randy was sitting beside her bed, bathing her face and reading his Bible. At her movement, he looked up and smiled at her. "It's OK. Jack's with Mara," he added before she could ask.

"They haven't come for us?" Dani croaked.

Randy raised an eyebrow and handed Dani the glass of water standing on her bedside table. "No. They haven't. Not yet, but we're getting ready to move out. You fainted ten or fifteen minutes ago. Mara said you are mentally exhausted."

"Then I've gotta get out of here before they do come," Dani mumbled, trying to sit up. She was overcome with a wave of dizziness. Randy reached out an arm and restrained her as easily as if she had been a child. She lay back on the pillows and glowered at him in frustration. "Shouldn't you be out helping the men?"

"There's time," Randy said simply.

After a long pause, Dani said, "You were right." She wiped her nose on her sleeve before he could hand her a tissue. "Everything you said. I've been running away from it because I couldn't face the consequences. I'm still not sure that I'm ready to face them. But I can see now that I have to try."

"Dani, with God on your side, you are strong enough to face anything. Our time left here is so short. You must make your decision quickly."

"I've already decided. I just never told anyone. I want to be baptized. I gave my life, for what it's worth, to God. And I want Jack to be dedicated."

Randy beamed. "I'll tell Pastor Reiss immediately. As soon as we find some water and are reasonably safe, there's going to be some serious dunking!"

Dani lay back on the pillows as he left the room. She felt as though a blanket of peace descended on her, and in a moment she fell into a deep and untroubled sleep.

* * *

Dietrich was furious and barely in control of his rage. He wickedly slapped Leaman repeatedly with the backs of his hands. "What on earth were you thinking? We're not out here hunting game, we're hunting Remnant Believers!"

Risking his own life, Leaman glared defiantly, though not understanding what had possessed him to take a shot at the deer. Maybe the relentless heat was affecting his reason. All of a sudden, he had felt the urge to kill something, and he honestly hadn't seen the girl or the car. He could have sworn it wasn't there; it was as if they didn't exist.

Dietrich turned away and stalked back to where he'd spent most of the day watching the farm. He watched Dani sneak around the farmhouse. A few moments later, the whole farm seemed to burst alive. *Now they knew! He had to move now!*

* * *

Dietrich had fewer men and far less protocol to follow than did Agent Roddrick, which gave him a few minutes head start. Agent Roddrick was afraid of this, and her fears were confirmed when she saw Dietrich's two Jeeps bounce out of the trees onto the dirt road. She shouted into her two-way radio.

"Let's move. Now! Now!"

Midnight Hour

* * *

No more than a few minutes after he had left Dani to rest, Randy saw the trouble. "They're coming! We don't have time to load all the horses," he yelled when he saw the dust. "We've got to move right now!"

A dozen heads whipped around. And then, despite their unmilitary-like backgrounds, men, women, and children alike snapped into action like a team of Navy Seals.

Pastor Reiss ran up. "This is useless! We're not going to escape! Certainly not with all the supplies we will need."

"Let's just leave with what is loaded. It's our only choice," Randy said on his way back inside to grab Dani.

"We've got cars," Dan said. "Some still have gas."

"But not enough room," Randy replied. "And I know you're not willing to leave anyone behind. Let's just go with the plans you have already made and head for the mountains."

Randy turned to Reiss. "Keep them praying, and let's trust God to watch our backside. I'll be right behind you with Dani, and save a horse for her to ride."

A look of determination came over Dan, and he marched outside. Mara set down the bag she had just picked up and grabbed Randy's arm. "I love you," she said. Then she kissed him hard and ran out after Pastor Reiss.

* * *

Dietrich smiled. *These people are so stupid*, he thought. *They don't even realize it's too late to try and escape!* He thought this repeatedly as he directed his men to flank the group of Remnant Believers as they tried to get their horses packed and moving.

Dietrich jumped from his Jeep before it stopped. His men followed his lead, aiming their weapons at the Remnant Believers.

* * *

Dan and Randy brought up the rear. The main body of Remnant Believers was a hundred yards or more ahead, moving remarkably quickly. Looking back, Dan shook his head in complete disbelief. "What are they doing?"

Randy couldn't figure it out, either. It looked comical, whatever had possessed Dietrich and his men. "I don't know. It certainly doesn't make sense from here."

"It looks as if they're just pointing their guns at each other."

Randy crouched beside Dan and studied the situation for some time. Finally, he shook his head. "It looks as if they see people who aren't really there."

That was pretty much what Dan had been thinking too. They gave each other a knowing look, then burst out laughing. As they jogged to catch up to the group, they joked about angels having an awfully good sense of humor.

* * *

Somehow, they managed to drag the trial out for another week. Amy was not sure where they came up with all the witnesses, some of whom she could not ever remember meeting. But it didn't take a genius to figure out why they prolonged the trial.

Television cameras captured every movement in the courtroom. Amy had heard rumors that the trial was so popular that advertisers were paying more for each thirty- second spot than they paid during a Superbowl game. She'd even heard it whispered, perhaps deliberately within her hearing, that thousands were joining the United Coalition of Churches as a direct result of the trial. This news was bitter, and she fought its poison, which threatened her with discouragement.

But finally it was over. Every witness exhausted, every angle probed. Amy was asked to stand as the jury read her sentence.

"We find the defendant," declared the foreman of the jury, "guilty as charged."

Midnight Hour

A roar of approval met this statement, and anyone wishing to speak was obliged to wait. Even the judge made no move to quell the noise in the courtroom. She merely waited for it to subside before pronouncing sentence. "Amy Cooper, you are hereby sentenced to death by lethal injection. This sentence to be carried out within thirty days. You will spend the remainder of your life in solitary confinement awaiting the fulfillment of this sentence. Dismissed."

And it was over. Just as quick as that. Amy felt no pangs of remorse, no fear, only a relief that it was finally over. She was ushered out immediately by guards who placed her strategically before the television cameras before leading her out. Amy didn't need to watch the news reports to know how she would look to viewers.

Pale. Wan. Painfully thin. Defeated.

But not really defeated. They could pronounce whatever sentence they wanted, but they could never defeat her, because God was in her corner. He was on her side. And no matter what it looked like from an earthly vantage point, she was not defeated and never would be. Even when the deadly chemicals were coursing through her veins and her heart was pulsing its last beat, she would not be defeated.

On the contrary. She had won.

Chapter Thirteen

Seconds to Midnight

Mara clutched her arms tightly around her and wandered away from the fire. They were deep in the Idaho wilderness, and it was a crisp, clear night. Their only horse nickered softly. The stars overhead looked far more peaceful and inviting than the world on which she stood. A few yards out, she turned around and watched Randy at work helping to build a couple of lean-tos for a family with three small children who had joined their group. The family's name was Warner. Pastor Reiss was putting the finishing touches on a lean-to for Dani and baby Jack. She smiled, and then the smile faded, and she walked farther out.

They had met up with nearly all the families who had left the farm surreptitiously in the days before being raided. They had shared stories of their escape, studied together and prayed, then said what they knew would probably be their final goodbyes here on this earth. Mara knew she had never in her life felt as depressed as she had since leaving the farm. And she wasn't the only one who felt this way.

Suddenly she felt Randy's arms wrap around her, his cheek next to her ear. "What are you doing out here?"

"Thinking. Looking at the stars . . ."

"They're pretty."

"I know. I wish . . ." Mara paused and took a deep breath.

"You wish what?"

"I wish things weren't so horrible. I wish I didn't feel so unworthy . . ."

"Oh?" Randy gently turned Mara around. He cupped her face in his hands and looked deeply into her eyes; he then drew her to his chest and held her tightly, and for a few moments, neither of them spoke.

"You've heard Pastor Reiss talk about going through the time of Jacob's trouble. I know that's what I'm feeling. I just don't feel worthy to represent God."

"I know. I feel the same way. Sometimes I think I don't deserve God's grace. How could I?" Then Randy smiled. "Amazing, isn't it?"

"Yes." Mara paused. "Randy, do you think we are safe?"

"To tell you the truth, Mara, I don't know. I think Dietrich is getting closer. When I've been out scouting, I've seen helicopters searching, and I know Dietrich is with them. He'll fly in and track us on foot for a while, and then he'll leave by helicopter."

"Where is he getting helicopters?"

"I'm sure the FBI and Dietrich have finally chosen to cooperate. I can only imagine that by now there is a fervent push to round up every last Remnant Believer on the planet."

Mara looked up at the sky again. "I find myself searching for Jesus every time I look at the sky." She heard Randy breathe deeply. He gave her a gentle squeeze. "What do you suppose is happening to Amy?" she asked.

"I don't know. But God does, and He is watching out for her . . . like He is for us."

Mara made Randy kiss her. "You have so much faith. That's one of the reasons I love you so much." She laced her fingers through his, and they walked hand in hand back toward the camp. "Randy? If Dietrich is closing in on us, what do you think we should do?"

"I've been thinking about that. They're searching in grids and finding evidence here and there that we're around. So I think if we turn around, we might be able to lose them for some time, hopefully before they realize they've completely lost us."

Before they wandered back into camp, Randy stopped and grabbed both of Mara's hands, turning her toward him. For a long time, he didn't say anything—just gazed at her with the most tender, loving look she had ever known. She didn't ask what was on his mind. The moment was too precious.

"Mara," Randy finally said, his voice full of emotion, "will you marry me?"

* * *

Pope Xavier sat contentedly back in a white overstuffed armchair in his suite. Before him paced the Holy Mother, her aspect dark and brooding. She gave him a stern and reproachful look, and he repented of his contentment.

"Mother, you are angry," he said petulantly.

"No, my little father, but you must not relax and rejoice yet. Our victory is not complete. No, not by any means."

"But things are going so well," protested Xavier, struggling to gain an upright position in the armchair. His girth betrayed him, and he fought against it with rising impatience. "Can we not take a little time to reap the rewards of what we have accomplished? After all, these Remnant Believers have been scattered and reduced like so many little fires to be extinguished."

"Nevertheless, they burn still," the Holy Mother pointed out. "And so long as they continue to burn, they raise a stench in my

Son's nose that He cannot tolerate."

Xavier hoisted himself out of his chair, puffing with exertion. "And we will stamp them out, Mother, I swear it!" In his zeal, he raised his voice to her, and she turned on him sharply.

"It is not enough!" she shouted. "They must be put out immediately. Immediately! Do you hear?" Her mood over, she smoothed her pale blue dress out with slender hands. "I want every Remnant Believer put to death immediately. They must all be dead by the end of the week. And then we shall have the sacrifice. Have you secured the child?"

"Not yet, Your Holiness," Xavier protested, "but soon. He is within our very grasp. But we did not want to move too soon."

"See that you do not," she admonished sternly. "We cannot afford any more bungling by your inept employees."

"Not my employees," he protested vehemently. "Were they in my employ, they would have been terminated long ago. It is because I am working with inferiors, Mother, that I cannot please you. Were I on my own, with power of my own, I would leave no stone unturned in an effort to make you happy."

She smiled then, a wispy smile that softened her face. "I know you would, my little father. For your heart is true and your motives pure. One day very soon you will be master of all that you see. When my Son arrives, He will see to it that you are ruler of all. Gavin Larson and his puppet, Thurgood, will answer to you. Then we will see progress."

He made a move as if to take her hands in his own, but she was gone. Vanished. A wraith that dissolved before his eyes. His heart ached with sadness that he would not see her again, perhaps until the next day. But the ache soon faded when he thought of all that she had said.

It was completely true that things would be different if he were in charge. As it was, he bowed to the power of Gavin Larson and President Thurgood, who between them didn't make up one good man, much less a godly one. It was time to take control of a situation that seemed to have eluded them both. He arranged to meet with them within the hour.

It was not hard. They had become accustomed to hearing him out now and acted quite easily on his command. It was just that they took so much time about everything. "The wheels of justice," he heard again and again, "grind dreadfully slow." Well, he was tired of slow. The wheels of justice would simply have to speed up for him.

* * *

The FBI helicopters are handy. Too bad Agent Roddrick is part of the package, Dietrich mused. He was glad that she was flying in the other one. He was getting tired of her constant stream of orders. If she thought she was going to track down the Remnant Believers they were after solely from the air, she was stupider than he had first given her credit for.

If not for him doing some tracking by foot, she could be at this for weeks longer. When hunting people, you had to be patient, observe their behavior, and learn how to predict their next moves. Dani Talbot had slipped through his fingers in the past, but each time, he had learned more about her, and each time he got out of the helicopters and tracked on foot, he learned more about the group she was with. And he knew how close he was. He was much closer to finding them than anyone realized.

* * *

As soon as Gavin entered the Oval Office, Thurgood nodded for the Secret Service agent to leave. Through the months, it had become routine, and although Thurgood still heard about the breach of policy from the head of his security detail, he managed to get his way.

"Sit down, Gavin," Thurgood gestured toward the couch on his right. "I just received word from Attorney General Soran that Director Aldridge has died."

Midnight Hour

Caught by surprise, Gavin's eyebrows opened wide. Then he burst out laughing, and laughed like a hyena for several minutes in front of President Thurgood. It was obscene laughter, feral in its origins but quickly sliding toward pure demoniac cackling. Nervously, Thurgood began to pace the Oval Office, and it was obvious that he dearly wished he had not been so successful in convincing the Secret Service he was completely safe with Gavin Larson.

Gavin got up and grabbed him by the shoulders. "Oh, calm down, Donald. I'm not crazy! Join me in relishing this moment!"

"I'm afraid you'll have to hold your celebration," Thurgood said dryly. "Xavier should be here at any moment. He claims he has a matter of extreme importance to speak to us about."

"Oh, he does, does he? *Hmmm*. I'm glad he's stopping by. I'd like to thank him for getting Aldridge off my back." Gavin patted Thurgood on the arm and went and poured himself some coffee. "I'm beginning to feel things will work out as I had planned after all."

"Oh?" Thurgood said. "And are there any surprises *I* should be aware of, Gavin?" He walked to the window and stared. "Did you know people are dying by the thousands in this city every day?" he said soberly. "A hundred thousand or more die daily across the country. Each day it's worse, so no one really knows."

Gavin took a sip of coffee, a faint, odd little smile on his lips. He heard the words, but they passed right through him without triggering the slightest bit of emotion. He realized at that moment that he truly had the ability to become the ruler of the world.

Thurgood continued lamenting. "You realize that all this is happening while I am president? If the focal point of the nation's, even the world's, anger was not the Remnant, I would probably be the one to blame. I have undoubtedly done the least of any president for this great country..." Thurgood turned and looked at Gavin with tormented eyes. "Instead, I have hidden myself. I have helped point the finger at the Remnant, and in the meanwhile, millions are dying of disease and the oppressive heat. California is still a shambles. And now the whole world is spiraling into what experts are predicting to be the worst drought in recorded history."

"Donald, your concern is touching. But you place too much responsibility on your own shoulders. This misery will soon end. When the Remnant Believers are all wiped from the face of the earth, this will seem like a mere bad dream. The world will have a new beginning." He slapped President Thurgood heartily on the shoulder. "And you, my burdened friend, will be recognized for guiding the United States through these dark times."

"I would hope you are right, Gavin. But . . ."

Thurgood's words trailed off at Pope Xavier's arrival. "Sirs," Xavier said, stepping forward to take their hands in an ardent handshake. "I trust you both are feeling well today."

Thurgood nodded distractedly and then sat down at his desk.

Gavin grinned absurdly and nodded. "Oh, yeah! Couldn't be feeling better!"

Xavier raised an eyebrow and looked at Thurgood.

"Gavin is rather tickled Kent Aldridge has died, I believe," Thurgood explained.

"You did it!" Gavin said. "You called it right on the head. Oh how I wish I could have seen Kent Aldridge's face the moment he knew he was going to die."

"Let me assure you, Mr. Larson, you would have found yourself oddly uncomforted by the spectacle," Xavier said softly. Yet there was a quality in the tone of his voice that caused President Thurgood to look at him curiously. It didn't register with Gavin at the moment, however, flying as high as he was.

"I very much doubt that. I think I would have been very comforted."

Before collapsing on one of the two blue couches in another fit of hysteria, Gavin ratcheted down his elation over Aldridge succumbing to Cartier's Disease. He put on a somber expression for the benefit of the other two men. "You two sure don't know how to enjoy a good moment, do you?"

Thurgood cast a strained, tired look at Gavin. Gavin noticed how frail the president was looking. His eyes roamed to the pope, and it was apparent the pontiff had put on considerable weight and had become considerably more pensive. Suddenly Gavin felt particularly alone in his quest, although this really didn't surprise him. He had spent a considerable amount of time hypothesizing the future and had known that eventually one would have to climb on the backs of the other two to become the ultimate authority.

"Now then, I have important news," Xavier said, launching into the reason he had come.

"From the Holy Mother?" Gavin asked laconically, raising one questioning eyebrow.

"Yes," Xavier lied, "from the Holy Mother. She has asked me to tell you that unless all Remnant Believers are scourged from the earth by this Friday, her Son will cause the sun to burn so brightly that the entire earth will be consumed."

"Can it get hotter than it already is?" Gavin muttered to himself.

Thurgood, however, leapt from his chair, overturning it in his anxiety. "You can't be serious, man!" he exclaimed, his voice hoarse. "Why, think what that means. Hundreds of thousands . . . we don't have the equipment, the means of disposal, the . . ."

"Permission," Gavin supplied sarcastically. "You can't simply destroy that many people all at once, on the whim of a ghost no one sees but yourself."

"Do you *not* see me, Gavin Larson," a sweet voice asked.

Trembling, the religious leader turned slowly. Although it was day, a brilliant glow filled the chamber where the three men met. Thurgood stood as though stricken, neither moving nor speaking. Gavin gazed with rapt awe at the beautiful figure standing in the room. Mary's robes glowed with a soft light that refracted like a prism and hummed with energy at each movement.

"Am I a ghost, Gavin?" Mary asked. "Do you not see me?"

Gavin staggered a few paces forward and then bowed on his face before the Holy Mother. "Holy Mary, Mother of God," he breathed. "I am not worthy. Forgive me. I did not believe."

Thurgood had remained silent but not unimpressed. He moved out from behind the desk and approached Mary, falling on his knees before her. "Donald," she said warmly. "Do you not remember me? When you lay so sick, near to death, you traveled down a long tunnel of light and met me there. I bid you return for yet a while longer, did I not?"

"You did," Thurgood whispered. "You did just that. You told me I had a work to do for you."

"And will you not do it?" Mary pleaded. "My little father takes liberties," she spared Xavier the tolerant look one might give a naughty child. "It has never been my intention to destroy the earth. But he is right about one thing. My Son is very displeased. Things are not moving fast enough. He wishes to return to claim His kingdom on the twenty-eighth of April. That is but two weeks from today. There remains only a week to sweep away the remainder of the resistance, the impediment to His return, and a week to ready our souls to receive Him. It is not too much to ask, I think."

"Mother, no, not too much," Thurgood said, "but what you ask will take time. We have located most of the Remnant Believers, but not all. Not nearly all. Even if we executed all those in custody, we would not be rid of them all."

"You can be," Mary said smoothly. "If you put all your resources into it. You can be rid of them all. There would not be one left on the earth if you were to concentrate all your manpower, all your technology, in rounding them up."

"It might be . . ."

"See to it. If you do not, I will take severe action to punish you. All *must* be ready for my Son. I will tolerate no delay."

In the next instant, she was gone. It seemed that the room had been drained of warmth, and Xavier shivered slightly. Gavin was slow to rise to his feet, seemingly transformed by the encounter. His eyes, so cynical before, were full of fear. Thurgood helped him to his feet, and the two of them made their way to chairs where they sank down gratefully.

"It can be done," Gavin murmured. "If I were to rally everyone. Every person true to our cause would have to be united, motivated properly. It *could* be done."

"By Friday?" was Thurgood's skeptical reply.

"If need be," Gavin responded, warming quickly to the idea. "Dietrich, I dare say, is close to having the child by this time. If we issued a general arrest warrant for any known or suspected Remnant Believer, called upon every resource in our power, we could have them all rounded up inside of a week. Then on Friday, we could order them all put to death."

"But the public," Thurgood protested.

"Will be told just what the good Father has told us." He looked at Xavier, who felt stirrings of importance. "They refused to listen to you before, and we lost most of California. Let them refuse to listen to you this time," he smirked. At first, he had been caught by surprise by the apparition, but his mind was working quickly.

"There is not a living soul who would dare go against any order this man issued," he went on. "Not after what happened last time. And if you and I stand beside him, present a united front, no one will dare defy us. It will all be over and done with before anyone can object."

An odd gleam came to Xavier's eyes, and Gavin smiled and winked at the pope. *Oh, you fools*, he thought. *Molech, you shall have your sacrifice.*

* * *

Less than four blocks from the White House in heavy darkness, Gavin stabbed relentlessly at the climate controls in his limousine and continued to sweat like a pig in the middle of the stalled traffic. The power was out in this grid, undoubtedly due to a million air conditioners greedily sucking power. "Is this the best this air conditioner can do?" he shouted at his driver through the vehicle's intercom.

"I'm afraid so, sir. This is the worst heat on record—"

"Oh, forget the blasted trivia! Just hurry up and get me home." He had already shed his jacket and was attacking the knot in his tie when his cellular phone rang. Digging it out of his jacket, he growled, "What is it?"

A lot of silence and static increased Gavin's agitation, then Dietrich's smug voice rolled almost lyrically over the connection. "I've got the baby!"

"In your hands?" Gavin asked cautiously, remembering full well how often Dietrich had failed in past months.

An unsettling silence, then, "There are only a few Remnant Believers left here, Gavin, and we have them surrounded and unable to escape. They seem to have given up. Do you want me to bring the boy to you?"

Gavin would have much preferred Dietrich in physical control of the baby, but time had become a precious commodity. He could be on a government jet to Idaho in minutes, and he did *not* want to waste precious minutes. He ordered Dietrich to get his hands on the boy, and he would be there as soon as possible. Taking a deep breath, he gained some measure of control and then dialed a number that got him in touch with Thurgood in a matter of only a few minutes. Amazing.

"Is Xavier still there?"

"No, he is not here at the moment."

Gavin felt better. It hardly amazed him that he was growing to despise the pope. As able as Xavier was at disguising his ambition, Gavin could smell it. But he intended to do something about that. Seeing the pope's "Holy Mother" about floored him at first. He felt he had managed an Academy Award performance of humility and reverence, yet even then his mind had been realizing a plan. Molech would be proud.

* * *

They had rested during the day this time, and it was rest that was very much needed, Randy thought. He regretted making everyone break camp to travel at night. But after discussing his plan with the group, everyone had agreed it was a sound idea. He still wondered how sure he was of it.

While everyone else had rested, he had taken their horse and gone ahead several miles to erect a false camp intended to help throw Dietrich and the FBI off their trail and give them some extra time. It had been a long hike, but he'd had much to think about. Mara's answer had been a passionate Yes, and he knew he'd never enjoyed a kiss more than the one that had sealed their engagement.

Dan dropped his gear in the middle of camp and stood beside Randy for a few moments.

"Dan, is this the best idea?" Randy asked.

"I think it's our only option."

"That's what I'm kind of afraid of. What if Dietrich sees it that way too?"

"Won't happen," Dan said as he slapped Randy on the shoulder and went off to help Dani. Ten minutes later, Randy was leading the group off into the deepening night, often doubling back. They were going to have to go slow, but they also needed distance too. He had to get them far enough away that the helicopters started their search going away from them. Was that possible?

* * *

"We can't be too far behind them," Agent Roddrick said, wiping sweat out of her eyes, and Dietrich agreed, although he knew that he and Roddrick were thinking quite differently about the situation. He squinted at the narrow, soulless eyes of the FBI agent, dirty clumps of hair, wet and sticky against her sun-blistered forehead.

This was the first she had spent time on the ground since their chase began, and he knew so much more about their quarry than she did that he could barely stifle a smart remark. He simply ignored her. He lifted a wide-brimmed straw cowboy hat and wiped his forehead as he walked around and thought about things.

"The ashes are faintly warm," Roddrick said, digging underneath the dirt someone had used to smother what could be described as a keyhole fire. "This fire couldn't be more than twenty-four hours old." She stood and brushed off her hands, staring around at the camp, her confidence returning.

Stupid woman, Dietrich thought. *Can't you see that this campsite was made by only one person? There are no footprints of children. No worn depressions in the earth where people had slept for several hours in the lean-tos that had been erected.* Dietrich smiled appreciatively. Ever since he had discovered that one of the men in this group of Remnant Believers was Randy Burton, he'd gained a lot of respect for the ex-FBI agent. He took another good look around at the painstaking work put into making the camp look as real as possible. Even the remains of the fire had bits of food in it. *It had to have been you, Burton. But even though you put a lot of work into erecting this campsite, you could not have done enough to fool me. I know too much about your group now.*

Agent Roddrick ran back to her Black Hawk helicopter and motioned for the pilot to fire it up. She waved for her agents and for Dietrich and his Freedom Society people to follow her lead. As the rotors started turning, Dietrich climbed inside his helicopter and grabbed his headset. When they were off the ground, he told his pilot to fly back the direction they had come and waited patiently for Roddrick's livid voice to assail his ears.

Midnight Hour

* * *

Dietrich enjoyed the verbal battle with Agent Roddrick. Almost as much as he enjoyed winning the decision about which direction to go. He knew he had gradually won the allegiance of every member of their combined forces—not simply on his own merit, however. Roddrick managed to repulse everyone with her caustic language. To avoid being tossed from her helicopter, she shut her mouth and accepted defeat. Dietrich liked her spirit and knew he should keep an eye on her.

He had allies, more now than just Leaman and the other men from the Freedom Society Gavin had sent with him. After leaving Burton's artificial campsite, they flew for another forty-five minutes in a grid before landing in a clear meadow for the night. There had been some discussion about flying to a Forest Service station, but Dietrich felt they were close to their quarry. So close, in fact, that he had called Gavin and told him the baby was as good as in his possession. He had no intention of wasting time flying away when his objective was so close.

Even at night, they were still hot.

"We're gonna die, you know, Roddrick," Dietrich taunted she who glared at him. "The mountains are gonna crash on us. That's what Remnant Believers think will happen to the wicked." He laughed. "Ever read the Bible? It's in there."

"If that's so, I'm making sure I take some Remnant Believers with me."

Dietrich stopped wiping his face. "When we catch up with this group, I don't want you killing any of them. This is my group. Do you understand? If it weren't for me, you wouldn't find them."

"You haven't found them yet, either," Roddrick snapped.

* * *

They had covered less ground in the dark than Randy had hoped for. Yet they were making far better time than they would have were their path not so easy to follow. He listened to Dan and Mara exchange comments about how God was enabling them to see. They had all spent enough time in the mountains during their lives to know that the night could be pitch black.

Dani and the three Warner children in their group were exhausted. During the night, they unloaded the packsaddle and divided up the food. The three men and Mara carried as much food on their backs as they could, and the rest was stashed. That freed up the horse for Dani and the kids to take turns riding. But they had lost valuable time. And it had cost them in supplies. Randy commented on it frequently, until Mara got tired of it.

"Haven't you realized yet that we nearly have as much food as we left the farm with? And how long have we been trudging around in the mountains? Long enough to have gone through our meager supplies twice or three times over!"

Exhausted, they crossed over a ridge to the western side. Randy was glad when the ridge was behind them; it gave them extra time to get into the valley and find a concealed campsite without worrying as much about being visible in the morning sun. Halfway down the slope, he glanced at his watch. The sky was quickly turning from a faded violet to a hazy azure, which told him the sun was going to be relentless for yet another day. And yet despite knowing the earth was being scorched daily, they were always comfortable. Even at night when things could cool down a lot, the drastic shift in temperature had not bothered them. *God is truly with us*, Randy thought.

They reached the valley about the same time as the direct sunlight. Dani came up beside Randy. *She certainly looks a lot better*, Randy thought. Little Jack was riding comfortably in a makeshift kid backpack Mara had constructed.

"The horse needs water," Dani said.

Randy agreed. "I've been praying for a small creek when we

got off the mountain, but I'm afraid there's just no moisture in these mountains." Dani glanced around. Randy noticed how tired she looked and decided there was no need to keep everyone moving. It would be best if they found some good cover and rested through the day. Later, he could take the horse and their water flasks and canteens to look for water.

* * *

Dietrich brought his binoculars to his eyes again, then motioned for the pilot to take them down into the valley. He'd gotten the two Black Hawks into the air at sunrise. No one had complained, not even Agent Roddrick, who had spent a miserable night trying to sleep under one of the birds. She was probably as anxious as everyone else to get on with the hunt. He opened a channel with Roddrick in the second helicopter and told her what he was doing.

"I don't see anything."

Dietrich smiled. "Neither do I," he said. "Maybe if you had some instincts of your own, you'd recognize it." Boy, he loved goading her.

* * *

Amy felt as though she were smothering. She had been in solitary confinement for what seemed like forever. During that time she had seen no one, spoken to no one, heard not a single voice. Indeed, the only sounds that reached her in her prison cell were the tap of the guard's footsteps when he, or she, brought the meals, if you could actually call what passed for food in this establishment meals.

The door was constructed with a square cutout on the bottom. Through this the plate of food was pushed and when she finished, it was through this hole she passed her empty plate back. One day, she had not passed her plate back after finishing her food and no more was brought to her until she had. She missed two meals that way and was tempted to just die of starvation and have it over with.

After all, she was doing no one any good where she was. She couldn't witness to a single soul. She had tried to witness to the guard once. For her pains, she had received a 50,000-volt jolt from the stun belt she was forced to wear as a security restraint. She had dropped to the floor of her cell in convulsions and lost consciousness.

She had not tried again.

And then a thought occurred to her. There were no *human* eyes to see her steadfastness. There were no *people* to witness to. But by her very faithfulness she was witnessing to countless angels and other beings about the character of God. By remaining true to the end, she was saying, and acting, that she believed God was true, just, and righteous, no matter what the circumstances were. She was putting her life completely in His hands and trusting Him not only with the situation but also the outcome.

So she returned her plate and began to eat again.

* * *

By the time they heard the rotors, it was too late. Two black helicopters shot over the mountaintop like wraiths, almost directly above them. Randy and Dan tried to usher everyone into more cover, but the pines were not quite thick enough. Too much granite. Mara ran to help Dani while Randy tried to grab one of the kids. He lost the lead rope out of his left hand, and their horse turned and galloped wildly from the chaos.

"Randy!" Dan yelled.

Randy wheeled to look for the helicopters. Why else had Dan yelled? But it wasn't the helicopters. His eyes found Mara, who was lying on a granite slab, clutching her leg. He rushed the little boy to his parents and returned to Mara.

"Is it broken?" He searched her face, afraid to hurt her but knowing he would trying to get her to cover. And they were too exposed out like they were.

"It's my ankle. I slipped on the pine needles. I don't know if it's broken or sprained." She gave him a pleading look. "Leave me here. All I'll do is slow you down."

"Funny."

"I mean it!"

Randy grabbed Mara by the shoulders and looked her straight in the eyes. "Even if I had half a notion to leave you here, it wouldn't matter. The only chance we have is if they don't see *any* of us. Now, hang on!" He pulled her arms up around his shoulders and swung his left arm under her legs. Careful not to lose his own footing, he loped after the rest of the group.

* * *

"Dietrich! Did you see movement?" Roddrick's excited voice pounded through the earphones.

"Where? What?"

Roddrick's helicopter swept right, away from the other helicopter and circled around.

"Follow them," Dietrich said, his eyes now intently searching the treeline. Finally, he thought he saw something. Yes, there it was again. Movement among the trees! Dietrich got on the radio to Roddrick. "I want you to stay above them. We're going to land, and I want you to flush them toward us."

"And what if they don't flush?"

"Then shoot one or two to get the others moving. That's what you've been wanting to do." Dietrich imagined the pleased look on Roddrick's face. It was a bone to throw her while he got into position to capture this filthy bunch of Remnant Believers.

As Roddrick's helicopter hovered over the trees, Dietrich's

landed in the meadow. He and his men jumped off, and the helicopter lifted off. In the distance, shots could be heard coming from Roddrick's helicopter.

* * *

"They're shooting at us!" Dan yelled. He looked up and screamed, "You devils! You're shooting at children!"

Randy left Mara behind cover with Dani and ran to pull Dan out of danger. The Warners and their three children were hunkered down behind a massive slab of granite rock that tilted toward the meadow, for the moment, safe.

"They're going to kill someone," Dan growled angrily. "So help me, if one of these children gets killed, I'm going to—"

"Then let's pray they don't," Randy said, squeezing Dan's arm. A shot splintered a tree over Mara and Dani. Another whined off a rock. Then a fresh flurry of slugs thumped around all of them. "They've got us nailed down, and there's no way we can get away without being seen," he said.

Dan glanced at the helicopter and looked around shrewdly, still hot and angry but letting his common sense retake control. "Maybe we ought to give ourselves up and let God work things out for us. I don't think we have any other options. Let's let God work."

Randy hesitated. Sweat got into his eyes, and he wiped the back of his hand over his face. He glanced Mara's and Dani's way, then over at the Warners. Everyone was terrified, and maybe he was most of all, because he dreaded getting someone killed. Dan was right. There just were no more options. This was the end of their run.

Randy slid to the ground and lowered his head. "Dear God, we can't hide anymore. Mara is hurt, and the children are tired. If we try to move, I'm afraid some of us will get killed. I ask for your strength to see us through whatever lies ahead. Though we are unworthy, we are not afraid of death. We know in whom we believe. In Jesus' name, Amen."

* * *

He remembered Agent Roddrick, and he was hardly surprised to see her again. There was no integrity left in anyone anymore, probably least of all Bureau agents who, like Roddrick, were abusing their power. Everyone seemed only to care about himself or herself. With narrow eyes, he surveyed the raw, blistered faces of their captors.

"Check him for weapons especially." Roddrick pointed with a H&K MP5 machine gun. Randy was searched immediately by Agent Miller, but he had no weapons. Despite the threat of being killed, he had not met a Remnant Believer anywhere who had been willing to kill to save himself or herself.

Dietrich walked over to Roddrick and spoke in low tones. After a moment, she nodded and stared through malevolent, yellow eyes at the captives, as if waiting for the command to devour them. Dietrich then turned, walked up to Dani, and yanked little Jack from her hands. Furious, Randy lunged forward, but had only gained a step before someone brought the butt of his rifle down on his head, dropping him to the ground.

On his hands and knees, Randy slowly shook his head. He heard Mara's voice asking him something, but she seemed extremely far away. As if in the next valley, Dani's screams echoed and echoed. A warning shot was fired into the air; then came silent fear.

Despite her ankle and regardless of the danger, Mara managed to get onto the ground beside Randy. She inspected the gash on his head. "How do you feel, honey?" she asked softly.

"It hurts. I feel sick." With no warning, he heaved, and Mara pulled his head tenderly to her chest and held him.

He made a move to get up, but a wave of pain and nausea swamped him. Still, he thought he must do something to stop Dietrich from taking Dani's baby. Slowly, breaking free of Mara and using her help to assist him to his feet, he stood and located Dietrich.

"Dietrich, you coward. Why do you want Dani's baby? Give him back to his mother."

Roddrick stepped up and ordered Randy to get on the ground or else she would kill him. Randy looked over at Dani apologetically and slowly knelt down beside Mara. Dani wilted to the ground, too, and began to cry softly.

Dietrich held the baby roughly in his left arm. He looked as though he didn't want to get too close to it for fear of catching something. He talked into his cellular phone with his free hand. Jack, miraculously, was quiet.

As soon as he hung up, Dietrich issued orders to Leaman, whom Randy distinctly remembered, and a few other men. Those men began to scout for rocks to haul to the clearing.

For two hours, the small group of Believers huddled together while armed FBI agents and Freedom Society members milled around with M16s, H&K machine guns, pistols, and shotguns while others carried in rocks. There was no way any of them could escape without some or all getting killed. Even if a few did manage to get away, the helicopters sitting in the meadow would limit their freedom to minutes. Randy gazed around at the faces of their group. When he got to Dan, he shook his head hopelessly.

"What do you think Dietrich wants with little Jack," Mara whispered.

"I don't know, Mara. I just don't know."

"I should have been more concerned when Dani told me the deal she had made with the Freedom Society. It just sounded so ridiculous and improbable." Mara's voice broke as she turned away and stared at the ground.

It was Dietrich's behavior after his cellular phone rang that alerted Randy that the waiting was over. A fist of fear punched him in the chest, and moments later, the distinctive *whomp-whomp* of yet more helicopters could be heard. Two swooped in like dragonflies and dropped neatly to the ground. Gavin Larson hopped out of the first, dressed in khaki's and a safari hat. He was fiendishly happy, although he was obviously broiling in the sun. *Get used to the heat, Gavin Larson*, Randy thought. *For you, it can only get worse.*

It took Randy a moment to recognize the man who stepped down out of the second helicopter. Greg Harrison's handsome face seemed to be part of another lifetime. He could hardly believe that only months before he had calmly watched the popular anchor smoothly narrate the heartbeat of the country. Camera and technical personnel swarmed out after him and quickly set up.

Flanked by heavily-armed Freedom Society members, Gavin strode directly over to Dietrich. He waved a hand toward the cameras in an all-encompassing gesture and a smug smile. His attitude made Randy's stomach flip-flop. Something major was about to go down, and he had a sinking feeling that they were the main attraction.

* * *

"Ah, Dietrich. You have finally impressed me." Gavin ignored Dietrich's loathing glare and reached for the child. "Let me see him." He inspected Jack as if he were a prime piece of meat and nodded his approval, then checked the sun, calculating time.

"Has everything been readied as I ordered," he asked.

"It has," Dietrich replied. "We have plenty of rocks."

"Good. Good. Then let's begin. I want to do this today."

Dietrich hesitated. "Gavin, I have followed your orders faithfully and without asking many explanations. However, I would like to know exactly why this child is so important to you. What are your plans for him?"

Gavin put his free arm around Dietrich's shoulders and led him toward the center of the clearing. He was aware of the intense stares he was getting from the Remnant Believers, as well as the curious looks from the motley crew of Agent Roddrick's team and Dietrich's Freedom Society people. He looked around and sniffed the air. "Dietrich, you are a unique man, a man who is committed only to survival and whoever has hired you. Although I have found your failures aggravating, I have also appreciated your loyalty. Finally, Dietrich, I believe it is time you should fully know what I have been planning and working toward." Gavin paused, an odd gleam in his eye. "My time has come to prove my loyalty to Molech, and in so doing I will sit at his right hand and be given many powers. I will have dominion over the world. Right now, Pope Xavier also believes he is headed for a position of spiritual supremacy, but he is a sad, weak old man who has been manipulated far more than he knows. The Catholic Church has been a useful tool of Molech's for hundreds of years. Through it, he has led billions of people to him."

Dietrich seemed to contemplate this. He stepped back from Gavin and said, "Will you still require my services?"

Gavin laughed. "Oh, Dietrich, yes! Yes! Remain loyal to me, and you will have more than you can imagine." Unexpectedly, his voice dropped to a cold, level pitch, and he said, "But if you turn against me, you will end up like these worthless people." Gavin's gesture took in all of the captive Remnant Believers. "They will all be dead before we leave this place."

"I understand. And how do we get the favor of this god of yours?"

Gavin grinned. He gripped Jack hard with both hands and jostled him. Jack began to wail, and Gavin laughed. "It is time for a ceremony that has been out of practice for a few thousand years. This child belongs to Molech now. He is a gift from me. With him, I will secure Molech's favor. Take the stones you have gathered and build a table, an altar, if you will, and pile brush and wood on top of it."

"And Xavier?" Dietrich asked. "What will happen to him? Surely—"

"I will destroy Xavier, with Molech's blessing."

* * *

The fear in Randy's chest swelled as he watched. He felt he knew what their captors were building, but he was afraid to say anything to Mara, afraid that he might worry her unnecessarily if she hadn't already come to the same conclusion. He sat with his right leg crossed underneath him and his arms and head resting on his left knee, watching for an opportunity for them all to escape. Impossible. He also noticed that Dan was working his way closer to him and Mara. After several minutes, Dan was close enough for them to whisper.

"What do you think, Dan?"

"I was going to ask you that same question."

Randy shook his head almost imperceptibly. "Looks like an altar. I wonder why." Mara heard him and immediately became curious.

"That's what I was thinking. An altar. Unfortunately, I think I know why. The way Gavin has pursued Dani's child, I believe he intends to offer him as a sacrifice."

A startled cry escaped Mara. "As a sacrifice!"

Dan glanced around to make sure they weren't drawing suspicion. He turned back to Randy and Mara and shrugged. "What else could it be? They're gathering fuel too. I would have to say this sacrifice will be made with fire. I remember that sacrifices were made to a pagan god named Molech in ancient Bible times. Even God's people, the Israelites, were known to have participated in such offerings to Molech." Dan paused as one of their guards walked close by, close enough to possibly overhear them. Mara's face had turned white, and Randy was just as appalled. Then Dan continued. "If this is something similar, then Gavin may be proving his allegiance to Molech. Children were the ones to be sacrificed. The act of going through the fire was a pledge to Molech. The ultimate pledge would be to go through the fire yourself, but, of course, that has its drawbacks. Better to sacrifice a child, I guess, and somehow take the credit."

"We can't let this happen!" Mara said.

Randy's eyes narrowed. "We won't, Mara. We won't." How they could stop it, he didn't know, but they would. Somehow. He looked at Dani, watched her as she kept her eyes glued to little Jack, and wondered about her.

"I think someone should tell Dani," Mara said.

Randy squeezed Mara's hand and nodded at Dani. "Does she look all right to you? She hasn't moved."

Mara watched Dani for a while and agreed. "She could be in shock. She has certainly been traumatized more than any of us. Maybe she has just shut herself down."

Maybe that's best, Randy thought. And the instant he thought it, Roddrick ordered their small group to stand. Two men with tattoos on their wrists threw the last armloads of fuel on top. Armed men bunched the Believers up, shouting as they followed Roddrick's orders.

Randy helped Mara to her feet. Dan grabbed Dani and held her around the shoulders. The Warners huddled together. Mom held one of the children. Dad had the other two squeezing him tightly around the neck. They were herded toward the altar.

Randy's eyes flitted about, trying to discover some kind of escape plan, but it was of no use. Since Gavin's arrival, there were as many as thirteen armed men and women. Yet, as he looked at little Jack, he knew he would not allow Gavin to sacrifice the child, even if he had to forfeit his life and the lives of his friends to keep it from happening.

"We might all die in the next few minutes," he whispered to Mara.

She squeezed his arm. "I know, honey. I understand." He felt her reluctantly let go, allowing him freedom to move. Gavin and Dietrich were on the opposite side of the altar, and to his left and forward of him, Roddrick was a cautious five yards away. Dan Reiss was closest to her.

Clutching Jack a bit too hard, Gavin said, "In the next few minutes, all of you, and millions of satellite viewers, indeed the entire world, will be privileged to witness my offering to Molech, the god I serve, the god I am leading the world to serve. Long ago, I was called in a vision to lead the world to god, to Molech, if you will. At the time, I did not realize how to go about my mission or to whom I had pledged myself, but I began my work in the position I held at the time as an aide to House Representative Donald Thurgood. When I became the head of the United Religious Coalition, I felt that the doors had been opened for me to use my influence to bring people of different religions together . . ."

Randy noticed Dan's face turn an angry red. "You're hurting that baby!" he snapped.

Gavin paused and stared at Dan. "What?"

"The baby. You're squeezing him."

Gavin smiled devilishly. "Don't worry. He'll be dead in a few minutes."

Dan took in a deep breath; the muscles in his neck and arms flinched. *He's coiling to attack,* Randy thought suddenly.

"Why? What was your purpose in uniting the religious world?" Dan asked, diverting Gavin's attention from the baby.

"Because, as I said, I was called to lead."

"And you never considered the consequences?"

Perplexed, Gavin narrowed his eyes. "What consequences? I will be rewarded. I will be given unbelievable powers and wealth. Those are not consequences. They are rewards for my commitment. And now, with this child, I will make another pledge to assure my place with my god."

"Your god, Gavin Larson, is the devil himself." Dan spoke slowly and clearly. "You have willfully led people from the one true God. Our God. The Lord of all universes and beings. Whatever you call your god, whether it be Molech or Vishnu or Brahma or Shiva or possessions or power or even the Flying Purple People Eater. It doesn't matter. What you are following is the devil, Satan. The only reward you will possibly have is hell."

Gavin glared, furious yet seemingly shocked by a sudden truth. It drove an odd kind of hate through his eyes, the kind of extreme anger that comes from knowing the truth but refusing to admit to it, and his eyes glowed like firebrands. He snapped orders for the stacks of fuel to be lighted. Two men poured on a flammable substance and lighted the tinder. Satisfied with the fire, Gavin turned back to Dan Reiss. "You fools. As soon as you watch this child pass through the fire, the rest of you will also be killed."

Mrs. Warner let out a startled gasp and covered her mouth. Dani continued to show little sign of emotion, surely in shock, her face twisted in despair.

Gavin stripped little Jack and held him toward the fire with both hands. The heat turned his delicate skin pink, and he began to cry then scream while Gavin raised his eyes and spouted a chanting kind of prayer. Little Jack's screaming wrenched Dani from her catatonic state. She saw her baby and dashed toward Gavin.

No warning. Everything broke loose as devils on molten wings encouraged death.

Someone fired a weapon, and Dani's body jerked. Randy knew she'd been hit, yet he couldn't do anything for her. His eyes swept back to Gavin. Larson coiled his arms.

"Randy, he's going to throw Jack into the fire!" Mara screamed.

Randy was already moving. *Too late,* he thought. Gavin tossed the baby, and Randy leapt over the altar. His arms reached out and snatched Jack's body, clutching him like a football. He twisted midair, protecting Jack as his own body plunged onto the inferno. He remembered rolling with Jack sheltered in his arms and then all went black.

* * *

When Dani moved, Roddrick lifted her H&K machine gun to cut her down. Although Dan Reiss was two yards away, he lunged as soon as he saw Roddrick move the weapon. But he could do nothing to stop the spray of slugs. Roddrick's finger squeezed hard on the trigger. Slugs sprayed in an arch and should have cut through Dan's belly. Instead, they ricocheted harmlessly off the stone altar. Mr. Warner ducked, pulling his children underneath his body. Bullets sprayed the area around him, but he was not touched.

Dan made a grab for the machine gun, but his strength was gone, and Roddrick's hate and fury overpowered him. She yanked the weapon free, her finger still pulling off rounds. Her firing was indiscriminate and killed several of her fellow agents and Dietrich's men.

* * *

A man who had made a living from death, and he had never really thought of his own. Dietrich had expected Randy Burton to do something rash, and he had been ready for it. He'd held a 9MM semiautomatic in his right hand, ready to dispatch Burton the instant he moved.

At first he thought someone had hit him in the side of the neck with a heavy limb. But when he turned his body toward Roddrick and saw the pastor jump for her, he discovered he couldn't speak.

You stupid woman, stop firing! Dietrich grabbed his neck. Warm, sticky fluid ran down his chest. An instant later, he fell on his knees. Roddrick smiled insanely as she knocked the pastor away and pulled the weapon back up. Dietrich hated the look of her, and he shot her in the face before he died.

* * *

She lost track of the time. Days and nights flowed into each other. She had no good idea how long she had been in solitary and how long she would remain there. And then one day the air circulation system quit working. The temperature in the enclosed cell rose rapidly. Amy grew weaker and weaker by the hour, the heat making her faint.

This is it, she thought. *I'm going to die here. Baked to a crisp. It will all end here. When I wake up, I'll see Jesus coming in the clouds to take me home.*

She lay against one wall and drifted in and out of consciousness. She remembered a time when she was little when her mother had left her and two brothers in the car to run into a store. It took longer than she expected, and the three children were crying and hysterical when she returned. The three of them were drenched in sweat and the youngest in a kind of stupor. He'd been fine, but the whole ordeal terrified Amy.

But will I really go with Him? Doubts assailed her. *What if I don't wake up when He comes? What if He takes the others and not me? I'm not worthy. I'm so sinful. I've done so many things wrong. I'm wicked. How can God accept me?*

She tried to think about Jesus, but seeing her own wretched condition next to His made her feel even worse. "Lord, God!" she cried out at last, unable to stand the evil forces pressing down on her. "Help me!"

Instantly a sense of peace and acceptance flooded her being. Moments later, a low murmur of sound and a draught of cool sterilized air wafted from the air ducts. It was an hour before Amy felt well enough to attempt to move, and when she did, her knees felt like overcooked noodles. Had she known, at that moment, that the entire country was experiencing a debilitating heat wave and power companies were routinely turning off people's air conditioning for several hours each day to conserve power, her courage might have been somewhat shaken. But mercifully, due to her solitary existence, this knowledge was kept from her.

Days of this treatment left her feeling as though everything that surrounded her was surreal. When they finally came for her, she blinked at them in surprise. It seemed like years since she had laid eyes on a fellow human being. She greeted them in a bewildered daze. "Hi. What's going on?" she asked stupidly.

She received no answer, but one guard grabbed her arm and the other held the door of her cell open while she was dragged through it. Her legs moved in different directions, and she bumped up against the guard, causing him to curse at her and jerk her arm. A burning flash shot through it, and she struggled to keep up with him.

Their feet made a hollow tapping sound on the scrubbed floor as they hurried her down the long corridor. Another pair of guards was stationed at the double doors leading out to a separate part of the facility. A loud buzzer sounded, and the doors opened. Amy and her guards passed through them.

She found herself in an enclosed chamber. One wall was glass and beyond it a sort of gallery where several people milled uneasily. She recognized Major Thule. Ray sat as close as he could get to the window and looked torn between guilt and anguish.

Amy pulled away from the guard a little and put her fingers against the glass. "I love you, Ray," she mouthed, knowing he couldn't hear her. His eyes filled with tears.

"Amy, tell them what they want to hear," he begged.

She shook her head sadly. "I can't."

He pulled away and turned his back to the glass. The guard, tired of the little melodrama, yanked her back. The people within the small chamber worked together with somber ease, anticipating each other's every move. Before she knew it, Amy was lying on the table while guards strapped her down.

Moments later a man she didn't know stood over her and looked down into her face. "Mrs. Cooper, I have been instructed to ask you if you are willing to recant?"

"No, sir, I am not," Amy replied. She was surprised at the feeling of calm, peace, and yes, strength that infused her system. "God is my strength and my refuge, and I trust in Him and Him alone."

"In that case, I am forced to proceed." She felt the stab of the needle as they hooked her up to the machine that would deliver the fatal dose of chemicals to her system.

Amy wasn't sure what she would feel. She imagined that she felt the poison flowing through her veins. It felt hot, like scalding water being poured over her arm. She waited for it to reach her brain, waited for the fogginess that would surely come, waited for death. But nothing happened.

The tension in the room was palpable.

"Why isn't anything happening?" she heard a guard murmur.

"The dose just isn't high enough yet," was the strained reply.

"But I've seen men three times her size die with half of that."

"Something is wrong," a voice said finally. "Maybe there is something wrong with the mixture."

"No." The voice was frantic. "I did it myself. There's nothing wrong."

"There obviously *is* something wrong. Give her more."

A buzz broke the tension, and Amy heard someone pick up a phone. "I'm sorry, Major Thule, but there seems to be some difficulty with the, er, the injection, ma'am; it's not working. We'll have it fixed. Probably too diluted. Please be patient."

They cursed and fumbled with chemicals and tubing. They checked the needle, then, to be on the safe side, they removed it and put it in again. "OK, let's try this again," she heard a voice mutter.

I'm prepared, Amy thought. *Are you?*

* * *

Pope Xavier was sulking in his room when he felt a slight shiver in the chair beneath him. Gavin had flown off in great secrecy hours earlier, and no matter how many questions he asked, no one would give him any information. He was, therefore, greatly agitated when, after Mary did not arrive at her usual time, he turned on the news and saw none other than Gavin Larson, preparing to sacrifice a baby to Molech!

Xavier watched agog as Greg Harrison covered the ghastly scene with barely controlled reserve. Before the show was over, he placed a frantic call to President Thurgood but was put on hold so long he gave up and turned again to the television screen. What in the name of all that was holy was Gavin trying to accomplish?

A cold fury took possession of him then, and he decided that he would have no more part with the American president or with Gavin Larson. He was God's mouthpiece on earth and would not be usurped by this arrogant upstart. He did not need them, and they could not push him out of the way. They had gone too far.

His face then, had anyone chanced to behold it, was gruesome in its appearance. His eyes shone with the cold light of a murderer, and he knew he would commit murder or any other necessary thing to destroy Gavin Larson or anyone who presumed to stand in his way. President Thurgood, and indeed Gavin Larson himself, were only in their present positions because of him. It was his grace and the Holy Mother's that had allowed them a part in their glorious plan. Now they had outlived their usefulness and must die by any means necessary.

In the last few moments before Gavin prepared to fling the squalling baby into the flames of the altar, Xavier was certain. He could kill the man in cold blood. He could kill him and not even flinch. He would allow nothing to stand between him and the Holy Mother's plan, not Gavin Larson, not Donald Thurgood, nothing.

She would reign supreme, and he would be at her side. That is how they planned it, and that is how it was meant to be. Larson and Thurgood had been merely crutches, and he berated himself for even thinking that he needed them. Now they were unnecessary. It was time to stand alone.

Xavier threw himself into the nearest chair with a self-satisfied smirk and watched in awe as pandemonium broke loose on the television. Shots rang out, and bodies dropped. A man hurtled across the screen, snatching the baby as it left Gavin Larson's hands. Blood spattered the camera lens before all went black and a message was put up about the station experiencing technical difficulties.

He sat in the chair brooding, allowing himself the luxury of self-pity, letting it feed his anger. "Mother!" he called loudly, his voice as demanding as a small child whose will has been thwarted. "Mother! I need you!"

"And I need you, my little father," the beloved voice answered.

Xavier turned, expecting to see Mary. Instead, he saw a figure that took his breath away. His heart skipped up into his throat, and his blood froze in his veins. The apparition was large, as large maybe as two men standing one on the other. It looked like a tired, sinister old man and drooped tiredly. His broad forehead sloped down to a pair of eyes that peered out slyly at Xavier. Those eyes were full of malice. Xavier felt himself shrink away.

"Come, my little father, don't you recognize me?"

"You are not the Holy Mother." Xavier was emphatic.

"We are one and the same," the apparition replied.

"Who are you?"

"Do you not know me?"

Xavier's thought flitted to Gavin's little speech on television. "Not . . . Molech?" he guessed.

The apparition seemed to grow impatient. "It doesn't matter. Call me whatever you wish. Molech is but a number of names men have given me throughout the ages. There is little time left. I need your help if we are to win this battle. Gavin Larson is of no further use to me. But you are. You must destroy them. Destroy the Remnant Believers. Or all will be lost."

"I? How can I?"

"Listen carefully. There is an air force base near Boise. The commanding officer is one of my most loyal followers. If you tell him, he will take his squadron out and annihilate this group of Remnant Believers once and for all. Make the phone call."

Xavier considered what he was about to do.

"If you do this, you will save the world," the apparition assured him.

"How do I know I can trust you?"

Unbelievably, the form before him shifted, and Mary stood before him, a stern look on her face. "Would you sooner trust me, my little father?"

Xavier, marveling, picked up the phone. "Instruct me," he requested. "Where shall I call?"

A crisp military voice answered the phone at Mountain Home Air Force Base. Xavier was immediately transferred to Captain Monroe. "Captain, this is His Excellency, Pope Xavier, and I have a request of the most urgent nature."

When he was finished, he replaced the receiver, astonished that he could coolly order the execution of a group of people he did not even know. His palms were not even damp. In his mind, he could hear the powerful engines of the jets firing up and exhilaration, like jet fuel, flowed icy cold through his veins.

* * *

When Randy returned to consciousness, Mara was holding him. The last thing he remembered was diving through the fire to save Dani's baby. He tried to smile at Mara's beautiful, anxious face. There was no pain, and he assumed it was because he was so badly burned that his senses were overloaded. Mara wiped a flood of tears from her eyes.

"Am I burned?"

Mara shook her head.

"No, not a singe. It's a miracle. Praise God!"

Mara bent over and kissed him passionately on the lips. "You saved Jack. Dani's got him, and she's going to be OK too.

"But she was shot," Randy protested feebly.

"I know, so was Dan, but they're fine. There's not a scratch on them.

Randy blinked and looked at the vast sky behind her. "Gavin. What happened to Gavin and the others?"

"Gavin is alive, I think. Dietrich is dead. He killed that woman FBI agent. There are lots of dead. At least half of them but none of us.

"It's a miracle."

"I know." She nudged him gently and motioned toward the sky where clouds roiled violently. "Look, He's coming."

Randy's eyes scanned the sky. There was a small cloud directly above him that he hadn't noticed a second before. But before he could think what that might mean to them, his ears picked up the mechanical thunder of jets. Seconds later they could see low-flying A-10 Warthogs bearing down on their position.

"Do you think they're coming to help us?" Mara asked dubiously.

"I think they're coming to wipe us out." Randy calculated the distance between the planes and their little group; then he compared it to the fast-growing cloud and prayed that that cloud brought with it deliverance.

* * *

"You have done well, my little father."

"I am eager to do more, Mother."

"Not now. Later you will do more, much more. For now I would like you to stay here. I will tell you when I need you again." Mary placed a sweet kiss on his forehead. Her breath was cool against his skin, and even his pout did not move her. Instead, she laughed gently. "My, but you are anxious. Do not worry.

There is yet much to be done, and you are in the seat of power now, you and you alone."

After she was gone, Xavier slumped into a chair, sulking at the inactivity forced upon him. His adrenaline flowed, electrifying his body. He was ready to go out and conquer the world for the Holy Mother and do it with only his bare hands! Why must he then be confined inside like a naughty child?

He was the supreme ruler of the earth! God on earth now reigned on earth! All was restored to its rightful place. He could not wait one more second to taste the fruits of his hard labor.

When he first felt the tremor, it drew a frown to his brow. Earthquake? Surely the Holy Mother would have warned him, protected him, if that were the case. What then? Before he could make it to his feet and across the floor, the carpet beneath him was heaving violently. He pitched forward, landing on his hands and knees and crawling frantically for the door. Timber groaned as rafters gave way. Plaster pelted him from the disintegrating ceiling. Shards of glass imbedded in his skin as the windows shattered under violent pressure.

He felt the floor tip beneath him as he slid ungracefully along the polished wood floor.

"Holy Mother!" he cried. "Save me!"

Instantly, he was outside the building. He watched as it crumbled. The wind was intense. It ripped at his clothes. Hail pelted from the heavens and bruised him. He staggered toward an overhang of the collapsed building for protection. Shielding his eyes, he looked up in the sky as the wind howled fearsomely.

What he saw made him scream in terror.

It seemed as if the whole heavens had burst open, unable to contain the glory pressing against them. Light surrounded thousands upon thousands of angels, and in the center of the great multitude of them was One whose eyes looked into Xavier's very soul. He could feel them. Even at this distance he could see the pity in those eyes.

His soul was bared, and in it he saw filth unimaginable.

Every good work he had done was exposed by its true motivation. Every thought he had imagined righteous and holy was revealed as polluted and twisted with greed and pride. He shrieked in disgust at his own condition, and at the same time he realized that the delusions he had cherished had become part of him. He could not separate himself from them now.

The light seared him, and guilt weighed him down so heavily that he staggered to stay upright. He *had* to stay on his feet. A chasm yawned before him, and within its depths he saw the only course open to him. His most pressing and urgent need was to escape from the presence of the Holy Lamb of God. He had no other thought.

Every step was a major accomplishment as he limped toward the jagged precipice. Looking back over his shoulder, his face was haggard and distorted with horror and fear. He threw himself gratefully over the edge, desperate to plunge into the darkness below.

"Mother, save me!" One last cry was torn from his lips as he embraced the unknown. He hurtled through space, free at last from the pureness of the Holy light.

* * *

Amy closed her eyes against the glare of the lights in the room. The burning sensation had gone, and she felt supercharged, as if she could bolt upward, breaking her restraints as if they were limp spaghetti noodles draped over her arms. She felt the tremor before she heard it.

There was a low rumble, and the surroundings quivered almost imperceptibly. The noise grew louder, as though a large plane was flying close to the building. The shaking began in earnest, and Amy was forgotten as everyone in the chamber scrambled to get out through the door. She heard the muffled sound of shrieking beyond the glass and Ray's voice screaming her name.

She tried to move, expecting to feel claustrophobic as the bands tightened on her, but to her amazement they were loose, and she easily pulled free of them. She sat up and looked around. Everyone was gone except Ray. He was trying to maintain his balance as the building heaved and tossed. Only the spot where Amy sat on the table that was to have held her for the execution remained calm, like a small island in a raging storm.

"Ray!" she called.

"Amy!" The glass between them shattered and the girders of the building screeched horribly as they twisted and collapsed onto themselves. "Amy, save me!" In the next instant, he disappeared into a yawning cavern that opened up as the floor split in two.

Above her the roof caved in, falling all around her, but not even the dust settled on her. Outside she could see that it was gloomy. Great bolts of lightning chased across the sky. Thunder claps split the air, and she felt it reverberate around her. The noise was deafening. She put her hands to her ears. Still, she heard a voice say:

"IT IS DONE!"

The earth now convulsed with such terrible heaves that Amy felt a jolt of fear course through her. Hailstones, many the size of grapefruit, fell around her. She clung to the edge of the table, her knuckles white. Finally, she could hold on no longer. But instead of sliding down into one of the gaping holes around her, she felt herself lift into the air.

Up she sailed, past the ragged roof of the building. Beneath her the entire structure caved in on itself and was swallowed whole by the greedy earth. As she gained elevation, she could see the panorama of the earth spread out before her. Mountains that had stood for years were leveled off and in some places completely engulfed.

It was then she noticed that she was not alone. Graves, as far as the eye could see, were spewing out the dead. The resurrected shone with radiance and embraced each other. She turned her attention ahead and saw Jesus riding to meet them. And with Him hosts of heavenly beings.

"Amy," a warm, melodious voice said.

"Yes?" She turned, wondering who addressed her in such a loving way. The tone was all the more touching, because she had not heard a kind word since she had last seen Brian.

A tall, radiant being was by her side. Long, golden hair flowed down his back, and silken wings were draped around his shoulders. He held out his hand to her. "I'm Thierry, your guardian angel. Come. There is someone who wants to see you."

She placed her hand in his and felt a pleasant jolt go right through her. They moved at an incredibly fast pace, but the journey wasn't at all stressful. When they stopped, Thierry led her up to a man leading two children. A man who was a stranger and yet very familiar.

"Brian? Brian! Is that you?!"

"Amy!" Brian, this new, recreated, beautiful man who in no way resembled the walking corpse she was accustomed to seeing, held out his arms to her, and she fell into them sobbing and laughing at the same time.

"Brian, it's so good to see you! And you look so wonderful."

"You don't look too bad yourself," Brian teased.

"I was so . . . heartbroken, when you died," Amy prepared herself to choke back the sobs that had wracked her with every thought of Brian's execution, but there were none. Instead, a sense of joy filled her so full that she thought she might explode with happiness. "It's so *good* to see you!"

Amy felt a strong, gentle hand on her shoulder. "There is someone else who wishes to see you," Thierry said quietly, indicating Jesus with his other hand.

Amy took Brian's hand and together with their angels leading them, they went forward to meet the Savior of the world. To hug Him, to thank Him, personally, for all that He had done for them. As they moved forward, Amy realized that simply thanking Jesus for all that He had made possible would likely take the rest of eternity.

And she couldn't wait for it to start.

* * *

Gavin Larson knew the Bible better than most Bible scholars. When he saw the cloud in the sky, he recognized it instantly and fell to his knees. The earth shuddered and heaved. He glanced up as the jets broke away and scattered like flies, the sky boiling behind them in a roiling storm. He clenched his fists until blood spurted from his palms and then tried to look heavenward, at the cloud, but he couldn't. He just couldn't. He looked at the Believers he had wanted to destroy. Their eyes were pointed heavenward, such peace on their faces. They stood erect and proud. They cried, they stretched their arms toward the sky.

Gavin couldn't bear to watch them any longer. He closed his eyes and wailed and bit his lips. Blood flowed down his chin and onto his chest. Even with his eyes closed, he began to see a light, and he covered his face. Still, the light became unbearable. He got to his feet, swaying against the heaving earth. Beyond the Believers, great granite rocks tumbled down the mountain.

No one noticed him run toward the rocks. The Truth was more than he could bear.

* * *

Dani stared around her, disbelieving what she saw. Time seemed to be standing still or maybe it had simply ceased to be. She clutched Jack closely and was relieved at the solid weight of him in her arms. His face, always beautiful to her, was so miraculously changed, that she was curious to see her own. Did she glow with a beautiful light like Jack and the people around her? Were the lines of worry and fatigue erased like those of everyone else? Did she radiate with joy and peace? She knew that she must.

Two angels flanked her: her own guardian angel, Arwen, and Jack's. Arwen gripped her lightly by the elbow. "Danielle, there is someone you must see." His voice was soft and musical. The lyrical way he said her name made her want to hear it over and over.

As she turned she saw a familiar face, and yet not so familiar. This face had no lines of pain. This body strode toward her confidently and with no trace of a limp.

"Daddy!" she shrieked happily. She shifted Jack to one arm and threw her free arm around her father's neck. It was impossible to control the tears of happiness that coursed down her cheeks, christening them all. Baby Jack squawked, and Dani pulled away slightly. She laughed self-consciously as Jack stepped back and for the first time saw his grandson.

"Who have we here?" he exclaimed.

"Daddy, this is little Jack."

Jack's eyes swam in grateful tears. "Oh, Dani," he said, choking with emotion. "I'm so *glad* you're here. How I prayed. You can't begin to . . . I'm *so glad* you're here. It's a miracle. A miracle. And my grandson. Baby Jack. May I hold him?"

Dani handed the baby to her father and stood watching them. Her father, someone she'd always considered reserved, stuffy even, blew raspberries at the baby and addressed him in a string of babytalk that sounded perfectly ridiculous and wonderful. He looked a little googley-eyed when he finally stopped playing with the baby and looked up at her.

"How I wish your . . ." He broke off suddenly and a shadow crossed his face. "Dani, do you know . . . have you seen . . ."

Dani guessed who he was wondering about. "Mom's not here, Dad. A lot happened after you died. Mom got involved in the New Age movement. Satan appeared to us as you. You, or rather, the apparition, told us lies, and Mom believed them. She . . . she killed herself to be with you—or what she thought was you."

Jack's eyes filled with tears, and he handed his grandson back to Dani. "I'm so sorry, Dani. For us, but mostly for your mom. I was really hoping that maybe . . . I know we each have to make our own decisions, but I wish she were here."

"Me too, Dad," Dani whispered.

"She was always searching . . ."

"She just didn't want to accept salvation as a free gift," Dani supplied simply. "She wanted to earn it or jump through hoops to win it. She just couldn't accept that it was free. I think she liked to think that salvation was like an elite club and only those who were well-connected could join. All the commoners were excluded."

Jack nodded. "I'm afraid you're right." He clutched her hand violently. "But you're here. And Jack. In spite of my mistakes. And I'm so glad."

Dani laughed. "Yes, we're here, and I'm glad too. Unbelievably glad. When I think of the narrow escape I had. . . . Well, I'm really grateful to be here. I'm thankful we have an eternity, because it will take me that long to express my gratitude to Jesus for His mercy."

Arwen interrupted them politely. "You will be happy to learn there are others here you are acquainted with. Brian Willis, Mara Benneton, Randy Burton, Lynn Burton, Alice Nolan, Dan Reiss . . ." He stopped as Jack let loose an exultant shout.

"When can I see them all?" he wanted to know.

"Dad," Dani chided him, teasing, "we have all of eternity, remember?"

Jack laughed heartily. "And I'm so glad!"

"You will have plenty of time for your reunion," Arwen assured him. "Right now everyone is assembling at the Sea of Glass. Come, follow me."

Jack took her hand, and Dani cradled Jack easily, as if he weighed nothing at all. They passed scenes of incredible beauty. The very air was alive with fragrance. Surrounding them were rolling hills of verdant green, lush and velvety as chenille. Snow-capped mountains thrust their majestic peaks high into a sky so blue its beauty would have been painful any place but heaven. Dani observed it all with quickened breath.

The terrain before them descended gently, leveling out when it reached the edge of the Sea of Glass. Dani didn't need Arwen to confirm the name of the place. No other location could have better matched its name. The water was so clear it mirrored the blue of the sky, remaining clear to the very bottom. It was vast, stretching across the plain, the shore of its opposite bank nearly beyond reach of their vision. Dani slowly realized that the distance she could see was phenomenal, making it even further to the opposite bank than she had first estimated.

Beautiful sea creatures could be seen, some of which Dani recognized from earth and some new ones that clearly existed only in heaven. Around the entire sea, men, women, children, and angels crowded. All of them raised their hands singing praises to the King.

Jesus stood on one bank flanked with angels. Their glory was an awesome spectacle, but as brightly as they shone, He shone brighter still. Dani swallowed back tears of gratitude and clasped hands with her father. Halfway down the shoreline, she could make out Randy and Mara, embracing and singing with the entire heavenly host, whose vocal ability so far-surpassed any choir she had ever heard that there was no comparison.

They were well into the second chorus before Dani realized that the young, vibrant woman standing next to them was Alice Nolan! And beside her, shining with radiance, was Lynn Burton. Before she could speculate further on their changed appearance, she was grabbed from behind and squashed in a bearhug that left her breathless.

"Dani! Jack!" The salt and pepper was gone from his hair, and his face shone like a beacon.

"Pastor Reiss!" Dani squealed. She surrendered Jack to Dan as he picked the baby up and held him high over his head.

"And look at this little guy. Just think, Jack, you'll get to grow up in heaven. What a privilege." He blew kisses up into the baby's smiling face before handing him back to Dani. "What an opportunity you have, Dani. You'll get to raise your son in the best possible environment. He won't grow up hearing stories about heaven; it will be his home address!"

He turned to Jack, and there were tears of happiness in his eyes. "I can't tell you what I felt when I heard the news that you had been shot. But I'm glad you missed out on the end. I think it would have been even harder for you to live through that than it was for us to go on living without you."

"When I look back at my life," Jack replied, "it seems like such a distant memory. The pain I felt there seems so trivial in comparison to the joy I feel now. Everything I went through was worth this. Everything and then some. It was all worth it."

"Every second," Dani echoed as she gazed out over the vast multitude. Around her the chorus of the song began again, and, startled, she realized that she knew the words even though she had never heard the song before. She lifted Jack slightly so he could see the wonderful things spread out in front of him.

Across the great sea her eyes met those of Jesus, and He smiled. She smiled back, shyly at first and then broadly as His own smile increased. She could feel His love even from a distance. Her mouth opened of its own accord, and praise poured from it. She sang with the others as joy swelled her heart to bursting.

"Hallelujah! For our Lord God Almighty reigns.
Let us rejoice and be glad and give him the glory!
For the wedding of the Lamb has come,
and his bride has made herself ready.
Fine linen, bright and clean was given her to wear."